THE
1970s

Other books in this series:

THE
1970s

Mark Ray Schmidt, Associate Professor of English,
University of Arkansas at Monticello, *Book Editor*

David L. Bender, *Publisher*
Bruno Leone, *Executive Editor*
Bonnie Szumski, *Series Editor*
David M. Haugen, *Managing Editor*

Greenhaven Press, Inc., San Diego, California

AMERICA'S DECADES

Every effort has been made to trace the owners of copyrighted material. The articles in this volume may have been edited for content, length, and/or reading level. The titles have been changed to enhance the editorial purpose.

Library of Congress Cataloging-in-Publication Data

The 1970s / Mark Ray Schmidt, book editor.
    p.   cm. — (America's decades)
Includes bibliographical references and index.
ISBN 0-7377-0308-3 (lib. bdg. : alk. paper) —
ISBN 0-7377-0307-5 (pbk. : alk. paper)
    1. United States—Civilization—1970– 2. Nineteen seventies. I.
Schmidt, Mark Ray, 1953–   . II. Series

E169.12 .A17 2000
973.92—dc21   99-047627
                                                                        CIP

Cover photo: 1. Archive Photos 2. C. David Rubinger/Corbis
Hollywood Book and Poster, 206
Jimmy Carter Library, 57
Library of Congress, 14, 126
National Archives, 28

©2000 by Greenhaven Press, Inc.
P.O. Box 289009, San Diego, CA 92198-9009

Printed in the U.S.A.

Contents

schools toward desegregation. This issue was used by
Nixon as he moved toward reelection in 1972.

Chapter 3: Environment, Energy, and Automobiles in the 1970s

Foreword

In his book *The American Century*, historian Harold Evans maintains that the history of the twentieth century has been dominated by the rise of the United States as a global power: "The British dominated the nineteenth century, and the Chinese may cast a long shadow on the twenty-first, but the twentieth century belongs to the United States." In a 1998 interview he summarized his sweeping hypothesis this way: "At the beginning of the century the number of free democratic nations in the world was very limited. Now, at the end of the century, democracy is ascendant around the globe, and America has played the major part in making that happen."

As the new century dawns, historians are eager to appraise the past one hundred years. Evans's book is just one of many attempts to assess the historical impact that the United States has had in the past century. Although not all historians agree with Evans's characterization of the twentieth century as "America's century," no one disputes his basic observation that "in only the second century of its existence the United States became the world's leading economic, military and cultural power." For most of the twentieth century the United States has played an increasingly larger role in shaping world events. The Greenhaven Press America's Decades series is designed to help readers develop a better understanding of America and Americans during this important time.

Each volume in the ten-volume series provides an in-depth examination of the time period. In compiling each volume, editors have striven to cover not only the defining events of the decade—in both the domestic and international arenas—but also the cultural, intellectual, and technological trends that affected people's everyday lives.

Essays in the America's Decades series have been chosen for their concise, accessible, and engaging presentation of the facts. Each selection is preceded by a summary of the

11

article's content. A comprehensive index and an annotated table of contents also aid readers in quickly locating material of interest. Each volume begins with an introductory essay that presents the broader themes of each decade. Several research aids are also present, including an extensive bibliography and a timeline that provides an at-a-glance overview of each decade.

Each volume in the Greenhaven Press America's Decades series serves as an informative introduction to a specific period in U.S. history. Together, the volumes comprise a detailed overview of twentieth century American history and serve as a valuable resource for students conducting research on this fascinating time period.

Introduction

To begin to understand America in the 1970s, we need to first look at the aggressive confidence that marked Americans in the 1960s. Whatever the task before them, Americans in the 1960s pushed ahead to reach their goals. Thousands of workers at NASA aggressively raced the Russians to reach the moon. Activists in the civil rights movement confidently worked to build a new nation of equality and opportunity. Political and military leaders confidently pursued a war in South Vietnam to defeat the Communists. Later, leaders in the peace movement aggressively worked to end the war in Vietnam. Americans had a habit of feeling sure of themselves and their goals.

In the 1970s, Americans' habitual confidence suffered many blows. In fact, during the 1970s, the people of the United States of America often doubted their ability to control their destinies. For example, the war in Vietnam continued with no apparent resolution in sight. Twice, Americans waited helplessly in long lines to buy a limited amount of gasoline for their cars. In the mid-1970s, the Watergate crisis made many Americans lose confidence in their leaders and their government. At the end of the decade, Americans felt weak as radical students in Iran occupied the U.S. embassy in Tehran and held Americans hostage for months. Yet, during this decade, two movements, the women's movement and the environmental movement, showed that Americans could still confidently shape their futures.

As the 1970s began, Americans were increasingly pessimistic about a military victory in Vietnam. The most powerful nation in the world was losing a war to the small armies of the Viet Cong (the Communists of the South) and North Vietnam. While in the 1960s the question was how to fight the war, in the 1970s the task became finding an "honorable" way out of Vietnam. President Richard Nixon's process of slowly pulling out of the region bred strong feelings of resentment, impatience, and anger in

America. Some people were impatient, wanting a quick withdrawal. Others resented the idea that America would, for the first time, lose a war. Either way, American confidence suffered.

Richard Nixon gives his farewell speech to White House staff after his resignation.

The civil rights movement also put a dent in American confidence. In the 1960s, the movement to improve race relations and the civil rights of blacks had been a dramatic saga of marches, protests, speeches, and landmark legislation. At the center of the movement was the personality, drive, and integrity of Martin Luther King Jr. The road toward equality was bumpy, but the civil rights movement seemed to be progressing. Then in 1968 King was assassinated, and no other single black leader emerged to unify the movement. Thus, in the 1970s the movement lacked leadership and direction. Another part of the problem was the discovery that the task of establishing racial equality was going to take longer than expected. In this aspect, the civil rights movement was similar to the conflict in Vietnam. America had begun both tasks with optimism in the 1960s, but in the 1970s the long, tedious years of struggle had worn down that optimism. The issue of equality in society continued in the 1970s, but the movement lost its momentum.

A third blow to Americans' confidence was the economic impact of two worldwide oil crises. To Americans, autos had served as symbols of freedom. Cars were associated with the American dreams of travel, escape, power, independence, and self-determination. If people could not buy gas for their cars, then somehow one of their fundamental rights had been violated by a foreign power. Thus, the first gas shortage and price increase of 1973 was a shock to most people. Six years later, when Americans were again comfortable gasoline consumers, a second emergency developed and gas was again in short supply and costly. Americans resented the limitations and consequent choices that the new situation demanded. Many turned to Japanese cars which sold for low prices and had the best gas mileage. Exchanging their dreams of big, powerful American-built cars for the less dreamy but practical imports was not an easy task for many people.

A fourth blow to American confidence was the Watergate crisis. It became clear that president Nixon's staff and associates had used government agencies to harass political enemies, had tried to corrupt the judicial system to protect friends, and that Nixon clearly lied to the people about his actions. Watergate did more than remove Nixon from office; it was a crisis in American culture.

In an effort to regain their confidence, Americans elected Jimmy Carter as president in 1976. He was a Washington outsider who promised a fresh start for the country. However, Carter's idealism and confidence was quickly lost. The economy was sluggish, unemployment was climbing, and the country seemed without clear direction. Then in 1979, Iranian student fundamentalists took over the U.S. embassy compound and held American diplomats and workers as hostages. Americans felt powerless as they watched television news programs which repeated the theme of "America held hostage." The programs showed the Iranian students joyfully marching around the embassy and burning the American flag. After months of unsuccessful diplomatic negotiations, Carter ordered a military operation to free the hostages, but when a helicopter accident in the desert killed troops and destroyed needed equipment, the mission was abandoned before reaching Tehran. For 444 days American confidence sagged under the crisis, which, more than any other single issue, worked to defeat Jimmy Carter in the 1980 presidential election. Republican Ronald Reagan offered Americans a convincing optimism about the nation's political and economic future.

In the midst of these disappointments, the women's movement and the environmental movement pushed ahead in the 1970s with surprising energy. The modern women's movement reflected the ideals of nineteenth-century feminists, but in the 1970s many of the early movement's dreams were realized. The introduction of the birth control pill in the 1960s had given women greater choice over when, and if, they were going to follow a career or become a mother. This trend continued in the 1970s, as women were increasingly accepted as full-time members of the workforce with long-term career plans. In addition, the number of women attending college in the 1960s and

1970s climbed significantly. Women graduates were motivated to look for ways to utilize their educations. In addition, the sluggish economy of the 1970s pushed many women into working: A single income was no longer enough to support many families. Court decisions (such as those dealing with abortion), new laws (such as those dealing with gender discrimination), and other factors also contributed to the confident march of women into new areas of American life.

Environmentalism also had a new popularity, a new optimism, and a new forcefulness in the 1970s. While building upon a heritage of conservation, the ecology movement developed in many directions affecting just about every area of American life. Some environmentalists confidently worked to save endangered species of animals, some worked to set aside national lands as permanent wilderness areas, others lobbied for new federal regulations to reduce water and air pollution, some worked to limit nuclear power plants, and others worked to change Americans' habits and values, through school curricula and mass media, as they related to environmental pollution. In spite of the wide-ranging goals of the two movements, and in spite of a lack of centralized leadership, both the women's movement and environmentalism spread quickly and effectively.

The 1970s are in many ways key to understanding the final years of the twentieth century and the opening years of the twenty-first century. Radical cultural changes took place in the 1970s. The women's movement changed the daily habits of the vast majority of Americans for years to come. Large numbers of women became permanent, full-time members of the workforce. This led to greater flexibility for workers' schedules, introducing flex time, maternity and family leaves, and home-based work. The 1970s environmental movement caused many shifts in Americans' personal, business, and political priorities. More businesses advertised that their products were safe for the environment. Government regulations of autos and factories began to clean up the smog in big cities. The 1970s also forced

American businesses to become more competitive in an emerging global economy. Americans were forced to develop more cooperative trade relationships with other countries, contributing to the free trade relationships which helped spur economic growth in the 1980s and 1990s. Finally, the 1970s led people to distrust the government's ability to guide the economy with price controls and other regulations. As a result, Americans were more willing to trust the market forces to guide the economy. Thus, the 1970s helped to set the stage for the period of deregulation during the Reagan years and the economic boom during the Clinton years.

CHAPTER 1

International Issues of the 1970s

AMERICA'S DECADES

Nixon's Plan to End the Vietnam War

Richard Nixon

In 1985 Richard Nixon published a book recounting his memories and impressions of the Vietnam War. The following selection gives his account of how he began developing a plan to bring the war to an "honorable" conclusion. Nixon mentions two groups of people in American politics: "hawks" and "doves." The hawks were political leaders and their supporters who wanted an aggressive military victory in Vietnam. Doves were political leaders and their supporters who wanted to move quickly toward peace in Vietnam by evacuating most, or all, American troops from the area. In this selection, Nixon also defends his decision to secretly bomb Communist positions in Cambodia, a neutral country bordering South Vietnam. Many Americans were angry when they later learned about the bombings because they saw them as an expansion, not a reduction, of the war.

I had begun a reappraisal of our Vietnam policy before I was inaugurated. During the transition, Henry Kissinger, whom I had chosen to be my national security adviser, began reviewing all the possible policies toward Vietnam and distilled them into a full spectrum of specific options,

with massive military escalation at one extreme and immediate unilateral withdrawal at the other.

Options for the War

At one end of the spectrum, some hawks argued that we
should go all out in pursuing military victory. Because I
could not allow my heart to rule my head, I ruled out this
option very early. Opinion polls showed that a significant
percentage of the public favored a military victory in Vietnam—but only a victory won by delivering a knockout
blow that would end the war quickly. Only two strategies
existed that might have won the war in a single stroke. We
could have bombed the elaborate system of irrigation dikes
in North Vietnam, though this would have resulted in
floods that would have killed hundreds of thousands of
civilians. Or we could have used tactical nuclear weapons
against enemy forces. Like Eisenhower in 1954, I gave no
serious consideration to the nuclear option. I also categorically rejected the bombing of the dikes.

By the time I took office in 1969, the only strategy for
pursuing a military victory that deserved serious consideration would have been to order a major escalation of the
conventional war. We could have resumed the bombing of
North Vietnam that Johnson had suspended in November
1968. We could have threatened to invade North Vietnam
and thereby tied down North Vietnamese forces along the
demilitarized zone. We could have crippled Hanoi's supply
lines by mining Haiphong Harbor. We could have authorized the hot pursuit of Communist forces into their sanctuaries in Cambodia and Laos.

While we had the resources to pursue these tactics and
while they might have brought victory, I knew it would
probably require as much as six months and maybe more
of highly intensified fighting and significantly increased casualties before the Communists would finally be forced to
give up and accept a peace settlement.

None of these options was compatible with political
reality.

If we had chosen to go for a knockout blow by bombing the dikes or using tactical nuclear weapons, the resulting domestic and international uproar would have damaged our foreign policy on all fronts.

I decided against an escalation of conventional fighting for three reasons. First, I doubted whether I could have held the country together for the period of time needed to win in view of the numbers of casualties we would be sustaining. As the close election results demonstrated, Johnson's bombing halt had been enormously popular, and though the Paris peace talks were stymied by North Vietnamese intransigence, the American people still had high hopes for their success. Second, having seen Vietnam paralyze American foreign policy for years, I was determined not to take actions in the war that would destroy our chances of developing a new relationship with the Soviet Union and the People's Republic of China. Third, I knew a military victory alone would not solve our problem. Assuming that we committed the forces and adopted the tactics needed to win militarily, what would happen after we had won? Unless the South Vietnamese were prepared to defend themselves, they would be overrun by the Communists as soon as we left.

For all these reasons, I decided against pursuing a purely military solution to the war.

Options for Peace

Other hawks suggested a different approach. They conceded to the doves that we should not have gone into Vietnam in the first place, but contended that now that we were there, we had no choice but to see it through. Our goal, they argued, should not be to defeat the enemy but to stay long enough so that after we withdrew there would be a "decent interval" before South Vietnam fell to the Communists. I believed that this was the most immoral option of all. If our cause was unjust or if the war was unwinnable, we should have cut our losses and gotten out of Vietnam immediately. As President, I could not ask any young American to risk his life for an unjust or unwinnable cause.

Some doves urged that we simply continue the policy we had inherited. They believed that if we vigorously pressed the peace negotiations in Paris and presented our adversaries with "reasonable" proposals, the North Vietnamese would eventually agree to a cease-fire and a negotiated settlement of the war on terms we could accept. In dealing with the North Vietnamese, I had very little faith in a policy that relied on the negotiating process alone. To seek peace at any price was no answer to an enemy who sought victory at any price. I was convinced that unless we backed up our diplomatic efforts with strong military pressure, the North Vietnamese would continue their strategy of talking and fighting until we tired of the struggle and caved in to their bottom-line demand: that the United States withdraw unilaterally and acquiesce in the overthrow of the South Vietnamese government in exchange for the return of American prisoners of war. I considered it unthinkable that we would fight a bitter war for four years, lose 30,000 men, and spend tens of billions of dollars for the goal of getting our POWs back.

Finally, other doves urged that we end the war quickly by announcing the immediate withdrawal of all American forces. A compelling case for this option could be made in political terms. Several of my political allies advised me to blame the war on Kennedy, who had sent 16,000 Americans to Vietnam, and Johnson, who had increased their number to nearly 550,000. If I brought our troops home, they argued, I would be a hero regardless of what happened to South Vietnam and its people.

I rejected this option, too. Had I chosen it, the conquest of South Vietnam by North Vietnam would have been inevitable. That was a result I would not accept. As Vice President, I had been a strong advocate of measures that might have prevented this tragedy. As a private citizen, I had emphatically supported the decision to intervene in the war, though I had disagreed just as strongly with the way my predecessors had handled it. As President, I continued to believe that the moral and geopolitical reasons behind our intervention remained valid. Neither my head nor my heart would permit me to sacrifice our South Vietnamese allies to the enemy, regardless of the political costs I undoubtedly would incur by not withdrawing from the war immediately.

As I studied the option papers before my inauguration, I realized that I had no good choices. But Presidents are not elected to make easy decisions.

Developing a New Plan

When Johnson administration officials briefed me about Vietnam before I took office, they presented no plan for how we should end the war. No progress had been made in the negotiations in Paris. No comprehensive American peace proposal had been announced. No plans existed to bring home any of our 550,000 troops in Vietnam. On the contrary, sending more troops had been under consideration.

In the first months of my administration, we put together a five-point strategy to win the war—or, more precisely, to end the war and win the peace. Our goal was not to conquer North Vietnam but to prevent North Vietnam from conquering South Vietnam.

Vietnamization. Since 1965, the United States had furnished most of the money, most of the arms, and a substantial proportion of the men to help the South Vietnamese defend their freedom. In the chaos following Ngo Dinh Diem's assassination, we had no choice but to take the lead role in the prosecution of the war. But as a result of this policy, the South Vietnamese military had developed an unhealthy, and unsustainable, dependence on the United States. Now we decided to train and equip South Vietnam's army so that it would have the capability of defending the country itself. This involved more than handing over our automatic rifles and the ignition keys of our tanks. The most optimistic estimates were that it would take at least three years to create a fighting force that could stand up to the North Vietnamese Army. Secretary of Defense Melvin Laird carried out this plan and dubbed it, appropriately,

"Vietnamization." Our whole strategy depended on whether this program succeeded.

Pacification. Our defeat of the Tet Offensive had produced a political vacuum in the countryside. Areas that the National Liberation Front had controlled for years were now up for grabs. We knew that whichever side won the race to take control of the hamlets would have won half the battle. We therefore abandoned the strategy of attrition, which had produced many casualties and few results, and replaced it with one of pacification. Our principal objectives shifted to protecting the South Vietnamese at the village level, reestablishing the local political process, and winning the loyalty of the peasants by involving them in the government and providing them with economic opportunity. General Creighton Abrams had initiated this shift in strategy when he took command of our forces in Vietnam in 1968. I reemphasized the critical importance of our pacification programs and channeled additional resources toward them.

Diplomatic Isolation. All of North Vietnam's war matériel came from the Soviet Union or Communist China. I had long believed that an indispensable element of any successful peace initiative in Vietnam was to enlist, if possible, the help of the Soviets and the Chinese. Though rapprochement with China and detente with the Soviet Union were ends in themselves, I also considered them possible means to hasten the end of the war. At worst, Hanoi was bound to feel less confident if Washington was dealing with Moscow and Peking. At best, if the two major Communist powers decided that they had bigger fish to fry, Hanoi would be pressured into negotiating a settlement we could accept.

Peace Negotiations. Our decision to forgo a quick military victory increased the importance of the negotiating process in Paris. I was far less optimistic than some of my advisers about the possibility of quick progress in the negotiations unless we coupled our diplomatic efforts with irresistible military pressure. Ho Chi Minh and his battle-hardened colleagues had not fought and sacrificed for twenty-five years in order to negotiate a compromise peace. They were fighting for total victory. But in the hope that I was wrong, I vigorously pursued the negotiating process. I had another compelling reason for doing so. I knew it would not be possible to sustain public and congressional support for our military efforts unless we could demonstrate that we were exploring every avenue for ending the war through negotiations. I insisted on only two conditions: I made it clear I would reject any settlement that did not include the return of all our POWs and that did not protect the right of the South Vietnamese people to determine their own future.

Gradual Withdrawal. The key new element in our strategy was a plan for the complete withdrawal of all American combat troops from Vietnam. Americans needed tangible evidence that we were winding down the war, and the South Vietnamese needed to be given more responsibility for their defense. We were not recklessly pulling out according to a fixed schedule. We linked the pace of our withdrawal to the progress of Vietnamization, the level of enemy activity, and developments at the negotiating table. Our withdrawal was to be made from strength, not from weakness. As South Vietnamese forces became stronger, the rate of American withdrawal could become greater. The announcement of the withdrawal program made another subtle but profoundly important point: While the French had fought to stay in Vietnam, the United States was fighting to get out.

Our new strategy in Vietnam sought to achieve the goal for which we had fought for four years. While the United States was going to end its involvement in the war, it would keep its commitments to South Vietnam. We would continue to fight until the Communists agreed to negotiate a fair and honorable peace or until the South Vietnamese were able to defend themselves on their own—whichever came first.

All five elements of our strategy needed time to take hold. I knew that we would have enough time only if the level of the fighting remained low. If the war heated up, American casualty rates and, in turn, domestic pressure to get out of Vietnam would increase dramatically. I also knew that the North Vietnamese would negotiate at the conference table only if we convinced them that they could not win on the battlefield.

In February 1969, while we were negotiating in Paris and preparing a new peace initiative to probe Hanoi's intentions, the North Vietnamese launched a savage offensive in South Vietnam. Communist forces killed 453 Americans in the first week, 336 in the second, 351 in the third. South Vietnamese troops were being killed at a rate of over 500 per week. North Vietnamese forces launched a direct attack across the demilitarized zone and indiscriminately fired rockets into Saigon.

These moves were a deliberate test. If there were any truly binding understandings given in exchange for the bombing halt in November 1968, the North Vietnamese were blatantly violating them. I believed that if we let the Communists manipulate us at this early stage, we might never be able to negotiate with them from a position of strength, or even equality. The only way we could get things moving on the negotiating front was to do something on the military front. I therefore concluded that retaliation was necessary.

Our first option was to resume the bombing of North Vietnam. Ideally, we should have dealt a swift blow that would have made Hanoi's leaders think twice before they launched another attack in the South. But I was stuck with Johnson's bombing halt. I knew that even though we could show that North Vietnam clearly had violated the "understandings," bombing North Vietnam would produce a violent outburst of domestic protest. This, in turn, would have destroyed our efforts to bring the country together in support of our plan for peace. I decided that the importance of our domestic unity outweighed the need to retaliate directly against North Vietnam.

Secret Bombings in Cambodia

Our second option was to bomb North Vietnam's military sanctuaries just inside Cambodia along the border with

South Vietnam. Cambodia was formally neutral. But its neutrality was a formality. We honored Cambodia's neutrality; North Vietnam trampled it. Since 1965, the Communists had established a string of bases on Cambodian territory because they knew that their forces in these areas would be immune to attack. North Vietnam in effect annexed these territories, expelling virtually all Cambodian civilians who lived in or near them. Once secured, the bases were stocked with thousands of tons of supplies shipped in through the Cambodian port at Sihanoukville. For four years Communist troops had struck across the border at American and South Vietnamese forces and then escaped back to the safety of their jungle sanctuaries. A classic example of this tactic was their offensive in February 1969. In March we decided to bomb one of these bases in retaliation.

We also decided to keep the bombing secret. We did this for two reasons: We wanted to avoid the domestic uproar that might result from a publicized air strike, and we

U.S. Marines unload equipment and supplies in the jungles of Vietnam.

wanted to avoid putting Prince Norodom Sihanouk, Cambodia's head of state, in a perilous political position.

I had first met Sihanouk sixteen years before. From the long talks I had with him when I visited Phnom Penh in 1953, I knew he was a clever, opportunistic survivor. His actions did not govern events; events governed his actions. What he did or could do depended largely on what happened in Vietnam. For years he had maneuvered to appease the North Vietnamese because he believed that they represented the side with the best chance of winning. In 1965, when South Vietnam was tottering on the brink of collapse, he severed diplomatic relations with Washington and acquiesced in the establishment of Communist sanctuaries and supply lines in Cambodia.

By the late 1960s, when the tide of the war had turned, Sihanouk began to grow deeply concerned about the Communist military presence in his country. He looked to the United States for help. "We don't want any Vietnamese in Cambodia," he told an emissary from President Johnson in January 1968. "We will be very glad if you solve our problem. We are not opposed to hot pursuit in uninhabited areas. You will liberate us from the Viet Cong. For me only Cambodia counts. I want you to force the Viet Cong to leave Cambodia." Also, in a press interview in December 1967, Sihanouk said that he would grant American and South Vietnamese forces the right to go into his country in "hot pursuit" of North Vietnamese and National Liberation Front troops, as long as no Cambodians were harmed.

As we considered the bombing of the sanctuaries in March 1969, we made these calculations. We knew Sihanouk would approve of the air strikes. But we also knew that he could not afford to endorse our bombing publicly, both because it would violate his formal neutrality and because it would risk provoking a North Vietnamese reprisal. If we bombed the sanctuaries secretly, we believed Sihanouk would probably remain silent. If we announced our bombing publicly, we believed he probably would feel compelled to protest our actions. Cambodian protests, in turn, would create pressure on us to stop the bombing. We therefore proceeded in secrecy.

On March 18, our first bombing run in Cambodia took place. It was a great success. We received reports that our bombs touched off multiple secondary explosions, which meant that they had hit ammunition dumps or fuel depots. Crew members observed a total of seventy-three such explosions in the target area, ranging up to five times the normal intensity of a typical secondary explosion. Politically, Hanoi's diplomatic foot-dragging ended as its delegate in Paris quickly took up our proposal to convene a session of private talks.

The Bombings Continue

Originally we had contemplated only this one attack. We were prepared to defend our action publicly if we received a formal protest. But none was made. Hanoi's leaders had no grounds for complaint, because they had for years denied that they had any troops in Cambodia. And Sihanouk, as we expected, assented to our bombing through his silence.

In April and May, I ordered air strikes against a string of enemy-occupied areas within five miles of the border. White House approval was required for each attack through August 1969; thereafter, I turned over general authority to conduct the bombing campaign to our commanders in the field. Our sorties, now conducted regularly against the sanctuaries, wreaked havoc with the enemy's logistics and forced the Communists to abort planned offensives. By curtailing the enemy's ability to attack within South Vietnam, the secret bombing saved the lives of many of our fighting men and bought us valuable time to press forward with Vietnamization.

In May 1969, leaks to the news media revealed our operations. Sihanouk's response to the stories showed that he was in favor of what we were doing. "Here it is," he said at a press conference, "the first report about several B-52 bombings. Yet I have not been informed about that at all, because I have not lost any houses, any countrymen, nothing, nothing. Nobody was caught in those barrages—nobody, no Cambodians." He added, "If there is a buffalo or any Cambodian killed, I will be informed immediately. But this is an affair between the Americans and the Viet Cong–Viet Minh without any Khmer witnesses. There have been no Khmer witnesses, so how can I protest?"

Criticism of Bombings

Some critics later contended that the secret bombing was an illegal abuse of presidential power. There was no substance to this charge. No reasonable interpretation of the Constitution could conclude that the President, as commander in chief, was forbidden from attacking areas occupied by enemy forces and used by them as bases from which to strike at American and allied troops. Congress was consulted within the limits imposed by the necessary secrecy of the operation. Richard Russell and John Stennis, the chairman and ranking member of the Senate Armed Services Committee, were informed and approved of our plans.

Former President Eisenhower was the only one outside of government that I informed about the bombing. When I briefed him on the operation at Walter Reed Hospital, he strongly endorsed the decision.

The charge that our bombing was illegal under the standards of international law also was without foundation. It is illegal to bomb a neutral country. But neutrality is more than pacifism. As the Hague Convention of 1907 stated, "A neutral country has the obligation not to allow its territory to be used by a belligerent. If the neutral country is unwilling or unable to prevent this, the other belligerent has the right to take appropriate counteraction." North Vietnam was using Cambodian territory as a staging ground for its aggression. South Vietnam and the United States therefore had the right to strike back at the North Vietnamese forces inside Cambodia.

By mid-1969, Sihanouk made it plain that he understood it was North Vietnam's actions, not those of the United States, that were endangering his people and threatening to pull his country into the war. In June he complained at a press conference that Hanoi had crowded so many Communist troops into one of Cambodia's northeast provinces that it was "practically North Vietnamese territory." A month later he invited me to visit Cambodia to mark the improving relations between our two countries.

Negotiations in Paris

While we applied pressure on the military front, we continued to push forward on the diplomatic front. On December 20, 1968, I had sent a message to Hanoi indicating our interest in a fair negotiated settlement. The message was sent through Jean Sainteny, a personal friend whom I had met at the home of Paul Louis Weiller in the south of France in 1965 and who had good relations with the North Vietnamese leaders. On February 1, 1969, in one of my first directives to the National Security Council staff, I had ordered a preliminary exploration of the possibility of a rapprochement with Communist China. We had also taken the first steps toward a detente with the Soviet Union. On April 14, Kissinger met with Soviet Ambassador Anatoly Dobrynin and presented a proposal for setting up a private negotiating channel with North Vietnam. . . .

What we needed most was time. No President has a limitless amount of time to invest in any policy. Because my predecessors had exhausted the patience of the American people with the Vietnam War, I was acutely aware that I was living on borrowed time. If I was to have enough time for my policies to succeed, my first priority had to be to gather as much political support as possible for the war from the American people.

Nixon's Appeal to the American People

In late October 1969, I began preparing a national address on the war in Vietnam to be delivered on November 3, 1969. . . .

My speech . . . addressed the questions of what a defeat in Vietnam would mean for South Vietnam, the world as a whole, and the United States. It summarized the reasons why we were in Vietnam.

I began by making the moral case for our intervention. Our original decision to intervene was justified because we were trying to stop foreign aggression: "Fifteen years ago North Vietnam, with the logistic support of Communist China and the Soviet Union, launched a campaign to impose a Communist government on South Vietnam by instigating and supporting a revolution." Our continued involvement was just because it prevented massive human suffering: A precipitate withdrawal of American forces would "inevitably allow the Communists to repeat the massacres which followed their takeover in the North."

I then explained that a unilateral withdrawal from Vietnam would be a disaster for the cause of peace in the world. Our acquiescence in aggression would encourage further aggression: "Our defeat and humiliation in South Vietnam without question would promote recklessness in the councils of those great powers who have not yet abandoned their goals of world conquest. This would spark violence wherever our commitments help maintain the peace—in the Middle East, in Berlin, eventually even in the Western Hemisphere." Peace could not be won through a withdrawal bordering on surrender. "It would not bring peace," I said. "It would bring more war."

After outlining my plan to end the war and the steps I had already taken to do so, I concluded by speaking about the consequences of a precipitate withdrawal for the United States. "The immediate reaction would be a sense of relief that our men were coming home," I said. "But as we saw the consequences of what we had done, inevitable remorse and divisive recrimination would scar our spirit as a people." I observed that while it was not fashionable to speak of patriotism or national destiny in these troubled times, it was clear that "any hope the world has for the survival of peace and freedom will be determined by whether the American people have the moral stamina and the courage to meet the challenge of free world leadership."

Appeal to the "Silent Majority"

I had spent hours writing the conclusion, in which I sought to go over the heads of the antiwar opinion makers in the media and to appeal directly to the American people for unity: "And so tonight—to you, the great silent majority of my fellow Americans—I ask for your support." I said that I had initiated policies that would enable me to keep my campaign pledge to end the war. "The more support I can have from the American people," I stated, "the sooner that pledge can be redeemed; for the more divided we are at home, the less likely the enemy is to negotiate in Paris. Let us be united for peace. Let us also be united against defeat. Because let us understand: North Vietnam cannot defeat or humiliate the United States. Only Americans can do that."

The speech was the most effective of my presidency. I had told the American people that our cause in Vietnam was just and that our policies would end the war in a way that would not betray our cause. Ours was not the easy way out, but it was the right way out. And the American people showed that they concurred.

The People Support the Plan

The minute I left the air after delivering what came to be known as the "Silent Majority speech," the White House switchboard lit up, and the calls continued for hours. It soon became the biggest response ever to a presidential speech. More than 50,000 telegrams and 30,000 letters poured in, few of them critical. A Gallup telephone poll taken immediately after the speech indicated that 77 percent of the public approved of it. Congressional opinion soon showed the impact of this outpouring of popular support. By November 12, 300 members of the House of Representatives—119 Democrats and 181 Republicans—had cosponsored a resolution of support for my Vietnam policies. Fifty-eight senators—twenty-one Democrats and thirty-seven Republicans—had signed letters expressing similar sentiments.

With this response, the American people demonstrated

that deep down they understood what was happening in Vietnam better than those who reported on the war in the news media. The American news media had come to dominate domestic debate about the purpose and conduct of the war in Vietnam and about the nature of the enemy. The North Vietnamese were a cruel and ruthless enemy, but news media coverage continued to concentrate primarily on the failings and frailties of the South Vietnamese and of our own forces. Each night's television news reported the fighting battle by battle and, more than in any previous conflict, showed the terrible human suffering and sacrifice of war. But it conveyed little or no sense of the underlying purpose of the fighting. News-media coverage fostered the impression that we were fighting in military and moral quicksand, rather than toward an important and worthwhile objective.

Public-opinion surveys showed that the American people were weary of the war but wanted peace with honor. In March 1965, the proportion who said that we had *not* made a mistake by going into Vietnam was 61 percent. By May 1971, when the pollsters stopped asking the question regularly, the same percentage believed that it *had* been a mistake to enter the war. But this did not mean the American people wanted to cut and run. In the New Hampshire primary in 1968, a large proportion of those who voted for the antiwar candidate, Senator Eugene McCarthy, actually favored military victory in Vietnam. When Johnson failed to provide a plan to win or end the war, the proportion of those who disapproved of his handling of the situation increased steadily, hitting 63 percent in March 1968. I came into office having promised to end the war and win the peace—to wind down the war without abandoning our allies. Over the four years it took to do so, the proportion of those who approved of my handling of the war averaged 52 percent.

The November 3 speech was a turning point in the war. The approval rating for our Vietnam policy shot up to 64 percent. Now, for a time at least, North Vietnam's leaders could no longer count on dissent in America to give them the victory they could not win on the battlefield. I had the public support I needed to continue a policy of waging war in Vietnam and negotiating for peace in Paris until we could bring the war to an honorable and successful conclusion.

The War of October 1973 and the Oil Embargo

Burton I. Kaufman

Burton I. Kaufman has extensively studied America's foreign affairs since World War II. In this selection he presents the complexity of the political issues in the Middle East during the early '70s. The nation of Israel, though small in size and number, had a strong military to defend itself against its Arab neighbors, who had sworn "to drive the Jews into the sea." Egypt's new president, Anwar Sadat, was determined to unify the Arabs so that territory lost in the 1967 Six-Day War could be regained. The goals of the United States were to support Israel's self-defense, to limit the Soviet Union's influence in the area, and to maintain good relations with moderate Arab leaders. While the tensions were far removed from the lives of most Americans, the war led to an oil embargo. When Arab nations stopped exporting oil, gasoline prices climbed in the United States, forcing Americans to suddenly realize how dependent they were on foreign oil and world events.

A fter the Jordanian civil war [1970], the White House became preoccupied with other foreign policy matters, most notably ending the war in Vietnam, making a new opening to communist China, and reaching a strategic arms

Excerpted from *The Arab Middle East and the United States: Inter-Arab Rivalry and Superpower Diplomacy*, by Burton I. Kaufman (New York: Twayne Publishers, 1996). Copyright ©1996 by Burton I. Kaufman. Reprinted with permission from The Gale Group.

control agreement (SALT I) with the Soviet Union. Despite much talk in Washington and Moscow about a new detente between the United States and the Soviet Union, the White House still assumed that the Soviet Union determined the policies of the radical Arab states (Egypt, Syria, and Iraq). The administration thus ignored the fact that even such conservative and moderate leaders as [Jordan's King] Hussein and King Faisal of Saudi Arabia insisted that the Arab-Israeli dispute—the overriding issue in Washington's relations with the Arab world—could not be settled until the problems of the occupied territories and a homeland for the Palestinians were resolved. It also remained insensitive to the economic, social, and religious dimensions of Arab politics that were to become increasingly obvious over the next 20 years.

During 1971 the State Department tried to arrange an interim agreement between Egypt and Israel providing for Israeli withdrawal from the west bank of the Suez Canal. But such initiatives lacked White House support, and as William Quandt, a member of the NSC [National Security Council] staff, later observed, they only "raised the level of Arab frustrations while reinforcing the sense of complacency felt in Israel and in Washington." Indeed, for the next two years, the administration refrained from undertaking any major new diplomatic effort to resolve the Arab-Israeli dispute.

A New Push for Arab Unity

Since the end of the civil war in Jordan, major political changes had taken place in the Arab Middle East that altered forever the calculus of Middle East politics and made developments in the region one of the United States' paramount concerns. Of most immediate consequence was the death of Egypt's President Gamal Nasser, who suffered a fatal heart attack just one day after negotiating a truce between the fedayeen and the Jordanian government. Although the Egyptian leader had lost much of the luster he enjoyed among the Arab people following the Six-Day War in 1967, he had remained the most important figure in the Arab world.

The new Egyptian leader, Vice President Anwar Sadat, seemed an unlikely prospect to fill the void created by Nasser's death. Lacking Nasser's charismatic personality, Sadat had been outside the mainstream of power in Egypt until 1969 when Nasser chose him as his vice president. He was allowed to become president by other members of Nasser's inner circle only because they believed he would be easy to control. Furthermore, there were others who viewed themselves as the rightful heir to Nasser's position as leader of the Arab world. Two of these were Colonel Muammar Qaddafi of Libya and al-Asad of Syria. Qaddafi had come to power in Libya in 1969 following a military coup against Libya's monarch, King Idris. In Syria, al-Asad assumed total control of the government in November 1970 after a successful coup against Salah Jadid, with whom he had nominally shared power.

Those who anticipated that Sadat would be weak and easily overshadowed by other Arab leaders were wrong. Instead, Sadat moved quickly to establish his legitimacy as Egypt's new head of state and to stake out a claim as one of the Arab world's commanding figures. Perhaps better than any other Arab leader, Sadat understood the unenviable task he faced. In the last few years of Nasser's life, Egypt had become increasingly isolated within the Arab world. Attacked as pusillanimous by the Palestinians, Egypt was also ridiculed by such radical Arab states as Syria, Iraq, and now Libya for not being more aggressive in the struggle against Israel. Relying almost totally on the Soviet Union for weapons, Egypt still seemed defenseless against Israeli attack. Islamic fundamentalists also objected to Egypt's ties to the Soviet Union. Weakened by war, distrusted by the conservative monarchies of the Arab Middle East, despised by more radical Arab regimes, and dependent on a superpower whose ideology was anathema to the Islamic faithful, Egypt was a country whose ties with the rest of the Arab world badly needed mending.

Even more pragmatic than Nasser, Sadat was willing to

work with both moderate and radical Arab states. "My clear and declared policy was that Egypt could not distinguish one Arab country from another on the basis of so-called progressive and reactionary or republican and monarchical systems," he later wrote. As Egypt's representative to Islamic conferences in the 1960s, he had cultivated good relations with a number of conservative and moderate Arab leaders, including King Faisal and King Hassan II of Morocco. As Egypt's new leader, he sought to develop similar relations with Qaddafi and al-Asad even though they were his rivals in the Arab world and called for a type of Arab socialism that conflicted with his more moderate political views. But Arab solidarity was not an end in itself for Sadat. From the time he became Egypt's new leader, he

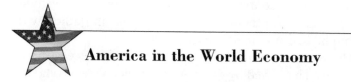

America in the World Economy

American industry and American dollars dominated the world economy after World War II. In the 1970s, that dominance was rapidly eroding.

In the seventies the world's economic structures underwent a drastic transformation as a result of a combination of trends and events that were unavoidable in some instances and wholly unpredictable in others. America's unquestioned domination of the international economy came to an end as postwar reconstruction in Western Europe and Asia was completed (with vast American aid), and West Germany and Japan became economic powers in their own right. This was formalized, in effect, when the United State accepted in 1971 the reality that the dollar no longer was the *only* currency that really counted in world trade and agreed to free the price of gold for the first time in nearly forty years.

Then came a series of "petro-shocks," demonstrating the West's—and America's—immense dependence on Third World oil producers. First, Libya and Iran joined in imposing higher was determined to end what had become Israel's de facto annexation of the occupied territories, preferably by diplomacy but by war against Israel if necessary. In contrast to other Arab leaders, he was motivated not so much by a desire to destroy the Jewish state as by a determination to regain for Egypt and the other Arab combatants in the Six-Day War the self-esteem and territories they had lost as a result of the conflict. Whether these aims were to be achieved through diplomacy or the resumption of hostilities, Sadat considered Arab unity essential.

Largely through Sadat's efforts, by 1973 the Arab world enjoyed a degree of solidarity it had not had since the 1967 war. Egyptian and Syrian military commanders worked closely with each other in planning the resumption of war against Israel. Following a decision by Sadat in 1972 to

prices on foreign producers extracting crude oil from their territories under antiquated concessions agreements. Then the 1973 Middle East War triggered the Arab embargo on oil exports to the West, causing havoc in the industrialized countries. Americans learned about long lines and shortages at gas stations, belatedly realizing that in its complacency the United States had relied on cheap foreign imports for more than one half of its oil consumption (it did so again in 1990).

Before long petroleum prices leaped tenfold, with the Organization of Petroleum Exporting Countries (OPEC) suddenly becoming a household name and a much feared and detested institution with extraordinary power in its hands. From one third in 1960, OPEC's share of world production rose to one half in 1975. Now the key word in international economics was "petrodollars," nobody quite knowing what to do with the uncounted billions of dollars sloshing back and forth between Third World producers and the great Western banks. For the United States, the "golden" years ended.

Tad Szulc, *Then and Now: How the World Has Changed Since WWII*. New York: William Morrow, 1990.

expel almost all of the Soviet advisers in Egypt, Saudi Arabia agreed to provide Egypt with economic and military assistance, including 20 fighter-bombers it had purchased from Britain. Jordan, which had been diplomatically isolated because of its policies toward the Palestinian fedayeen, was allowed back into the fold. By the fall of 1973, Sadat had achieved enough of a united Arab front that he felt able to renew hostilities against Israel.

Moving Toward War

Before deciding on a new war, however, the Egyptian president looked to the United States for help in getting Israel to withdraw from the occupied territories. That was one reason he decided to evict the Soviet advisers from Egypt despite the Friendship Treaty he had signed with Moscow just a year earlier. Although he was also dissatisfied with a sharp drop in the level and quality of military aid Egypt was receiving from the Soviet Union—due in large measure to Moscow's quest for detente with the United States—and, as a devout Muslim, found it distasteful to be closely tied to the leader of the communist world, he intended his action first and foremost as an overture to Washington.

In February 1973, the Egyptian leader sent his security adviser, Hafiz Ismail, to the United States for talks with Richard Nixon and Henry Kissinger, but the discussions were unproductive. Ismail warned that Israel's continued occupation of Arab territories would mean another war. Nixon and Kissinger replied that before Israel would withdraw from the occupied territories, it would have to receive guarantees as to its security. Ismail rejected this proposal for a quid pro quo. As the Egyptian journalist Mohamed Heikal put it, Ismail was annoyed by the White House's efforts to reduce the Arab-Israeli dispute "to a simple equation between sovereignty and security." He was also displeased to read en route home to Cairo a *New York Times* report that Nixon had decided to sell Israel 36 Skyhawk and 48 Phantom jets.

Convinced that the United States would not exert sufficient pressure for the Israelis to withdraw from the occupied territories, Sadat prepared for war. Although the preparations were undertaken with great secrecy, Sadat warned the White House repeatedly of renewed hostilities with Israel. During a summit meeting with Nixon in June, Soviet leader Leonid Brezhnev also warned of an impending conflict unless Washington and Moscow convinced Israel to give up the occupied territories. Notwithstanding Sadat's having unceremoniously kicked the Soviets out of Egypt a year earlier, the Egyptian leader, in need of arms, had patched up some of his differences with Moscow. He had even approved a five-year renewal of an agreement allowing the Soviet navy to use Egyptian ports. The Soviets had responded by resuming arms shipments to Egypt. Yet Brezhnev did not want a resumption of hostilities in the Middle East, which could undermine his efforts at detente with the United States. "I could not sleep at night," Brezhnev even told Nixon in expressing his concern about the possibility of another Arab-Israeli conflict. But while Nixon sensed the need for movement on the occupied territories, he was distracted by the developing Watergate scandal and the events leading to the forced resignation of his vice president, Spiro Agnew. And Kissinger simply did not take the Egyptian and Soviet warnings seriously. He later attributed his miscalculation to Sadat's diplomatic finesse. The Egyptian leader "was moving toward war, using an extraordinary tactic that no one fathomed," he later commented. "If a leader announces his real intentions sufficiently frequently and grandiloquently, no one will believe him." Kissinger had believed that time was working against Egypt, and that given Israel's military superiority and the cool relations between Moscow and Cairo, Sadat would have no other recourse but to seek a political settlement to the Arab-Israeli dispute.

War Begins

He was wrong. In September, Kissinger replaced William Rogers at the Department of State. On 6 October, he faced his first major crisis as secretary of state when on Yom Kippur, the most sacred day in the Jewish religion, Egyptian forces crossed the Suez Canal and attacked Israeli forces on the canal's west bank. Simultaneously, Syrian armies struck against Israel's lightly defended fortifications on the Golan Heights. The Israelis were caught completely off guard. Despite having one of the world's best intelligence services, Israel had learned of the impending attack only 10 hours before it took place, hardly enough time to mobilize against it. The United States was also surprised, so certain was the White House that Sadat had been bluffing in warning about impending hostilities.

Taking full advantage of the element of surprise and employing tremendous artillery and tank firepower, the Egyptians destroyed the Israeli defense line along the Suez Canal (the Bar-Lev Line), which had been thought to be impregnable, and advanced five miles into the Sinai. Syrian troops and tanks broke through Israeli defenses on the Golan Heights. As Israeli planes sought to destroy the bridgeheads the Egyptians had established across the canal, they were met by a massive barrage of SAM missiles, which in the first day of battle brought down 30 Skyhawk and several Phantom jets. Within the first three days of fighting, the Israelis lost about 60 aircraft, or about one-half the 120 Israeli planes that were downed during the conflict.

Most of Israel's air effort, however, was directed against Syrian forces on the Golan Heights, which posed the most immediate danger to Israeli territory and security. There, too, the Israelis suffered large losses, as Syrian air defenses shot down 30 Israeli aircraft in just the first afternoon of fighting. On the ground, Syrian forces also made impressive gains, forcing the Israelis from most of their defensive lines. On 7 October, Syria committed its armored divisions to the battle. As late as 9 October, four days into the fighting, the Syrians still held strategically important parts of the Golan Heights and nearly forced the Israeli Seventh Armored Brigade to withdraw from the battle, which would have allowed a major Syrian breakthrough.

By this time, though, Israel had fully mobilized its forces and gained mastery of the air, shooting down 70 Syrian aircraft in air-to-air combat. In control of the air, Israeli planes destroyed an estimated 400 of the more than 1,000 Syrian tanks involved in the fighting. Israeli ground forces recaptured the territory they had given up in the first four days of the battle. Israel also began strategic bombing, hitting at Syrian power stations and oil refineries and even attacking the headquarters of the Syrian air force and defense ministry in Damascus. By the end of the first week of the war, the Syrians were in retreat across the 1967 cease-fire line. . . .

The Syrian withdrawal across the 1967 cease-fire line, however, allowed Israel to concentrate its military effort on the Egyptian front, where the fighting raged on. During the first week of the war, Egyptian forces continued to cross the Suez Canal, and on 14 and 15 October, Egyptian armored divisions, which had been brought across the canal just two days earlier, launched a major assault in hopes of seizing the strategic Sinai passes of Mitla and Giddi. But this proved to be a grave mistake, for Egyptian forces had been trained essentially for one operation—to cross the canal on a broad front, destroy the Bar-Lev Line, and wait for a cease-fire. By moving eastward into the Sinai, away from Egypt's highly effective air defenses, Egyptian troops were subject to a pounding from Israel's superior air force. They were also met by four Israeli armored divisions. In the largest tank battle since World War II, fought over two days (14 and 15 October) and involving more than 2,000 tanks, Egypt lost an estimated 200 tanks and Israel about 60; both sides also suffered large losses in other armored vehicles and guns. Egypt failed to achieve any of its military objectives, and after the battle, the war shifted clearly in favor of the Israelis. . . .

The United States Misreads the Situation

Even after it had become apparent following the outbreak of hostilities on 6 October that a full-scale war was being fought and that the Egyptians and Syrians were inflicting heavy casualties on the Israelis, the White House and Pentagon had anticipated a decisive Israeli victory. "Every Israeli (and American) analysis before October 1973 agreed that Egypt and Syria lacked the military capability to regain their territory by force of arms," Secretary of State Kissinger later recounted. In his view, the United States' most important task was to warn the Soviet Union against getting involved in the fighting. Indeed, an Israeli victory would make clear to the Arab states the futility of relying on the Soviet Union to come to their rescue and of seeking a military solution to the Arab-Israeli dispute. "If we played our hand well," Kissinger commented, "the Arab countries might abandon reliance on Soviet pressure and seek goals through cooperation with the United States." Washington would, therefore, support a cease-fire based on the 1967 ceasefire lines, but it would be in no hurry to have it implemented. It would also oppose Israeli conquest of any new territory, which would antagonize friendly Arab states and make a final Mideast peace settlement all the more unlikely.

Not until 9 October did the White House gauge the full extent of what was taking place in the Middle East; in fact, just the day before, the CIA had erroneously reported that Israel had crossed the Suez Canal on both its northern and southern ends and had virtually recaptured the Golan Heights. But reality set in the next day when Israeli ambassador Simcha Dinitz informed Kissinger about the extent of his country's losses and requested an emergency supply of military equipment. That afternoon the secretary of state met with Nixon. They agreed to ship military supplies to Israel and to guarantee to replace Israeli losses of equipment.

U.S. Arms Lead to Oil Embargo

Either because of bureaucratic delays or as a subtle means of pressuring Israel into a cease-fire, the airlift to Israel was slow getting started. But on 12 October, Israeli ambassador Dinitz delivered a note to the White House from Prime Minister Golda Meir warning that Israel was in danger of losing the war unless the United States began a full-scale airlift of military equipment to Israel. Nixon responded affirmatively to Meir's urgent request and for the first time used American cargo planes to deliver goods to the Israelis.

The American airlift of equipment to Israel resulted in an Arab boycott of oil to the United States. Despite the friendly relations that existed between Washington and Riyadh, Saudi Arabia had warned the Nixon administration on several occasions in 1973 that it would stop oil shipments to the United States if Washington continued to pursue a pro-Israeli policy. This marked a significant change in Saudi policy from just a year earlier when King Faisal rejected pressure from Sadat and other Arab leaders to brandish the oil weapon. Recalling the failure of the 1967 oil embargo and the significant losses in revenues that had resulted from his country's cutback in oil exports, Faisal had doubts about the impact of another boycott. The United States, he believed, would not need Persian Gulf oil until at least 1985. Ever fearful about the spread of Arab radicalism and the threat it posed to his own throne, he also looked to the United States to protect his interests.

A year later, however, Faisal held a different view. Sadat was able to persuade him of the importance of Arab solidarity in forcing Israel, which Faisal hated as much as any Arab leader, to give up the occupied territories. He also concluded that the United States was already dependent on Persian Gulf oil, so that an oil embargo, coupled with cutbacks in oil production, might command a change in America's pro-Israeli policy. With the purchasing power of the dollar (the currency by which oil prices were set) deteriorating as a result of two recent devaluations, there was also an economic incentive to cut back oil production. "What is the point of producing more oil and selling it for an unguaranteed paper currency?" the Kuwaiti oil minister asked. The Saudis wondered the same thing.

By reducing oil production, the oil-producing countries might also force a substantial increase in profits. In 1970, Libya had taken advantage of the world's growing oil consumption and of new entrants into the competition for Middle East oil production—most notably Occidental Oil, which in 1966 had discovered a massive new field in Libya—to force an increase in the profits it received for its oil: Libya simply insisted on an increase and then required Occidental and the other oil companies in Libya to cut their production until they agreed to its terms. When the Shah of Iran demanded an even higher share of the profits for his oil, a game of leapfrog began in which members of the Organization of Petroleum Exporting Countries (OPEC) were able to jack up oil prices and their share of profits. In 1973, it seemed to Saudi Arabia and other oil-producing countries that cutbacks in production tied to increases in prices might have the same result.

Concerned about the possibility of an oil embargo, executives from ARAMCO and other oil companies with interests in the Middle East warned of the dire economic hardships it would cause and urged the White House to follow a more pro-Arab policy. Kissinger—who because of Nixon's preoccupation with the Watergate scandal now made most of the major foreign policy decisions—understood the risks involved in providing military assistance to Israel, but he could not chance an Israeli military defeat. On 19 October, the White House asked Congress for $2.2 billion in aid for Israel. The next day, King Faisal responded by announcing that Saudi Arabia was cutting its oil production and embargoing oil to the United States.

By the time Faisal imposed the oil embargo, the war had turned decidedly in Israel's favor. Together these two developments persuaded Kissinger that it was time to promote a cease-fire agreement. Pressured by the Soviet Union and sensing that the tide of battle had turned, Sadat indicated on 18 October his acceptance of a cease-fire. But on the verge of surrounding Egypt's Third Army, Israel was in no hurry to stop the fighting. Kissinger cooperated with the Israelis to the extent that he stalled negotiations with the Soviet Union over joint sponsorship of a UN resolution calling for a cease-fire. But on 22 October, the Security

Council adopted Resolution 338 mandating a cease-fire. The secretary of state was exultant. "[W]e had achieved our fundamental objectives," he later wrote. "We had created the conditions for a diplomatic breakthrough. We had vindicated the security of our friends. We had prevented a victory of Soviet arms. We had maintained a relationship with key Arab countries and laid the basis for a dominant role in postwar diplomacy."

Tensions Grow, Then Cease-Fire

But even though Israel and Egypt agreed to a cease-fire, the fighting continued. Using an alleged Egyptian violation of the cease-fire agreement as a pretext, the Israelis completed their encirclement of the Egyptian Third Army and blockaded the city of Suez. For Washington and Moscow, the October War now entered its most critical phase. Kissinger was irate at the Israelis. Throughout the war, he had been guided by the same view that he had always held as a member of the Nixon administration—that Israel needed to be militarily strong but not so unassailable that it could dictate its own terms for the Middle East or act contrary to American interests. By its action, Israel violated that premise.

On 24 October, Moscow responded to the resumption of fighting by calling for the United States and the Soviet Union to send a peacekeeping force to the Middle East. Brezhnev threatened to send in Soviet forces alone if Washington did not participate in a peacekeeping mission. The CIA reported that the Soviets had seven airborne divisions on alert. Under no circumstances was the United States prepared to allow the Soviets to introduce military forces into the Middle East. Another basic premise of Kissinger's Mideast policy had been to keep the Soviet Union out of the region.

Accordingly, the White House issued DEFCON III (Defense Condition 3), placing all of America's military forces on alert worldwide, including its nuclear forces. Kissinger also sent Brezhnev a letter signed by the president stating that sending Soviet troops to the Middle East would be a violation of an agreement on detente that Nixon and Brezhnev had signed during their meeting in June. Meanwhile, the Pentagon prepared to send American paratroopers to Egypt to confront Soviet forces if necessary.

The military alert served its purpose. The Soviets backed down from their threatened military action. But the situation remained highly volatile, and Kissinger was determined not to allow Israel to undermine the diplomatic objectives he had already achieved by continuing the fighting. At a press conference on 25 October, he urged the warring parties to stop the conflict immediately, promising that after a cease-fire, the United States would "make a major effort to bring about a solution [to the Arab-Israeli conflict] that is considered just by all parties." Shortly thereafter, the UN Security Council called for both sides to return to the 22 October lines as stated in UN Resolution 338 and provided for a UN observer force to oversee a cease-fire on this basis. Under intense pressure from Washington, Israel agreed to this latest cease-fire, finally ending the fourth Arab-Israeli war.

Camp David Accords and Middle East Tensions

Sandra Mackey

Sandra Mackey is a writer/commentator on the Middle East. Based on her travels and her studies of the region, Mackey has published several books and written for various news agencies. She points out that American actions and policies in the Middle East were often poorly developed. When America quickly came to Israel's aid in the 1973 war, the first oil embargo resulted. When the United States tried to assist a peace agreement between Egypt and Israel, other Arab nations felt their only option was to reject American offers to negotiate other peace agreements. When the United States tried to ignore the Palestinians, Arab nations refused to cooperate in any peace process.

Israel benefited enormously from the Palestinians' campaign of terror that raged between 1968 and 1972. Golda Meir's statement in 1971 that the Palestinians were not a people and therefore had no claim to a homeland was never seriously challenged in the United States. The following year, the massacre of Israeli athletes at the Munich Olympics so offended civilized society that it gave weight to Israeli arguments that the Arabs are the products of a backward, brutal culture. With a galaxy of political figures like the tough but somehow motherly Golda Meir, the eru-

Excerpted from *Passions and Politics: The Turbulent World of the Arabs*, by Sandra Mackey (New York: Dutton, 1992). Copyright ©1992 by Sandra Mackey. Reprinted with permission from the author.

dite Abba Eban, and the dashing Moshe Dayan who knew and understood the West, Israel carried on its media blitz in the United States. Israel, the bastion of democracy, the United States' indispensable ally against the encroachment of the Soviet Union into the Middle East, was imperiled. Thus it was morally and politically incumbent on the United States to feed and arm it. Americans listened, unaware of just how much the Arabs feared Israel and its American-supplied military might.

It was not long after the debut of high-profile international terrorism in 1968 that Lyndon Johnson completed his term as president. Hounded by Vietnam, he left office without ever addressing the turmoil in the Middle East that was constantly stirred by the United States' unrestrained support for Israel and its chess game with the Soviet Union.

Nixon/Kissinger Years

He was succeeded by Richard Nixon, the cold warrior with a passion for foreign policy, who came into office looking at the Arab world and seeing Russians instead of Arabs. The Soviet Union was still ensconced in Nasser's Egypt, running the Egyptian military as its own. To Nixon's credit, he reasoned that the United States could best get rid of the Soviet presence in the Arab world by addressing the grievances that had opened the door to the Soviet Union in the first place. Thus in November 1969, the Nixon administration reaffirmed the Johnson administration's policy of opposition to Israel's alteration of the status of Jerusalem and declared that "there can be no lasting peace without a just settlement of the problem of those Palestinians whom the wars of 1948 and 1967 made homeless." These statements were widely interpreted to mean that the Republican administration wanted better relations with the Arabs. This was confirmed by a slowdown in new arms sales to Israel, which was followed by the June 1970 Rogers Plan, aimed at ending the war of attrition between Egypt and Israel along the Suez Canal.

The Rogers Plan was Nixon's first foray into Middle

East politics. Conception and execution came largely from William Rogers, who as secretary worked out of the State Department. In the Nixon administration, this was the light side of Nixon's foreign policy apparatus. Origination, direction, and to a great extent implementation of foreign policy came from the duo in the White House—the president and his national security adviser, Henry Kissinger. . . .

The Middle East, overshadowed by the ongoing agony of Vietnam, moved up on Nixon's foreign policy agenda when Anwar Sadat expelled the Russians from Egypt. And then came the October War in 1973. Although Sadat had made numerous attempts to engage the administration in a Middle East peace effort, Nixon and Kissinger failed to consider Sadat's war as an act of diplomacy. Interpreting Israel's forced retreat in the Sinai as a threat to the United States' strategic position in the critical Middle East, Nixon ordered American planes to fly to the battlefield to resupply Israel's losses. The immediate result was the Arab oil embargo and an end to the industrialized world's cheap energy.

Mistakes in war were followed by mistakes in peace. Nixon and Kissinger ignored the possibilities of a comprehensive peace created when the Arab armies for a time held Israel to a standstill on the battlefield. In this brief illusion of victory, the Arabs had regained their honor and lifted some of the psychological burdens of the past. If the United States were ever to address the Arab world as a whole and force concessions on both sides, this was the moment. Instead, Henry Kissinger, the czar of foreign policy in both the Nixon and Ford administrations, married the United States' global concerns to the interests of Israel.

Rather than bringing all parties to the peace conference, which would have required Soviet participation, Kissinger adopted a step-by-step approach in which a series of bilateral negotiations would bring Israel and Egypt and Israel and Syria to the bargaining table as the first level of a process aimed at uncoupling the Arab states from each other and into agreement with Israel. Kissinger won disengagement agreements between Egypt and Israel and Syria and Israel. Then the process stalled. Ignoring or perhaps never fully appreciating the power that the issue of Israel exercises over Arab unity or the symbolic function the Palestinians serve in that unity, Kissinger's strategy in essence ruled out the search for a comprehensive settlement of the Arab-Israeli dispute. One of the central motivations of that strategy was to shut the Palestine Liberation Organization out of any role in deciding the issues of the region of which the Palestinians are such an integral part.

The man [Kissinger] who became secretary of state in Nixon's second term held a formalistic view of the international system. Diplomacy took place among states. Whatever else they might be, the Palestinians were not a state. In Kissinger's view, to even raise the issue of Palestinian participation in peacemaking would derail the entire process. Believing in addressing only those issues which promise success, Kissinger argued that no one had found the answer to the Palestinian problem and no one would. Consequently, he embraced Israel's position that the PLO be neither recognized nor permitted any role in negotiations that might take place between Israel and its Arab adversaries. . . .

Carter Years

When Jimmy Carter became president in 1977, the United States' Middle East policy had reached a dead end. But the instability in the region, which threatened to spill over into war with all of its ramifications for the American stake in the Middle East, had not. From the standpoint of American strategy against the Soviet Union, the Nixon/Kissinger policy of excluding the Soviets from the Middle East had proved self-defeating. Soviet arms continued to flow into Arab countries, and the Russian bear continued to growl its threats, precisely because the United States had blocked to it all responsible avenues of participation in the affairs of the region. Carter initiated a change. A joint statement on the need for a comprehensive settlement of the Arab-Israeli conflict issued by U.S. Secretary of State Cyrus Vance and Soviet Minister of Foreign Affairs Andrei

Gromyko indicated that the United States was cracking the door of the Middle East to the Soviet Union.

Carter then turned to the issue of the Palestinians. The Palestinians were not only at the center of the Arab-Israeli dispute, they were also an important component of the war in Lebanon that had begun in 1975. Anwar Sadat told the new president that the Palestinian problem remained the "core and crux" of Middle East instability and that the Arab-Israeli conflict could not be resolved apart from it. For the Palestinian issue, as always, involved more than the Palestinians per se. It reflected the psychological wounds of all Arabs generated by their unequal contest with the West and with Israel. To get the Arabs to the negotiating table, the Palestinians had to be included in any peacemaking process. This was one reality. The other reality was that, because of the promises that Kissinger had made to Israel, no one in the administration could speak directly to the PLO, the closest thing the Palestinians have ever had to a government.

Jimmy Carter became the first American president willing to sustain an attack on the domestic front over the issue of the Palestinians. In 1977, the year he took office, Carter dropped a pregnant code word into the United States' diplomatic vocabulary. It was "homeland." The president, commenting on the stalemate in the Middle East, stated that a condition for peace was "a homeland for the Palestinian refugees." With that one word, Carter seemed to set the United States on a new path. But the Palestinians themselves refused to give him the help he needed. In the summer of 1977, the United States, supported by Egypt and Saudi Arabia, made an effort to persuade the PLO to accept, even if only partially, UN Security Council Resolution 242. In return, the United States pledged its willingness both to support the idea of an "independent Palestinian entity" on the West Bank under UN supervision and to reassess its military aid policy toward Israel. The American and Saudi assessment that Arafat could deliver the PLO was wrong. The offer was rejected. . . .

Camp David Agreement

Keeping one eye on the domestic front and the other on the Soviets, Carter doggedly pursued the only promising scenario in the Middle East—negotiations between Egypt and Israel. In August 1978, Secretary of State Vance delivered letters to Anwar Sadat and Menachem Begin inviting them to meet Carter at Camp David. But the Camp David Accords that emerged were not an American formula but rather the acceptance of the Begin plan of the previous December. In their intense desire to win an agreement, Carter and Sadat failed to pay heed to the old British diplomatic maxim "Never negotiate on the other fellow's draft." The result was the great flaw of Camp David—the failure to address the problem of the Palestinians. In his meetings with the Israelis, Carter had pushed hard for Palestinian autonomy in the occupied territories as a transitional step that would lead to a Palestinian entity tied in some type of confederation to Jordan. As the negotiations ended, Carter thought he had Begin's assent on the principle of autonomy and a freeze on Jewish settlements in the occupied territories for five years while the autonomy talks were under way. But according to Carter, the day after the terms of the accord were announced, Menachem Begin reneged on his pledge to suspend building settlements. In a letter delivered to the president, Begin claimed the freeze applied only to the three-month period between the Camp David agreement and the signing of the peace treaty between Egypt and Israel. Unhappily, the Camp David Accords, which were to lay the foundation of a comprehensive peace settlement between Israel and the Arabs, failed to impede Israel's drive to absorb the West Bank and Jerusalem. By extension, the crucial element in the conflict in the Middle East was left unaddressed—the Palestinians, the icon of Arab unity.

Despite the great rejoicing that greeted Carter, Sadat, and Begin when they came off the mountain, thoughtful Israelis recognized the basic flaw in the agreement. Former

Menachem Begin of Israel (left) and Anwar Sadat of Egypt (right) shake hands after agreeing to the Camp David Accords.

foreign minister Abba Eban, writing in *Foreign Affairs,* said, "The harsh truth is that on the most crucial and complex issue—that of the Palestinians and the West Bank—the Camp David signatories did little more than postpone their confrontation by the kind of semantic dexterity that is quick to wear out." Nonetheless Carter moved the parties on to the Egyptian-Israeli peace treaty in March 1979.

By the following August, domestic politics began to exert their force on Carter's empathetic approach to the Arab world. Andrew Young, the ambassador to the United Nations, went quietly one evening to the New York apartment of Zuhdi Terzi, the PLO's UN observer. He was seen. The friends of Israel howled in protest that the promises made by Kissinger had been broken. Carter caved in. Young resigned. In the aftermath, the president who had spoken so warmly of the Palestinian "homeland" upon entering the White House was moved to say, "I am against any creation of a separate Palestinian state. I don't think it would be good for the Palestinians. I don't think it would be good for Israel. I don't think it would be good for the Arab neighbors of such a state."

Nonetheless, Carter continued to press on toward Middle East stability with what he had—an Egyptian-Israeli peace treaty. It had broken the Arab front, theoretically enabling other Arab states to follow suit. It was from this viewpoint that Carter and his advisers believed that peace could be achieved without a region-wide peace conference requiring Soviet participation. But the result was precisely the reverse. Rather than a triumph, the Egyptian-Israeli treaty had left the Arab world bitterly divided and the United States savagely condemned. The Saudis argued with some justification that the United States had so polarized the Arabs that the Soviet Union had been handed its best opportunity in years to reestablish itself in the Middle East. Thus, far from correcting Kissinger's flawed strategy, Carter ended up completing it. And just as Sinai II had cost the American taxpayer billions of dollars, so the Egyptian-Israeli treaty with its huge grants of aid to both sides would cost the same taxpayers billions of dollars more. George Ball, a former deputy secretary of state and ambassador to the United Nations who is an outspoken critic of American foreign policy in the Middle East, said at the time, "We bought the sands of Sinai for an exorbitant price from Israel, then paid Egypt a large price to take them back."

No matter how well intended, the mistake of the Egyptian-Israeli peace treaty was that it tried to sever one Arab state from another. In solving one problem, the state of war between the neighbors on the Sinai, it increased the immediacy and danger of a host of other problems. Arms expenditures, for example, of both Israel and Egypt actually increased after the peace treaty. Sadat, having isolated himself from his Arab environment, needed to cater to the desires of his armed forces for billions of dollars' worth of the latest and most sophisticated American equipment. Israel responded by gathering in its share of American military hardware. Yet as serious as the arms race was, even more important for the United States' position in the Arab world was the image that emerged of a powerful Western country dividing one Arab from another in the interests of Israel. It all happened precisely at the time that the Iranian revolution struck at the very foundations of American policy throughout the Middle East.

Revolution and Hostages in Iran

George Lenczowski

An expert on the Middle East, George Lenczowski teaches political science at the University of California at Berkeley. The following selection explains America's relationship with the shah (a title similar to "king") of Iran, particularly as Iran moved toward revolution and as the shah's health declined. In January 1979 the shah escaped Iran, and Ayatollah Ruhollah Khomeini, a religious leader, took power. In November 1979 a mob attacked the U.S. embassy in Iran's capital, Tehran, and held the Americans there hostage for 444 days. As Lenczowski points out, the hostage situation caused many people to view President Jimmy Carter as a weak leader and the United States as a feeble power.

E ver since Nixon's presidency, Iran had enjoyed a special, almost unique, status in U.S. foreign policy. In conformity with the Nixon Doctrine, Iran had become a virtual American surrogate in the Persian Gulf area. Iran's willingness and, as was believed in Washington, ability to replace Britain as the guardian of the Gulf's security were welcome from the American point of view. Nixon's decision to give Iran a blank check for arms supplies was translated into a consistent U.S. policy, of which Iran took full advantage by becoming one of the principal recipients of American weapons and by modernizing and enlarging its military establishment. The shah of Iran, Mohammed Reza Pahlavi,

Excerpted from *American Presidents and the Middle East,* by George Lenczowski. Copyright ©1990 by Duke University Press. Reprinted with permission from the publisher.

was, in American eyes, virtually identified with his country. His periodic consultations with a succession of American presidents since Truman had established him as a friend and ally whose foreign policy priorities, especially his resistance to Communism and Soviet imperialism, had found admiration and approval in Washington. . . .

Carter and the Shah

Jimmy Carter's advent to the presidency in 1977, as one observer noted, was a blow to the shah. This was because of Carter's frequently emphasized two goals of foreign policy: human rights and arms reductions. Insistence on human rights meant that authoritarian or repressive practices, even those engaged in by U.S. friends, would be viewed with a jaundiced eye by the new administration; and a policy of more careful scrutiny on the quality and quantity of arms supplied to foreign recipients would mean possibly severe limitations on the shah's ambitious military modernization program. In fact, soon after Carter's advent to power Iran's ambassador in Washington, Ardeshir Zahedi, voiced in private conversations his concern that the presidential human rights slogans were likely to cause confusion and disarray in Iran. This was so, as the ambassador knew well, because of the characteristic trait of Iranian political mentality—namely, to seek or suspect foreign clandestine inspiration of any significant event in Iran. A call for respect of human rights could easily be interpreted as American disapproval of the shah's domestic policies and as encouragement to the opposition.

For a number of years opposition in Iran was muted and almost clandestine. It had taken the shah a decade, since his countercoup in 1953, to consolidate his power and silence the dissidents. After launching his White Revolution the shah became the only and supreme wielder of power. Opposition to his rule did exist, but it was virtually equated with treason and subversion and, as a political force, was disorganized and ineffective. The shah did not conceal his role as the sole source of authority but preferred to have it known as royal authoritarianism rather than a dictatorship. There was, in his mind, a difference between these two notions: a king had a legal and historical legitimacy, a dictator ruled by naked force. Moreover, objectively, a dictatorship had a proclivity toward totalitarianism, that is, penetration of the all-powerful state into every area of individual and collective life, aiming at complete control of all human activities. By contrast, his royal authoritarianism tolerated a good deal of individual or collective freedom. Such matters as religion and its practice, education of one's children, pursuit of economic gains, ability to travel abroad and have foreign contacts, freedom to emigrate, and freedom to form clubs and associations were left to individual choice with no intrusion by the state, provided they were not a manifestation of political opposition.

Politically, however, the shah was not only supreme but was an "activist" aiming at a rapid transformation of Iran, a country lagging behind the West in many areas, into a modern industrial state, high in production and consumption, militarily strong, and culturally advanced. In the earlier days of his reign the shah had benefited from the advice of some experienced counselors who had the courage to tell him which policies or decisions were useful and safe and which were not. But as the shah advanced in age, experience, and power, while his erstwhile advisers died out or faded away, he became less tolerant of open or implied criticism; instead of independent advice, he began receiving words of praise and adulation. Surrounded by "yes" men, he was the constant object of obsequiousness, genuine or faked. Those praising his moves were often engaging in the time-tested Iranian exercise of "takieh" (or "ketman"), that is, a behavior calculated to conceal one's true feelings and to pretend that there was loyalty, conformity, and devotion where none of these existed.

Growing Tensions in Iran

So long as the economic boom, generated by huge oil revenues since 1973–74, lasted the shah could proceed successfully with his policies of modernization, development, and building a powerful military apparatus. But when a recession began in 1975–76, cracks appeared in the ostensibly stable structure. A number of negative aspects of the regime became increasingly visible. Urban construction demand had brought about disquieting demographic dislocations: the village poor flocked to the cities and crowded the peripheral shantytowns in unsanitary conditions, aggravating the conspicuous contrasts between the wealth of the upper classes and the poverty of the migrants. Corruption, always a bane in the Third World, became rampant and involved members of the royal family. Western-educated entrepreneurs, with easier access to the government and the imperial court, were amassing quick fortunes and becoming objects of envy by traditional bazaar-based merchant classes. Prosperity and development brought to Iran dangerously large numbers of foreign technicians and managers, including some 35,000 Americans whose relatively high standard of living provoked the resentment of the Iranian populace. Inflation hurt the masses. Popular alienation from the regime grew apace; individual or small group acts of violence (including some assassinations) began to multiply, to be met with severe (but apparently not very effective) acts of repression by the shah's secret police, the SAVAK. Opposition to the regime began to crystallize by 1976–77 into a coalition composed of four discernible elements: (1) the National Front liberal-democratic intelligentsia, mostly consisting of professional classes, bureaucrats, and students, all still full of nostalgia for the past idealism of the Premier Mohammad Mossadegh era of the 1950s; (2) the bazaar merchants and their numerous artisan retainers and acolytes; (3) the Leftists of various brands (Tudeh Party, Mujahedin-e-Khalq, etc.); and (4) the Shiite clerical strata, consisting of the mullas and led by the *mojtaheds* (jurisprudents), of whom the highest ranking carried the title of ayatollahs. These groups had little in common with each other; their ideologies and political objectives were often mutually incompatible. But together they formed a formidable negative coalition with one common denominator: hatred of the shah and his regime.

While President Carter was aware of some violations of human rights in Iran, he was also impressed by the progress and development achieved under the shah's rule. Broadly, his attitude toward the shah in 1977, the first year of his presidency, could be described as ambivalent. It is fairly certain that he was not well informed of the depth and scope of opposition to the shah and was not cognizant of the influence that the words or policies of an American president were bound to have on the attitudes of the Iranians and of the shah himself. . . .

The Rebellion Begins

The circumstances in Iran very soon took a turn for the worse. In early January 1978 an article in the popular Teheran daily *Etelaat* (apparently planted by the Ministry of Information) attacked Iran's religious leadership, singling out Ayatollah Ruhollah Khomeini with allegations of immoral conduct and treasonous lack of patriotism. The reaction to the article was immediate. Under the aegis of religious leaders violent riots erupted in the holy city of Qum and other urban centers. Iranian security forces responded harshly. Their fire caused the death of a number of demonstrators. It is the Iranian Shiite custom to mourn their dead in forty-day intervals. These mourning processions invited further clashes between the aroused populace and the security forces, resulting in new victims and thus perpetuating the cycles of violence which in due time spread to such major cities as Tabriz and Isfahan.

In the meantime the principal target of the government's hostility, Ayatollah Khomeini, in exile in Najaf (Iraq) since the 1960s, took full advantage of his sheltered asylum to wage an unrelenting propaganda war against the shah, by preaching to the numerous Iranian pilgrims visiting Najaf and Kerbela the need for resistance to the regime, and by sending hundreds of cassettes with tapes of his inflammatory speeches to Iran. These speeches and sermons were subsequently broadcast in Iran's mosques, inciting the people to rise in revolt against the godless and corrupt monarchy and calling upon the soldiers to disobey orders and desert.

The Shah Is Inconsistent

The Iranian government's response was inconsistent. On the one hand it used its security forces in harsh reprisals. These forces confronted the rioting mobs with lethal weapons because they lacked the nonlethal riot control equipment generally available to police in the Western world. On the other the shah began making conciliatory moves toward the opposition. . . .

The shah oscillated between an urge to introduce a strict military regime and his frequently expressed (to foreign envoys) reluctance to use massive force against his own subjects. He was clearly looking for guidance from Washington while suspecting it of working for his downfall. Moreover, he suffered from an incurable disease—lymphatic cancer—which he kept to himself as a deep secret. This perhaps could, at least partly, explain his changing moods, switching from bouts of depression to unwarranted optimism. In the fall of 1978 the shah appointed a new prime minister, hitherto chief of the Imperial General Staff, General Gholam Reza Azhari, to head what was popularly referred to as "the military government." Actually, most of the ministerial portfolios were, after a brief period, entrusted to civilians and, to avoid bloodshed, the shah opposed repressive measures against the dissenters on a massive scale. Moreover, General Azhari was a rather mild-mannered man, suffering from a heart ailment, who could hardly fit the definition of a rigid military leader. Furthermore the shah, as is often the case of more timid individuals, distrusted his own military chiefs and, to protect himself against a possible conspiracy, insisted that the commanders of the army, navy, and air force report to him separately rather than act jointly. . . .

As for the president himself, he seemed never to make up his mind whether insistence on human rights in Iran or

Iran's strategic value to the United States should be given priority. This question certainly transcended conceptual theorizing because the United States had a vast array of means to influence the course of events in Iran, perhaps decisively. These means included public presidential pronouncements, private advice to the shah, arms supplies policies, sales of riot-control equipment, training and upgrading Iran's military forces, or even using clandestine methods (as had been done in 1953 during the Mossadegh crisis) to effect changes in Iran. As the crisis worsened, Carter became more inclined to support the shah against his adversaries and on a few occasions sent him direct messages and once called him on the telephone. Thus in the fall of 1978 the president informed the shah "that whatever action he took, including setting up a military government, I would support him."

Later, as the year was drawing to a close, Carter still persevered in his policy of amity to the shah, but as he himself stated, this friendly attitude was almost always conditioned by advice that the shah should liberalize and reach accommodation with the dissidents. "Personally and through the State Department," he wrote, "I continued to express my support for the Shah, but at the same time we were pressing him to act forcefully on his own to resolve with his political opponents as many disputes as possible." As [the president's national security adviser Zbigniew] Brzezinski described it in his memoirs, "The Shah was never explicitly urged to be tough; U.S. assurances of support were watered down by simultaneous reminders of the need to do more about progress toward genuine democracy; coalition with the opposition was mentioned always as a desirable objective.". . .

November and December 1978 as well as January 1979 witnessed numerous—almost frantic—activities of the U.S. government to salvage what remained of the Iranian royal authority and American interests. A special task force on Iran was formed, directed by David Newsom, undersecretary of state. To supplement these efforts Brzezinski, with Carter's approval, established telephone communications with Iran's Washington ambassador, Zahedi, who spent some time in Iran in the fall of 1978. (This direct contact was highly resented by [Secretary of State Cyrus] Vance and [the U.S. ambassador to Iran, William] Sullivan.) Various emissaries were sent to Teheran to evaluate and report on the situation, which, especially during the holy month of Moharram (December), worsened appreciably. American visitors included Secretary of the Treasury Michael Blumenthal, Robert Bowie of the CIA, and Senator Robert Byrd. In late November former Under Secretary of State George Ball was invited by the president to study and report on the Iranian situation. His recommendations were more in line with Sullivan's and Vance's thinking: he favored gradual transfer of power from the shah to the opposition and urged opening of U.S. contacts with Khomeini. Although Ball's report was rejected by the White House, Vance chose Theodore L. Eliot, former ambassador to Afghanistan, to contact Khomeini in Paris. However, before Eliot could set out on his trip, his mission was canceled by the White House, and Sullivan was instructed to inform the shah that the U.S. government no longer intended to have any talks with Khomeini.

This ostensible stiffening of the American attitude was, within a few days, countermanded by a new message to be relayed to the shah that "the United States government felt it was in his best interests and in Iran's for him to leave the country.". . .

The Shah Escapes

The shah, accompanied by his family, left Iran for an extended "leave" on January 16, 1979. Formally, a regency council took over his duties. For the military there remained only three alternatives: (1) to support Shahpour Bakhtiar [premier of Iran], (2) to seize power by a coup (for itself or for the shah), or (3) to surrender to the opposition. The first alternative, as we have seen, was most unlikely; the third assumed that the opposition would emerge victorious; hence Brzezinski (and some Iranian generals) favored, until the very last minute, a military coup. [U.S. Air Force general Robert] Huyser, though not successful in ensuring the army's support for Bakhtiar, nevertheless succeeded in persuading its leading generals not to stage a coup.

Thus a sort of psychological vacuum occurred. On February 1, 1979, Khomeini returned triumphantly from Paris and on February 10–11 a mutiny of *homofars* (air force technicians) resulted in a popular uprising that put an end to the monarchy in Iran. The military leaders capitulated, and some offered their services to the revolution. Appearing as supreme leader of Iran's Islamic Republic, Khomeini promptly appointed Mehdi Bazargan, a respected and pious figure of the liberal opposition, as prime minister. In spite of an attack on and temporary occupation of the American embassy by a frenzied revolutionary mob (during which Ambassador Sullivan comported himself with cool professionalism, thus avoiding bloodshed), the U.S. government recognized Bazargan's government and continued regular diplomatic relations with Iran. In contrast to the early predictions of American experts, religious leaders in Iran not only assumed full authority but actually emerged as executives and active participants in the new government. Moreover, there was no question of introducing democracy. Khomeini as the supreme leader (*fakigh*) established a medieval-type religious totalitarian state that soon attracted the world's attention by its acts of intolerance, vengefulness, and repression, expressed in numerous imprisonments, torture, and executions. In fact the excesses of the shah's secret police paled in comparison with the cruelties of the new regime. A major exodus, by legal or illegal routes, of the Iranian secular intelligentsia and managerial class took place, while the religious leaders engaged in confiscations of private property, occupation of private homes, coercive measures toward women wearing Western dress, and haphazard distribution of available funds among the "deprived" classes. Revolutionary *komiteh*s terrorized the population, seconded by the Revolutionary Guards (*pasdaran*) and youth volunteers (*basij*). Universities and schools were "Islamicized" as well as the military academies. Production in many sectors of the economy decreased, and some rationing was introduced.

In spite of the basically anti-American and anti-Western stance of the Khomeini regime, a semblance of normalcy returned to Iranian-American relations. A special Pentagon emissary, Eric von Marbod, concluded with Bazargan's government a "memorandum of understanding" calling for termination and restructuring of major arms contracts—an important step that prevented untold complications likely to ensue if the matter had been left unattended.

The highest point in this process of normalization was reached when, at an anniversary celebration in Algiers on November 1, 1979, Brzezinski met and conversed with Premier Bazargan and two other Iranian ministers (all three laymen).

The Hostage Crisis

The gradual resumption of normalcy in U.S.-Iranian relations, however, suffered a complication when the exiled shah was admitted to the United States in November 1979 to undergo treatment in a New York hospital. The shah had been invited to live in the United States at the time of his departure from Iran and had he accepted the offer at that time probably no crisis would have occurred. But he delayed his arrival, choosing to stay in Egypt, Morocco, and the Bahamas for periods of time, until he found himself in Mexico, where his physical condition worsened. The White House and the State Department were aware of a danger to the American embassy in Iran should the shah be admitted to the United States. But his swiftly deteriorating health and the lack of appropriate medical facilities in Mexico led two prominent Americans, David Rockefeller and Henry Kissinger, to urge the president to permit his entry for humanitarian reasons and out of respect for the American tradition of political asylum, especially to a former ally now in need. Whatever misgivings he had had, Carter concurred with their judgment and agreed to the shah's admission.

By the time the shah came to the United States the mood in Iran had changed. Iranian revolutionary leaders had developed a suspicion that the American government might be plotting to restore the shah to power. As soon as the shah arrived in New York, Iran's militants (a street rabble and some fanatical students) on November 4 assaulted the American embassy in Teheran and captured a total of sixty-six individuals. The only staff members who avoided capture were Bruce Laingen, the U.S. chargé d'affaires, and two aides, who just happened to be in the Ministry of Foreign Affairs at that time, where they remained as virtual prisoners. There is no definite evidence whether the attackers were working entirely on their own initiative or had been abetted and instructed beforehand by Khomeini and his religious aides. Their action took the Bazargan government by surprise; Acting Foreign Minister Ibrahim Yazdi assured chargé Laingen that the captives would be released within forty-eight hours. Contrary to the expectations and promises of Yazdi and Bazargan, Khomeini's son Ahmad arrived at the U.S. embassy and in the name of his father praised the captors for their deed. As soon as Khomeini's attitude became known to Bazargan, he tendered his resignation and along with him Yazdi was also relieved of his duties. Thus the slender influence that secular democratic liberals had had on Iran's political process came to an end, and the religious figures, noted for their Shia fundamentalism and hatred of the "American Satan" and Western values, emerged dominant and monopolized most of the commanding posts in the Islamic republic.

What followed was a saga of Iranian cruelty, duplicity, violation of diplomatic rules, and utter disregard of elementary human rights on the one hand and, on the other, of American indecision, confusion, vacillation between the use of diplomacy and force to rescue the hostages, and of serious humiliation suffered by the U.S. government and military establishment.

By the norms of the civilized world Iranian behavior was

noted for its barbarity and cynicism. Khomeini's regime soon released the captured women and, in a move calculated to exploit American racial dilemmas, the black male employees as well. But the white male captives underwent all sorts of indignities and ordeals, with Iranian captors repeatedly pointing loaded guns at their heads, blindfolding and chaining them, keeping them bound and stretched on bare floors for hours, etc. The hostages were also threatened with a possible trial on spy charges. At the same time the Iranian regime formulated far-reaching demands: that the shah should be extradited to Iran and that his wealth abroad should be seized and returned to the revolutionary authorities. It is interesting to note in this connection that, according to available information, in anticipation of a similar move against itself the Soviet government sternly warned the Khomeini regime that any act of violence committed against the Soviet embassy or personnel in Iran would be met with a swift and strong retribution. There is no record of any Iranian attack on Soviet institutions or employees during the Khomeini era.

The American government tried to resolve the dilemma by diplomatic means, through the use of various intermediaries (because diplomatic relations were in due time broken and the Iranian embassy expelled from Washington). "We . . . asked the Algerians, Syrians, Turks, Pakistanis, Libyans, P.L.O., and others," wrote Carter, "to intercede on behalf of the release of our hostages." In mid-November Carter issued orders to stop U.S. imports of Iranian oil and to freeze some $12 billion of Iranian funds on deposit in the United States. Further sanctions followed. The administration also made efforts to remove the shah from U.S. territory and find a place for him abroad. The matter was complicated by the refusal of President Lopez Portillo to readmit the shah to Mexico despite his earlier offer to do so when the shah was leaving for New York. Eventually, after presidential aide Hamilton Jordan made a trip to Panama, its "strongman," General Omar Torrijos, offered the shah asylum on the island of Contadora, which the deposed ruler of Iran finally reached after a transitional stay at Lackland Air Force Base in Texas.

As negotiations with the Khomeini regime about the hostages dragged on through a variety of emissaries, certain Iranian leaders appeared anxious to reach a settlement, both to relieve the economic pressure caused by American sanctions and to restore some of Iran's reputation which had become grossly tarnished in the international community. But whenever it seemed that an agreement for the release of the hostages was in sight, Khomeini would throw his support to the militants' extreme demands and the contemplated deal would be called off.

Using Force

Exasperated, Carter and his advisers finally decided to resort to force. A seemingly ingenious plan of rescue was prepared, involving precise synchronization of moves among various branches of U.S. military and intelligence services. A special team, code-named "Delta," under the command of Colonel Charlie Beckwith, was to fly to a desert destination not far from Teheran from a gathering point on Masira Island in Oman and, through intricate maneuvers, rescue the hostages between April 24 and 26, 1980. Unfortunately, the planning was not flawless: it did not foresee a possible loss of any of the few helicopters to be employed in the action. So, when one of them was accidentally destroyed in the course of the operation (with several men killed), the rescue mission was aborted. To Carter it was a major blow to his and American prestige and possibly contributed to his failure to be reelected to the second term. Moreover, the whole episode further accentuated the simmering feuds within the administration and led to the resignation of Secretary Vance, already frustrated by his disagreements with the president and Brzezinski.

A month before this tragic failure, the shah, fearful for his safety in Panama, had left for Egypt, his plane refueling in the Azores. He claimed that Torrijos had been planning, in response to Iranian demands (and possibly for gain), to extradite him to Iran. Although Carter in his memoirs asserted that the shah's claim was false, there is reason to believe that it was true because Torrijos had informed a French intermediary in negotiations with Iran that he would detain the shah in Panama under certain conditions. Moreover, acting on his own authority, Carter's chief of staff, Hamilton Jordan, gave instructions to stop the shah's plane in the Azores until further orders. These came somewhat later, rescinding the original instruction, and the shah left without further impediment. His hasty departure from Panama in a chartered plane had been arranged by certain private American friends. In late July the shah died in Cairo.

Profitable Negotiations

In early September an emissary from Khomeini expressed—via West Germany—interest in resolving the hostage crisis. Later that month a war broke out between Iraq and Iran, thus causing Khomeini's regime to be more amenable to serious talks about the fate of American captives. Such talks were conducted in the fall of 1980 by Deputy Secretary of State Warren Christopher and Khomeini's delegate, Taba-Tabai, with the aid of Algeria. They resulted in a tentative agreement which covered four principal areas: (1) hostages to be released, (2) Iranian assets in the U.S. to be unfrozen, (3) Iranian claims on the shah's personal assets to be resolved in U.S. courts, and (4) Iranian claims and U.S. counterclaims regarding corporate and financial problems to be subjected to decisions of the International Court of Justice at The Hague. Even though Iran's revolutionary parliament approved these points in early November, the Iranians procrastinated with formal signing and, shortly before Christmas 1980, demanded that the United States transfer to Algeria $25 billion as a guarantee against the settlement of future claims and counterclaims. Although through the summer and the fall the president had vacillated between use of force and compromise (for example by ordering the aircraft carrier *Constellation* to sail from the Philippines to the Persian Gulf and then canceling his orders), this time he rejected Iran's demand as ridiculous and unacceptable and, in anticipation of a breakdown in further talks, prepared to declare a state of emergency or to ask Congress to declare war on Iran.

Ultimately, on January 19, 1981, the agreement was signed but, with a typically mean streak, Khomeini delayed the release of the hostages until 12:30 P.M., January 20, that is, thirty minutes after Carter relinquished his office as president. Thus came to an end one of the most heartrending and humiliating chapters in America's history.

Even at the time of the crisis it seemed clear that Khomeini, while satisfying his irrational craving to hurt and humiliate America, used the hostage crisis to consolidate his Islamic revolution. Although the captors inflicted much physical and psychological suffering on the hostages, they did not kill any. In fact, depriving the American captives of their lives would not have served Khomeini's purpose; it could have aroused so much indignation among the American people as to lead to war against Iran and elimination of the Khomeini regime. Hence Carter's hesitant policy, geared above all to the safeguarding of the hostages' lives, and his reluctance to use force or the threat of it, though understandable perhaps lacked political realism.

Carter became a victim of indecision as to which principle should receive priority: a principle of restraint, which was consistently advocated by Vance and which, it could be claimed, helped extricate the hostages from captivity, or a principle of placing broadly conceived national interest and honor above all other considerations, as promoted by Brzezinski. There is no doubt that, to Khomeini and other radical militants around the world, the hostage crisis revealed an element of vulnerability in the United States and other democracies, demonstrating that terrorist methods could be used successfully to achieve their objectives.

CHAPTER 2

National Issues of the 1970s

Busing and Nixon's Southern Strategy

James T. Patterson

James T. Patterson, a historian at Brown University, explains two key political issues of the early 1970s: busing and Nixon's political goals. School desegregation had begun in the 1960s, but many schools remained predominantly white or predominantly black. In the '70s, the federal courts were demanding that schools develop aggressive plans to end segregation. Increasingly, the courts dictated the busing of students from one neighborhood to another. As Patterson points out, such "forced busing" was resented by many people. Because of his values, and because he wanted to win the favor of many voters, Nixon acted to hinder busing programs. In addition, Nixon attempted to appoint to the Supreme Court southerners who would not support the future expansion of busing. Nixon's "Southern Strategy" was an attempt to win the votes of southern whites, who had traditionally voted for Democratic candidates.

While liberals could derive some satisfaction from the rise of feminism, affirmative action, and environmentalism between 1969 and 1972, they remained as hostile as ever to Nixon. Indeed, political polarization not only persisted but also sharpened under the watch of the new administration.

Some of this was predictable, given the implacable social and political divisions that had arisen in the 1960s. Some of it, however, stemmed from activities of the Nixon administration, which proved highly partisan in many ways. Nowhere was this more clear than in the area of race relations.

Nixon's Southern Strategy

On racial issues Nixon and his gruff and conservative Attorney General, John Mitchell, were moved mainly by political considerations. Despite rhetoric to the contrary, they were less interested in moderating interracial fears than they were in protecting themselves against the appeal [to both northern and southern working-class whites] of George Wallace, who was expected to run [for president] again in 1972. This meant placating conservative white voters in the South and border states and bringing disaffected Democrats—those who had shown enthusiasm for Wallace in 1968—into the GOP fold.

Nixon and Mitchell sought especially to win over southerners who were bucking desegregation of the schools, an issue that rose again to the center of public debate after 1968. In that year the Supreme Court had indicated, in *Green v. County School Board of New Kent County, Va.*, that it had finally lost patience with southern resistance. Striking down so-called freedom-of-choice plans, which perpetuated segregation, it placed the burden of proof on schools to come up with workable plans for change. "A dual system," it said, "is intolerable." Mitchell, however, sought to abet southern resisters by deferring guidelines, created by the Johnson administration, that would have terminated federal funding to segregated schools. Mitchell also opposed extending the Voting Rights Act of 1965, due otherwise to expire in 1970, on the implausible grounds that it was no longer needed. In August 1969, with schools about to open, HEW [Department of Health, Education, and Welfare] Secretary Finch sided with Mississippi segregationists who sought to postpone court-ordered desegregation. These and other actions highlighted the politically motivated Southern Strategy of the new administration and infuriated proponents of desegregation, including civil rights lawyers in the Department of Justice.

Nixon's efforts to put off desegregation of the schools ran up against determined and mainly successful opponents. The NAACP's Legal Defense and Education Fund brought suit that halted federal aid to segregated schools. Meanwhile, the Supreme Court rejected further obstruction of desegregation. In October 1969 it ruled unanimously in *Alexander v. Holmes Board of Education,* "The obligation of every school district is to terminate dual school systems at once and to operate now and hereafter only unitary schools." The enunciation of "at once" and "now" brought a few teeth, at last, to the doctrine of "all deliberate speed" that "Brown II" had set forth fourteen years earlier. In the 1968–69 school year 32 percent of black schoolchildren in the South had attended schools with whites. By 1970–71 the percentage jumped to 77 percent, and by 1974–75 it was 86 percent. Nationally, the change was less significant. School districts continued to figure out ways to maintain de facto segregation. So did state universities, especially in the South. Still, the changes in Nixon's first term seemed promising: between 1968 and 1972 the percentage of students attending schools that were 90 to 100 percent minority in enrollment decreased from 64.3 percent to 38.7 percent.

Having been rebuffed by the judges, Nixon resolved to counter-attack by naming a southerner to the Supreme Court when a vacancy arose in late 1969. His nominee, Clement Haynsworth, was a South Carolina federal judge. Liberals, however, fought back by airing reports that Haynsworth had a record of hostility to unions and civil rights. They also cited conflicts of interest in some of his rulings. Nixon fought tenaciously but to no avail. When the nomination reached the floor of the Senate, seventeen Republicans joined the majority of Democrats to defeat the nomination, 55 to 45. Mitchell snapped, "If we'd put up one of the twelve Apostles it would have been the same."

The President then tried again, this time in January 1970, by nominating to the High Court G. Harrold Carswell, a former Georgia state legislator who had become a federal circuit judge in Florida. Carswell, however, suffered from greater liabilities than Haynsworth. As a legislator in 1948 he had said, "Segregation of the races is proper and the only practical and correct way of life. . . . I have always so believed and I shall always so act." Some of his judicial decisions had reaffirmed these beliefs. Nixon's advisers warned him that Carswell did not have a chance. The President nonetheless persisted until early April, when the Senate defeated him again, this time rejecting Carswell, 51 to 45. Pursuing the Southern Strategy to the end, Nixon called a press conference and stoutly defended his nominees. "When you strip away all the hypocrisy," he said, "the real reason for their rejection was their legal philosophy . . . and also the accident of their birth, the fact that they were born in the South."

Busing as a Tool

Having made his case, Nixon then nominated Harry Blackmun, a moderate from Minnesota, to the opening. The Court, however, persisted in pursuing a liberal course on matters of race. In March 1971 it rendered the *Griggs* decision that toughened affirmative action guidelines. A month later it decided, again unanimously, in favor of county-wide court-ordered busing of students in and around Charlotte, North Carolina, as a means of achieving desegregation in the schools. The decision affected 107 schools and many thousands of students, of whom 29 percent were black. Many liberals were delighted, hoping that busing would compensate for racially separate housing patterns. Busing indeed helped Charlotte to maintain one of the most desegregated school districts in the nation.

Elsewhere, however, court-mandated busing became one of the most controversial issues of the 1970s, provoking passionately contested reactions, especially in the North. Many of those who protested busing had moved to all-white or mostly white neighborhoods in part to ensure that their children would not have to go to class with lower-class blacks. (Some wanted to avoid blacks of any class.) Cherishing the creed of "neighborhood schools," they were outraged that judges and government bureaucrats—some of them people without children in the public schools—were telling them what to do. Indeed, the majority of Americans rejected court-ordered busing, damning it as a desperate and divisive approach to complicated problems. A Gallup poll in October 1971 revealed that whites opposed busing by a ratio of 3 to 1. Even black people disapproved, by a margin of 47 percent to 45 percent. The issue of "forced" busing, already volatile before 1971, enormously abetted public backlash thereafter, fomenting violence in Boston and other cities.

Nixon was philosophically opposed to court-ordered busing. Moreover, he was quick to recognize the political advantage of catering to popular resistance. For these reasons he clamped down hard when officials in HEW and the Department of Justice tried to hasten desegregation. He wrote [John] Ehrlichman, "I want you personally to jump" on those departments "and tell them to *Knock off this crap*. I hold them . . . accountable to keep their left wingers in step with my express policy—Do what the law requires and not *one bit more*." Publicly, he declared his determination to "hold busing to the minimum required by law." Congress, he said, should "expressly prohibit the expenditure" for school desegregation of "any . . . funds for busing." In March 1972 he called for a moratorium on all new busing orders by federal courts until legal issues, then under appeal, could be resolved. Vigorous opposition to court-ordered busing became a main theme of his campaign for re-election in 1972.

Nixon's stand helped to tie up efforts for court-ordered busing between 1971 and 1974. Meanwhile, the retirements in late 1971 of Supreme Court justices John Marshall Harlan and Hugo Black enabled the President to add two more judges of his choice to the Court. His nominees were Assistant Attorney General William Rehnquist, a Goldwater Republican, and Lewis Powell, a Virginia attorney who had been president of the American Bar Association. Both were confirmed, thereby pushing the ideological bent of the Court to the right.

The Civil Rights Movement Loses Momentum

In 1973 and 1974, with popular feeling high against busing, the new Court rendered two key decisions that gladdened conservatives and depressed liberals. In the first in 1973, *San Antonio Independent School District v. Rodriguez,* the Court affirmed by a vote of 5 to 4 the widespread American practice of local financing of schools—a practice that resulted in large disparities in per student spending. The "right" to an education, the judges said in rejecting Mexican-American complaints, was not guaranteed by the Constitution. The second, *Milliken v. Bradley,* was announced less than a month before Nixon left office in August 1974. It involved schools in Detroit and its suburbs and was also decided by a vote of 5 to 4. In this case, as in the *Rodriguez* decision, all four of Nixon's appointees were with the majority. The judges overruled a lower court ruling in 1971 that had ordered the merging of school districts so as to promote metropolitan desegregation of predominantly black Detroit and fifty-three suburban districts, most of them white-dominated, outside the city. The suburban districts, [Chief Justice Warren] Burger reasoned, had not willfully segregated or violated the Constitution. District lines, therefore, could be sustained, separating Detroit from its environs.

The *Milliken* decision was pivotal in the postwar history of race relations, for it badly hurt whatever hopes reformers still maintained of overturning de facto segregation of the schools and of slowing a dynamic that was accelerating in many American urban areas: "white flight" of families to suburbs. Flight in turn eroded urban tax bases, further damaging schools and other services in the cities. A "white noose" was tightening around places like Detroit. Justice Thurgood Marshall, appalled by the Court's decision, declared, "Unless our children begin to learn together, there is little hope that our people will ever learn to live together. . . . In the short run it may seem to be the easier course to allow our great metropolitan areas to be divided up into two cities—one white, the other black—but it is a course, I predict, our people will ultimately reject. I dissent."

Marshall was prophetic about the further racial polarization of urban areas in the future. Many black ghettos grew even more desperate, virtually isolating an "underclass" that lived there. By 1974, however, the judges were hardly alone in abandoning ghettos to their fate. The *Milliken* decision reflected the backlash that had grown since the mid-1960s and that Nixon, Mitchell, and others in his administration had done much to stimulate. For these reasons the cause of racial desegregation continued to stall in the early 1970s. Black leaders who seemed threatening, such as the Black Panthers, were silenced, sometimes violently. Other black leaders remained divided and demoralized. The civil rights revolution, which had inspired grand expectations in the 1960s, reeled on the defensive in the 1970s and thereafter.

The Creation of Magnet Schools and Integration

Christine H. Rossell

Christine H. Rossell has extensively studied school desegregation. This selection gives a brief history of court decisions and plans used in various schools to reach the goal of racial integration. In the early '70s, forced busing of students from one area of a city to another was the preferred method of integration. Busing was hated by many people for various reasons: costs, time wasted, and particularly the fact that federal courts were dictating to local school districts what to do and how to do it. Later in the '70s, the courts began to approve plans that emphasized magnet schools. Such schools offered special programs to entice students from the whole school district, making racial integration more palatable.

From a legal standpoint, black Americans have voting rights and equal access to public accommodations. Discrimination in housing, employment, and education is illegal. Indeed, the entire framework of legalized discrimination has been swept away. At the very heart of this transition in the legal basis of American race relations and the status of black Americans is the *Brown v. Board of Education* decision of 1954. It is hard to find an intellectual who does not revere the *Brown* decision. Even J. Harvie

Wilkinson, a leading conservative in the Reagan administration's Justice Department, writes, "No single decision has had more moral force than *Brown;* few struggles have been morally more significant than the one for racial integration of American life."

The impact of the *Brown* decision has been far wider than school desegregation. Indeed, shortly after this decree federal courts at all levels were citing *Brown* in cases challenging different forms of official segregation. Against segregated beaches in Baltimore, golf courses in Atlanta, and public housing in Michigan and Missouri, *Brown* was invoked again and again to show that state-sanctioned segregation must be expunged from the laws. *Brown* eliminated the status of black Americans as "official pariahs." It set forth, as a goal of the American people, the elimination of discrimination and thus of segregation.

School Desegregation Begins in the North

The means by which this would be accomplished, however, continued to evolve over the next four decades. From 1954 to 1970 desegregation was largely token and voluntary throughout the United States. In the North, desegregation was accomplished through political rather than legal demands because no northern states had segregation laws— the few that had had them in the past had abolished them after the Civil War. The demand for school desegregation in the North, of course, generated serious political conflicts. In each case the outcome depended on the political power of the various groups involved: the black civil rights leaders, black and white elected officials, the school board, the school superintendent and administration, the mayor, the civic elite, and black and white "grass roots" organizations. The demand might be in the form of a letter, a demonstration at a school board meeting, or a lawsuit, and it could be made by black parents of children attending an overcrowded school, a civil rights group, or a group of white parents whose children attended a racially changing school.

In the early 1960s, when demands for school desegregation were first being made in the North, most "professional" school administrators believed that desegregation was not a proper or a necessary function of the schools. First, they argued that school segregation was a function of segregated neighborhoods "freely" chosen by whites and blacks. Second, they claimed that desegregation placed an unreasonable burden upon the schools because it was a purely social, not educational, program.

Thus, desegregation in the North began as a bitter conflict over the proper role of the schools, with both sides seeing themselves as advocates of moral right. The American school system had had a long history of pretending to resist the intrusion of politics and interest groups in the pursuit of a universal, high-quality public education in which all students are treated the same regardless of their community, class, or social origin. School administrators argued that the role of the schools was to educate, not to remedy social ills created by the private actions of individuals in the larger society. In response, civil rights leaders accused the school systems of narrow-mindedness and racism.

The outcome of this conflict in the North was the same as in the South—the school districts did nothing or at most instituted a freedom-of-choice plan voluntary in nature, small in scope, and burdensome only to the black children willing to travel long distances at their own expense in order to reap its benefits. In the North these plans were called "majority-to-minority" desegregation plans. A child could transfer from any school in which his or her race was in the majority to any school in which his or her race was in the minority. Significant numbers of black students—as much as 25 percent of the black student population in a school district—got on a bus at their own expense to go to a white school across town because their parents believed what most Americans believe: that education is a means of upward mobility.

School Desegregation Begins in the South

Desegregation in the South during this period consisted of court-approved "choice" plans, some very similar in concept to the northern plans. They took three forms: pupil-placement laws, freedom-of-choice plans, and "incremental desegregation" plans. Pupil-placement laws initially assigned students to the schools designated for their race. Requests for transfers were then considered on an individual basis, in light of various "nonracial" factors. These included the "psychological effect" on the student of attending the requested school, the "psychological qualification" of the student for the curriculum at the requested school, the possibility of disruption within the school, and the possibility of protest or economic retaliation by whites against blacks in the community. Little desegregation was accomplished by these plans. Because the initial assignment was on the basis of race, the courts began in the early 1960s to find them unconstitutional.

School authorities then replaced pupil-placement laws with freedom-of-choice plans. Most of these plans required every pupil to exercise a choice at the beginning of each school year, thus eliminating the automatic initial assignment of pupils to schools for their race. Although a pupil's choice could be denied only on grounds of overcrowding, the actual number of black students enrolling in desegregated schools was minuscule. A Student Non-Violent Coordinating Committee 1965 report explains why:

> One of the easiest ways for school boards to comply . . . is to adopt a so-called "freedom-of-choice" plan. The method is simple . . . get a few Negroes to sign up to attend white schools, and then let the local citizens "encourage" them to withdraw their applications. An even better way is to reject all Negro applicants because of overcrowding, bad character, improper registration, or any other excuses. . . . But, if by chance a few Negroes slip through—go directly to the parents' employers or the local welfare agent.

Virginia relied on its state pupil-placement board to keep integration to a minimum. The state board assigned all pupils to schools in accordance with three criteria that could be used to keep black students out of white schools:

1. Orderly administration of the public schools.
2. Competent instruction of the pupils enrolled.
3. Health, safety, education and general welfare of the pupils.

As a result of such tactics, almost 94 percent of southern black students were still in all-black schools in 1965. Consequently, the Office for Civil Rights (OCR) collaborated with the Justice Department in tightening up guidelines for freedom-of-choice plans. The mechanics of the choice process were broken down into 25 "problem areas." One area involved the method of making choice forms available to black parents. Typically the forms were sent home with students. Parents were often afraid to have their child bring a form back to his or her principal that indicated that he or she wished to transfer to another school. In some districts black teachers were pressured to select black schools for their black students. In order to solve these problems, OCR created a new requirement that forms must be mailed to parents from school headquarters and parents must be permitted to return the forms by mail. Still the plans did not desegregate.

The *Green* Decision

It was that fact that caused the Supreme Court finally to bite the bullet in 1968 in *Green v. County School Board of New Kent County [Virginia]*. Although *Green* is much less well known than *Brown*, current debates over race and schools probably owe their intellectual origins to *Green*, not *Brown*, because it was in *Green* that the Court finally decided that eliminating racial discrimination was not enough to establish a unitary system (that is, a system in which there were no white schools and no Negro schools, but "just schools"). The actual requirement was not "just schools," but schools that were racially mixed to a greater degree than would occur merely as a result of ending discrimination.

Green thus marked the end of the period of "nondiscrimination" remedies and began the period of "affirmative action" remedies. Plans were not only to be judged by their effects, but it was assumed a priori after *Green* that the most effective plan would be one that *required* black

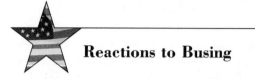

Reactions to Busing

While a majority of Americans in the 1970s began to support school integration, they hesitated to support busing.

It is offensive to American ideals that a person, because of his or her birth, should be assigned to a slum school with antique facilities, an atmosphere of violence, a weak academic program, and a teaching force that has lost all hope. It is offensive whether the reason for the assignment is that the person is Black, or that the mother of the family must support four children without the help of the father, or that the family recently emigrated from a peasant background and speaks broken English. But it is also offensive if the reason for assignment to the slum school is to achieve racial balance, if being born in a suburb would have kept the student from being so assigned. The difference is that, in some circumstances, considerations of equal treatment may balance that offensiveness for the judiciary that must remedy the effects of segregation.

It is also offensive to American ideals that members of one race should be treated as social lepers, as contaminating whatever school they are in and turning it into a slum school. Any public act that implicitly or explicitly concedes to White people the right to treat Black people as a contamination, to be bottled up so as not to infect the student bodies of safely White schools, is rightly seen as an intolerable exercise of racist sentiment. But it is nearly as offensive to use White children as merely a means, as an inoculation against racial insults, by substantially lengthening their school day by busing them for no apparent educational advantage to themselves though the administrative, legal, and social benefits of busing may sometimes make such a policy judicially worthwhile.

Arthur L. Stinchcombe and D. Garth Taylor, "On Democracy and School Integration," in *School Desegregation: Past, Present, and Future*, 1980.

and white students to transfer from their formerly one-race schools to opposite-race schools. This conclusion was drawn on the basis of empirical observation by the Court that forbidding discrimination and allowing voluntary transfer plans had not dismantled the dual system of black and white schools. As the Court noted of the two-school New Kent County system:

> The New Kent School Board's "freedom-of-choice" plan cannot be accepted as a sufficient step to "effectuate a transition" to a unitary system. In three years of operation not a single white child has chosen to attend Watkins school and although 115 Negro children enrolled in New Kent school in 1967 (up from 35 in 1965 and 111 in 1966) 85% of the Negro children in the system still attend the all-Negro Watkins school. In other words, the school system remains a dual system.

No Incremental Desegregation

Green was followed by *Alexander v. Holmes* which prohibited incremental desegregation, including grade-a-year plans and other proposals that delayed desegregation. Grade-a-year plans are phased so that one additional grade is added to the plan each year. For example, the first year's plan might begin by desegregating 12th grade; the second year's plan would add the 11th grade, so that 11th and 12th grades were desegregated; and so forth. A grade-a-year plan might also start with the lowest grade and work its way up. Regardless of the starting point, such plans could take up to 12 years to be fully implemented.

Alexander put an end to delayed desegregation plans, forcing the district courts to order immediate massive desegregation in the middle of the school year for all school boards in active litigation in the Fifth Circuit. Between 1970 and 1971 the public schools of the Deep South were substantially integrated by court orders based almost exclusively on segregation statistics.

The Fifth Circuit carefully avoided using loaded terms

like "busing" and "racial balancing." Nevertheless, extensive transportation was required in most of these cases solely on a showing of insufficient racial mixing in the local schools. Although the court was silent on the extent of permissible remedies, these plans usually included the pairing or clustering of schools and the redrawing of attendance zones. In a typical pairing of a K–5 black school and a K–5 white school (that is, schools with kindergartens and grades one through five), all students would go to the white school for grades K to 2 and to the black school for grades 3 to 5. In a three-school clustering, all students would typically go to one school for grades K and 1, another school for grades 2 and 3, and a third school for grades 4 and 5. These plans also included the redrawing of attendance zones so that some schools were integrated while continuing to have contiguous attendance areas.

Swann Gives Specific Suggestions

Plan characteristics were not specified in *Green* or *Alexander*. Nor was the degree of integration that would have to be achieved or any deviation that might be allowed in individual cases. The school districts simply did what was necessary to achieve court approval of their plans, and that usually meant adopting the plaintiff's plan. It was not until *Swann v. Charlotte-Mecklenburg Board of Education* in 1971 that the Supreme Court specifically addressed the issue of permissible remedies. *Swann* represented an innovation in the determination of both violation and remedy. The Court found that a school board that had racially motivated institutional practices, such as locating black schools in the middle of black neighborhoods and creating segregated feeder patterns, was guilty of de jure segregation even when the state segregation law had long since been rescinded. This finding foreshadowed the beginning of findings of unconstitutional segregation in the North. The major permissible remedies discussed in *Swann* were: (1) racial balance; (2) nondiscriminatory one-race schools; (3) altering of attendance zones, and pairing, clustering, or grouping of schools; and (4) transportation of students out of their neighborhood to another school in the district.

With regard to racial balance—the extent to which each school must reflect the racial composition of the school district—the Supreme Court held that mathematical ratios were permissible but not required. It found no constitutional requirement to have every school in every community reflect the racial composition of the school system as a whole, although that was "a useful starting point in shaping a remedy."

One-race schools are not unconstitutional per se, but the burden in a previously de jure segregated school system is on the school authorities to show that "such school assignments are genuinely nondiscriminatory." With regard to the pairing of schools and altering of attendance zones, these and other techniques were to be judged by their results. They are permissible if they desegregate schools, even if they are "administratively awkward, inconvenient, and even bizarre in some situations and may impose burdens on some."

Busing—the transportation of students from one part of the district to a school in another part of the district to achieve desegregation—was a permissible tool for dismantling a dual system where "feasible." Although the Court declined to provide any specific guidelines for future cases, it did state that busing was to be limited by considerations of time and distances, avoiding plans that would "either risk the health of the children or significantly impinge on the educational process." In one court case the time limit was defined as anything over 45 minutes; in another it was a bus ride of two and one-half hours per day for 1st- and 2nd-graders. In 1977 the federal district court in Los Angeles, California, allowed busing distances taking an hour each way.

No Passive School Segregation

The principal question after *Swann* was whether—or, more realistically, when and how—the requirement of racial balance would be extended to racially imbalanced school systems outside the South. The question was answered in 1973 when, in *Keyes v. School District No. 1, Denver, Colorado,* the first "northern" case to reach the Supreme Court, the Court found the requirement of racially balanced schools applicable to a school district that had never had a law mandating segregated schools. The Court still could not bring itself to state openly that it interpreted the Constitution as requiring integration. It continued to insist that the only requirement was the elimination of de jure segregation. However, de jure segregation was defined as encompassing almost any action a school board might take that resulted in racially imbalanced schools. Under *Keyes,* when intentionally segregative actions are found to have affected a "substantial portion of the schools," the burden of proof shifts to the defendant. The failure to desegregate a segregated school, even when that segregation results from neighborhood segregation and private acts of discrimination, is then seen as intentional segregation unless the school district can prove otherwise. In short, the concept of de jure segregation soon became so all-inclusive that it was almost impossible for a northern school district accused of de jure segregation to defend itself.

Forced Busing as a Tool

As a result of these decisions, mandatory reassignment or "forced busing" plans were implemented all over the United States between 1970 and 1976. They were accompanied by protest demonstrations, white flight, and, ironically, a reduction in racial prejudice. Indeed, if one focuses on racial attitudes, the end appears to justify the means. . . .

In *Arthur v. Nyquist* [1976], the federal district court found the school board of Buffalo, New York, guilty of intentional segregation. In a second, unpublished decision, the court approved implementation of a plan that relied primarily on magnet schools in black neighborhoods and on majority-to-minority transfers to white schools to desegregate the elementary schools (grades K–8). In *Amos v. Board of Directors of the City of Milwaukee,* the federal district court found the Milwaukee school board guilty of intentional segregation and, in a series of subsequent decisions, approved a plan similar to Buffalo's that relied primarily on magnet schools to desegregate black schools and on majority-to-minority transfers to desegregate white schools. This decision was followed by court-approved magnet school plans in other school districts, such as San Diego, California, Houston, Texas, and San Bernardino, California, and was preceded by modest magnet school plans adopted by school boards in predominantly white school systems in the West, such as Tacoma, Washington, and Portland, Oregon.

The courts have also allowed mandatory plans to be dismantled and replaced with magnet school plans. In 1988 in Savannah-Chatham County, Georgia, a federal district court approved the dismantling of the mandatory assignment plan implemented in 1970 and 1971 after *Alexander*. The court opinion gave the following reason:

> During the first year [of the 1971 mandatory reassignment plan], approximately forty-two percent of all white students assigned to a black receiving school failed to enroll in the school to which they had been assigned mandatorily. This "white flight" continued over the years as the school district, which had been a majority white district prior to the 1971 plan, became predominantly black. It became increasingly clear that the mandatory plan under which the school system had been operating since 1971 was unsuccessful in eliminating the last vestiges of the prior dual system and in achieving a unitary system in compliance with the mandates of the Court.

The mandatory assignment plan was ordered to be replaced by a magnet school plan with three essential features: (1) "revised attendance zones designed to maximize desegregation through emphasis on a neighborhood school assignment plan"; (2) "magnet programs at eleven predominantly black inner city schools in order to desegregate those schools"; and (3) "a majority-to-minority transfer option to desegregate predominantly white schools." In approving the school district's primarily voluntary plan based on magnets and majority-to-minority transfers, the court stated that "the law does not require that a desegregation plan be mandatory in any way, only that it be effective."

Coming Full Circle?

Thus, we see desegregation remedies coming full circle. The first desegregation plans after *Brown* relied on the voluntary transfer of students. These plans did not desegregate school systems, either because blacks were intimidated from transferring to white schools or because, when they attempted to transfer, they were told there was no room for them. As a result, in 1968 the courts began to approve only plans that relied on mandatory reassignment, using such techniques as pairing and clustering and the redrawing of attendance zones.

The court opinions did, however, occasionally point out that voluntary plans per se were not unconstitutional. In *Green* the Supreme Court held: "'Freedom-of-choice' is not a sacred talisman; it is only a means to a constitutionally required end—the abolition of the system of segregation and its effects. If the means prove effective, it is acceptable, but if it fails to undo segregation, other means must be used to achieve this end." In *Swann* the Court held that "an optional majority-to-minority transfer provision has long been recognized as a useful part of every desegregation plan. . . . In order to be effective, such a transfer arrangement must grant the transferring student free transportation and space must be made available in the school to which he desires to move." Thus, voluntary plans and other plans involving race-neutral assignment policies were to be evaluated in terms of their results. Where freedom of choice offers a real promise of achieving a unitary, nonracial system, there should be no objection to allowing it to prove itself in action.

What appears to have changed since 1968 is not the courts' willingness to approve "unworkable" voluntary plans, but their opinion as to whether such plans might work. The growing belief that voluntary plans *can* work is founded on a number of remarkable social changes that have occurred in the intervening years: (1) the overwhelming acceptance by whites of racial integration of the schools; (2) the overwhelming rejection by whites of "forced busing" to achieve this; (3) the public perception of continuing white flight from mandatory reassignment plans; and (4) the creation of magnet school plans that appear to provide an incentive for whites to act in accordance with both their self-interest and their support of integration. The belief on the part of the courts and school district policymakers that magnet plans might work, however, is a relative judgment based on a comparison of voluntary plans with mandatory plans that seemed not to work because they gave whites no incentive to comply.

The Struggle for Black Equality

Harvard Sitkoff

The mid- to late 1960s was a time of racial tensions but also a time of major progress toward racial equality. After the death of Martin Luther King Jr., the civil rights movement continued, but it lacked unity and clear direction. Harvard Sitkoff gives a list of areas in which progress was being made in the 1970s: the number of blacks elected to office, higher levels of education for blacks, and increases in income for some blacks. He also lists a number of troubling issues in the '70s: an alienation of blacks from the political process, continuing segregation in many schools, and declining economic opportunities for some blacks.

In a gloomy, troubled mood, Afro-Americans thus entered the next to last decade of the twentieth century. A quarter of a century after *Brown*, the United States remained a deeply divided and unequal society. The black struggle had brought significant changes. It achieved substantial progress. Black America in 1980 was radically different from what it had been in 1954. Yet the full promise of the civil-rights revolution was unrealized. Prejudice, discrimination, and segregation, both subtle and blatant, continued to poison social relations. Neither the franchise nor the demolition of legal racism had resulted in equality or justice. The ghetto was still a time bomb, its people social dynamite. Despite all that the movement had accomplished, the hardest and most paramount tasks lay ahead.

"Anyone looking for the civil-rights movement in the streets is fooling himself. Politics is the civil-rights movement of the 1970s," said the black mayor of Atlanta. "Politics is our first hurrah. It's where things are today." Indeed, the right to vote and the opportunity to hold public office has been one of the most visible changes in Afro-American life since *Brown*; more than a symbol of first-class citizenship, political participation has also produced important, tangible gains for blacks. Fewer than one in four adult blacks in the South could register to vote in 1954; over two-thirds were on the voting lists in 1970. Because of that turnabout, white officials found their traditional race-baiting rhetoric and practices no longer politically profitable. A onetime militant segregationist, Senator Strom Thurmond of South Carolina quickly realized the political wisdom of sending his child to a desegregated school. Even George Wallace saw the light. The former leader of Alabama's white supremacist forces appointed blacks to high state positions, crowned a black homecoming queen at the very university he had once sworn to deny to black students, and in 1979 sat on the podium applauding the inaugural remarks of Birmingham's first black mayor. By 1980, Mississippi, the state that had most violently and thoroughly resisted the civil-rights movement, claimed more black officeholders than any other state.

The number of black elected public officials in the South rose from fewer than a hundred in the year of the Voting Rights Act to some 500 in 1970, 1,600 in 1975, and nearly 2,500 in 1980. Equally impressive, the national total jumped from 300 in 1965, to 1,400 in 1970, 3,000 in 1975, and 4,700 in 1980. The number of black mayors of towns and cities leaped from none in 1965 to eighty in 1970 and to 120 in 1980, including Atlanta, Dayton, Gary, Detroit, Los Angeles, New Orleans, Newark, Richmond, and Washington, D.C. In the main, cities with black mayors spent more per capita for education and social services, and directed a higher proportion of their budgets toward the needs of the disadvantaged, than those headed by whites. Black mayors, overall, also did more than their white counterparts to establish affirmative-action programs in municipal agencies and to enforce a less biased, less brutal, law-enforcement system. The slightly over one thousand blacks who served on city councils and in the state legislatures in 1980 had a similarly incremental yet important effect on policies and priorities.

At the national level, blacks held eighteen seats in Congress in the late 1970s. They had held none between 1901 and 1928, only one in the following fifteen years, and just two between the end of the Second World War and *Brown*. In 1970, the congressional black caucus was established. Augmenting its presence were scores of blacks in sub-Cabinet-level leadership positions and in highly visible offices filled by the President. By the end of the decade, Carter had appointed two black Cabinet officers, two black ambassadors to the UN, a half dozen black ambassadors to foreign countries, a black Solicitor General, a black Secretary of the Army, a host of black United States attorneys and United States marshals, and numerous black justices to the federal district courts and the United States courts of appeals.

"You don't have to demonstrate when you can pick up a phone and call someone," claimed Andrew Young. Yet politics has not proved a panacea. It has not changed the basic inequalities between blacks and whites. Excessive black loyalty to one political party has been fatal. The Democrats take black votes for granted and do not adequately reward them. Yet, given the steady rightward drift of the Republicans, few blacks conceive the GOP to be a viable alternative. Blacks, moreover, remain on the fringe of national politics. Despite impressive gains, blacks held fewer than one percent of the nation's half a million elective offices in 1980, and just three percent of them in the South, where they constituted 20 percent of the population. Over half the hundred counties in the South with majority black populations still had no elected black officials. Whites in power there used all manner of subtle disenfranchising devices to sap black political strength.

Blacks, nationwide, participated in politics more infrequently than whites. Some explained this as a consequence of poverty; the poor, regardless of color, vote less than the middle and upper classes. Others thought it was due to black alienation from the political system. Still others considered it a legacy of past exclusion, when blacks became conditioned not to vote or join political organizations. Whatever the reasons, blacks in the 1970s engaged in less political activity than whites. Just one half of the 14 million blacks who could have voted bothered to register in 1972. Two years later, only a third of those eligible voted in the congressional elections. Barely 42 percent of voting-age blacks went to the polls in 1976, compared to a national turnout of 55 percent of eligible voters, and even fewer sought to exercise their franchise in 1980. Most important, black politics has not provided jobs for the jobless, adequate housing and health care for the poor, or quality integrated schooling. In Greene County, Alabama, where blacks control the entire political structure, the average black family income is about $2,500. Seventy percent of black homes in rural Alabama have no indoor flush toilet. Despite a black mayor and a phalanx of black officials, Newark in 1980 remains as spiritually and physically dilapidated as it was in 1967. Although the blacks in South Carolina constitute a quarter of the population—and are well represented politically—over half are in the most menial and lowest-paying jobs, and fewer than 5 percent are in managerial or professional positions. Atlanta and Detroit, with its official posts heavily black, have few jobs for their black youth and the highest unemployment rate for adult blacks in the country.

More black students attended segregated schools in 1980 than at the time of *Brown*. Only in the South has there been some progress. The passage of the Civil Rights Act of 1964 and the Elementary and Secondary Education Act of 1965, combined with an increasingly tougher stance by the federal courts and government officials responsible for implementing desegregation guidelines, brought significant results below the Mason-Dixon line. The proportion of Southern blacks in desegregated schools rose from 2 percent in 1964 to 14 percent in 1966, 16 percent in 1967, 20 percent in 1968, and 58 percent in 1970. The following year, President Nixon warned federal officials to stop pressing for desegregation or find other jobs. Two years later, the Supreme Court began its about-face by barring the busing of Virginia schoolchildren across city-suburban lines. Resegregation commenced. White flight to the suburbs, tracking, segregated private academies, and segregated church schools resulted once again in fewer than half the black students in the South attending desegregated schools in 1980. Significantly, much of the South's integration is rural. In Southern cities, where the population is growing, the late 1970s witnessed rapidly decreasing desegregation. The urban South appeared more and more similar to its Northern counterpart, where over two-thirds of the blacks went to schools at least 90 percent black. The absence of any considerable move toward residential desegregation, the refusal of the courts to order busing to eliminate de facto segregation, and the rejection by virtually every white suburb of suggestions to redraw attendance zones across school districts in order to foster integration, insured the continuance of the trend toward greater racial isolation in education.

Striking changes did come in the educational levels of blacks. Although sometimes of questionable quality, black schooling has steadily increased in quantity since *Brown*. Then, about 75 percent of blacks aged five to nineteen were enrolled in school. Over 95 percent were in 1980. The median school years completed by blacks aged twenty-five to twenty-nine rose from 8.6 in 1954 (3.5 years fewer than whites), to 10.8 in 1960 (about 2.5 years fewer than whites), to 12.7 in 1972 (only .4 of one year less than whites). In 1980, about 75 percent of black students were finishing high school, compared to 85 percent for whites. Two decades earlier, only some 40 percent of young blacks finished high school. In addition, 20 percent of blacks aged eighteen to twenty-four enrolled in college in 1980, compared to 26 percent for whites. The percentage of black high-school graduates going to college (31.5 percent) had nearly caught up with that of whites (32.2 percent). In 1954, 75,000 blacks attended college; 234,000 did so in 1963; about a half million, 7 percent of the total college population, attended in 1970; and over a million blacks did so in 1977, constituting 10 percent of the total college enrollment. This substantial progress was due largely to the increased availability of financial aid, the growth of community colleges, and greater access to predominantly white universities. Where 82 percent of black college students in the South enrolled in all-black institutions in 1965, 43 percent did in 1976. Still, at the end of the 1970s, blacks lagged considerably behind whites in graduating from college and being awarded baccalaureate degrees. Nearly six of ten black college students went to two-year rather than four-year institutions of higher education in 1980.

Perhaps the least change of all since *Brown* came in residential segregation. Despite court rulings and legislation outlawing racial discrimination in housing, such discrimination persisted. The index of residential segregation rose in nearly every American city between 1960 and 1980. Whites of every class continued to resist housing integration if it involved anything other than token numbers of blacks. Twelve percent of the population, blacks in 1980 accounted for less than 6 percent of the suburban population, barely an increase of 2 percent in more than twenty years. And most black suburbanites lived in all-black suburbs, usually the older, run-down industrial suburbs deserted by whites. The majority of America's 25 million blacks in 1980 had been confined to the inner cities of a score of metropolitan areas, mainly Atlanta, Baltimore, Chicago, Cleveland, Detroit, Los Angeles, Newark, New Orleans, New York, Philadelphia, St. Louis, and Washington, D.C., fulfilling the prophesy, and not heeding the warning, of the National Advisory Commission on Civil Disorders in 1968: "Our nation is moving toward two societies, one black, one white—separate and unequal."

Two unequal societies also developed within the black cities: a black middle class struggling to move upward or to maintain a tenuous grip on their precarious new status, and a sinking, permanent black underclass mired in poverty and despair. Those who justified a diminution of public and private efforts to end racial inequality overemphasized the extent of progress made by the black middle class and obscured the magnitude of the predicament of those left behind. They trumpeted the news of the absolute gains in the number of jobs for blacks, of the decline of the percentage of black families below the poverty line, and of the narrowing of the income gap between black and white workers, especially female wage earners. They made much of the proliferation of blacks in well-paying positions and in occupations never before open to them.

A far different picture, and a more accurate gauge of black economic progress, emerges from the statistics on median family income. In 1954, black families earned approximately 53 percent of what white families did. It gradually inched up to 60 percent in 1969, then to 62 percent in 1975. But it plummeted to 57 percent in 1979. Blacks had gained four percentage points in a quarter of a century. At that rate, racial equality in family income would come in 250 years. Median income in 1979 stood at $9,242 for black families and $16,740 for white families. Undeterred by this dismal prognosis, critics of plans for programs by the federal government to correct the imbalance argued the need to factor out of these all-inclusive national averages anomalies based on age, geography, and sex. They preferred to stress the fact that stable black families in the North earned incomes nearly equal to those of whites. That was true. But such families constituted a minority of black families, and a dwindling minority at that.

Blacks did earn less in the South, both absolutely and relative to whites, than in the North. In 1975, when the national median income for all black families was $8,779, 62 percent of that for whites, the same amount in the South was $7,696, 59 percent of that earned by Southern white families. But half the blacks in the country lived in the South in 1980, and that percentage is not slackening. "Freedomland" lost its luster in the 1970s, and for the first time in the twentieth century blacks reversed the pattern of migration from South to North. The Northern states experienced a net loss of 64,000 blacks between 1970 and 1975, and 104,000 between 1975 and 1977. Similarly, the black working population is proportionately younger than the white, and younger workers earn less than older ones, thus further depressing the overall median earning of blacks; and there is little likelihood of that trend changing in the near future. In 1970, the median age for white Americans was twenty-eight years and 21.2 for blacks, and the greater fertility rate for blacks in the seventies promises a still greater differential. Add to that the fact that lower family income necessitates more blacks entering the job market at an earlier age than whites, and the probability of blacks narrowing the income gap dims appreciably.

The dramatic increase in one-parent black families affected the relative economic decline of blacks more than any other factor. While the proportion of white families with more than one wage earner rose steadily in the seventies, the proportion of such black families decreased from 57 percent in 1969 to 46 percent in 1979. While the proportion of white families headed by a woman has hovered at about 10 percent since 1965, the comparable figures for blacks jumped from 23.7 percent that year to 34 percent in 1974, 37 percent in 1976, and 40 percent in 1980. A devastating half of all one-parent black families lived below the poverty line in 1978, compared to fewer than a third of such white families. Most important, nearly two-thirds of all black families living in poverty were headed by women, and the number of those families continues to soar, as does the number of children in such families. One in three blacks lived in poverty in 1980, compared to one in ten whites, and in all likelihood the number of black poor, both absolute and relative to whites, will mushroom.

The Watergate Crisis

Harold Evans

Harold Evans has written a number of books about American popular culture, particularly as seen through the media. In this selection, Evans points out that President Nixon's administration was marked by suspicion and secrecy. In 1972, Nixon's friends and personal staff were working hard to win Nixon's reelection. As part of their efforts, they broke into the Democratic Party offices in the Watergate building to get information. When the burglars were arrested, the White House tried to cover up the facts.

Watergate did not proceed out of any rational political calculation, but directly—and inevitably—from the twisted, paranoid psyche of Richard Nixon. That was not all there was to Nixon. His supporters, to take Haldeman's metaphor, saw a brighter side of the multifaceted quartz crystal: a man of high intelligence and original mind, gifted with strategic vision, industrious, a friend of the arts, protective of those he loved, a man with the fortitude to stand up for America and the coolest of judgments in a crisis; in October 1973 at the nadir of his struggle over the tapes he mediated in the Yom Kippur war with daring foresight.

But in Watergate it was the dark side of the crystal that caught the light.

The details of the mystery famously encapsulated in Senator Howard Baker's hammerlock question "What did the

Excerpted from *The American Century*, by Harold Evans. Copyright ©1998 by Harold Evans. Reprinted with permission from Alfred A. Knopf, Inc.

President know and when did he know it?" are in an important sense irrelevant. Nixon probably did not know that soon after midnight on June 17, 1972, four Cubans and an ex-CIA man wearing sunglasses and surgical gloves were going to break into the headquarters of the Democratic National Committee (DNC) at the Watergate hotel complex. But Nixon had set these and other malefactors in motion as certainly as if he had wound up a set of clockwork soldiers. His churning emotions, his habits of isolation, his appetite for the covert, his impatience with "bureaucratic" procedures and, above all, his choice of the men around him guaranteed gross legal and ethical transgressions. In the vernacular of political warfare, the attempt to replant a bug on the phone of Lawrence O'Brien, the DNC chairman, was among the lesser games. Nixon knew firsthand of the major offenses that came before the botched break-in—the "White House horrors," in the phrase of his Attorney General John Mitchell. The program of illegal wiretapping, the burglary at the offices of Daniel Ellsberg's psychiatrist, the political manipulation of the IRS, the corrupt pressure on corporate executives and labor leaders for millions of dollars in campaign money in return for executive favors, all transcend the incident at the Watergate. . . .

Nixon's Fears and Secrets

Three features characterized the administration: the nature of what they felt they needed to keep secret, the compulsive interest in other people's presumed secrets and the indiscriminate response directed at anyone who spilled the beans—or was remotely suspected of doing so. The list of suspects grew with every leak, so that fewer and fewer people were allowed to participate in policy making (on Vietnam, the number got down to seven, none of them in the cabinet). The secrecy invited penetration. Those on the outside inevitably wanted to look in. Perhaps that was all there was to the mysterious affair of Navy Yeoman Charles Radford. It was discovered in 1971 that Radford, a link between Kissinger's National Security Council and the Pentagon, had been filching highly sensitive documents from Kissinger's briefcase. He had been copying them—not for the Soviets but for the chairman of the Joint Chiefs of Staff, Admiral Thomas Moorer. It never became clear why the Chiefs thought it necessary to spy on the NSC. They resented Nixon's attempts to curb defense spending, worried about the China opening and arms talks with the Soviets. Whatever the motive, the spying from within aggravated the feeling that nobody was to be trusted.

Even before the leaks proliferated, Nixon was suspicious. One of the first things he did upon taking office was to order the FBI to bug the phones of 37 people. He had already planned a wiretapping program with Hoover, in April 1969, and Kissinger had already supplied a number of names, when the *New York Times* shook the White House on May 9, 1970. It revealed that the administration had been secretly bombing Cambodia since March 18. The intensified wiretapping program that followed was the top of the slippery slope. . . .

Political Sabotage Campaign

The grand moment that epitomized the Nixon era was on January 27, 1972, when Mitchell, still the chief law officer of the United States, sat puffing his pipe in his office in the Department of Justice, entertaining the idea of financing a vast law-breaking enterprise—on behalf of the President, who had sworn to uphold the Constitution. Liddy made the pitch to Mitchell; the President's counsel, John W. Dean III; and Jeb Magruder, a former cosmetics marketer who was deputy to Mitchell at CREEP [Committee to re-elect the President]. With the help of elaborate charts from a friendly CIA artist, the incomparable Liddy set out a $1 million program he called Gemstone. It envisaged kidnapping hostile demonstrators at the Republican convention, drugging them and dumping them over the border in Mexico; sabotaging air conditioning at the Democratic convention; hiring call girls to entrap Democrats, whose pillow talk would be bugged; staging faked demonstrations; and conducting electronic surveillance of Democratic campaign offices. As Attorney General, Mitchell ought to have arrested Liddy on the spot. Later he claimed to have been appalled, but his main problem with Gemstone seems to have been Liddy's million-dollar price tag. Liddy was allowed to go away and come back with a cheaper plan. In a meeting at Key Biscayne, Florida, on March 30, 1972, Magruder presented

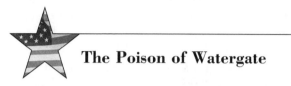

The Poison of Watergate

Charles Colson, an adviser to President Nixon, was convicted and sent to prison for his involvement in the Watergate cover-up. He tells how the Watergate crisis poisoned the atmosphere of Washington for months.

Now Watergate's hateful venom was rushing through the veins of Washington. There was a pervasive fear, a sense of impending doom, an atmosphere of recrimination reminiscent of McCarthy days. Usually-smiling secretaries were harried and irritable. White House staffers were worried and fearful. Tempers quickly flared even among friends who could normally discuss their differing views on controversial issues with civility. The press reporting was harsh, attacks personal and bitter, political rhetoric increasingly shrill. As the debate became more rancorous, thoughts of violence were spawned in a few warped minds. The FBI was called in to investigate three bomb threats against my home and car which followed TV appearances.

The workings of government were becoming paralyzed; senior policymakers were without direction; option papers went to the White House, but no decisions were returned. There were few in Washington not absorbed in the drama being played out in the Senate Caucus Room [where the Watergate hearings were held]; TV sets were on all day in many government offices.

Charles W. Colson, *Born Again*. Old Tappan, NJ: Chosen/Fleming H. Revell, 1976.

Liddy's final plan, which included the kidnappings and the bugging of the Democrats' Watergate headquarters and their main convention hotel, the Fontainebleau in Miami Beach. Mitchell would always deny approving this. But there was clearly pressure from Haldeman and Nixon himself to approve it, and according to Magruder, Mitchell finally said, "Okay, if they say do it, go ahead." By April 1972, according to Haldeman's own records, "Gordon Liddy's intelligence operation proposal ($300[,000]) has been approved."

Break-ins at the DNC offices, supervised by Liddy and Hunt, failed farcically on May 26 and May 27, but late at night on May 28 their team succeeded. Eugenio Martinez and Bernard Barker photographed documents and James McCord and Virgilio Gonzalez planted wiretaps on the phones. It was on a return visit on June 17, to improve the sound quality, that McCord's telltale tape on a door lock led to the detection and arrest of the burglars at 2 a.m. Hunt and Liddy fled their command room in the Howard Johnson motel across the street, leaving behind them a trail of clues that suggested it was more than "a third-rate burglary," as Nixon's press secretary, Ron Ziegler, promptly made out. The clues were soon followed to the White House by the tough trial judge, John J. Sirica, chief judge of the U.S. District Court, and brilliant reporting in the *Washington Post*. But the burglars also left enduring mysteries in which the shadows of CIA spymasters and double agents, call-girl rings, stool pigeons, blackmailers, Greek colonels, Howard Hughes, an informant still known only as Deep Throat and the enigmatic figure of the 37th president mocked the seekers of a cleansing single truth.

The Cover-Up

In the words of Haldeman in his 1978 memoir, Nixon was involved in the cover-up from day one. That is an understatement. He took over personal direction of it in March 1973, but he was its driving force throughout as the press, the courts and Congress tried to unravel the implications of what the President's men had wrought. He continued the cover-up of his own role through his own memoirs and to the end of his life—and beyond. By his legal actions, thousands of hours of White House tapes and thousands of documents have remained out of the reach of scholars. What is in the unpublished material will darken or relieve the shadows; but what we know is conclusive about Nixon's active and relentless determination to obstruct justice. Nixon partisans have found this as hard to admit as he did. His talk-out was that Haldeman and Ehrlichman ordered John Dean and others to protect the wrongdoers and that when he learned all the facts he insisted on a full investigation and prosecutions. If the cover-up touched him at all, it was out of his loyalty to subordinates. Paul Johnson, the conservative author, in his 1983 book *Modern Times,* portrays Nixon as the victim of a media putsch to overturn the electoral verdict of 1972, the "imperial press" replacing the "imperial presidency." Johnson writes: "Whether Nixon was actually guilty of an attempt to interfere with the course of justice, as alleged, and whether such an attempt, if made, was covered by a legitimate interpretation of raison d'etat, was never established." In fact, Nixon operated every possible stratagem to derail the investigation. He coached grand jury witnesses in perjury about what he and his staff knew. "I don't give a shit what happens, I want you all to stonewall it, let them plead the Fifth Amendment, cover up or anything else, if it'll save it—save the plan." He doctored transcripts of such tapes, not only to remove expletives, but to change their meaning. He raised hush money for the burglars. He lied and lied about his own knowledge. He cited reports clearing the White House staff that never existed; all previous statements were "inoperative." He refused to honor subpoenas for evidence. He suppressed and altered evidence. He ordered Assistant Attorney General Henry Petersen not to investigate the Ellsberg break-in: "Keep the hell out of it!" In the "Saturday night massacre" of October 1973, he fired Archibald Cox, the special prosecutor, over the objections of Attorney General Elliott Richardson and his deputy, William Ruckelshaus, who both resigned; Cox had insisted on having tapes of White House conversations. Decisive proof of Nixon's intent was there in his own words in a taped conversation released on August 5, 1974. In this "smoking gun" tape of June 23, 1972, six days after the break-in, he conspired with Haldeman to use the CIA to back the FBI off the investigation on the false grounds that it involved national security having to do with Cuba. The 42 tapes released by the House Judiciary Committee in April 1974, the Haldeman secret diary published posthumously in 1994, the Kutler-edited tapes of 1997 and the testimony of participants give a cumulative and corroborative picture of Nixon obsessed with the cover-up. In the famous conversation of March 21, 1973, in which his counsel John Dean warns him that there's a cancer close to the presidency— the cancer of blackmail and perjury—Nixon reiterates no fewer than 13 times the importance of paying off Hunt because he knows of too many seamy things. Dean says it might need $1 million to pay off everyone. "You could get a million dollars," Nixon replies. "You could get it in cash. I know where it could be gotten." Nixon has in mind Thomas Pappas, a Greek with ties to the fascist regime of colonels who had asked him to keep a sympathetic ambassador in place. Later, Nixon and others attempted to suggest he did not really mean to pay hush money. Although Nixon did murmur, "It's wrong for sure," at the end of the March conversation, it is also clear on the tape that this is a reference to promising clemency to the malefactors. He specifically approves hush money. That night, through Mitchell, an unmarked envelope containing $75,000 was delivered to Hunt's lawyers.

The sympathetic biographer Jonathan Aitken tap-dances through all this. He concedes Nixon was "less than helpful" in assisting the course of justice, but portrays him as trapped by his treacherous counsel Dean into believing he had to do what he did to protect Mitchell. Dean was certainly a malign figure, but the person Nixon was concerned to protect was himself. Leonard Garment, Nixon's former law partner and presidential counsel in 1973, remarks in *Crazy Rhythm* (1997) that the transition from bungled break-in to cover-up took place "without even the whisper of gears shifting" precisely because Nixon's sense of personal jeopardy was so great. The break-in could have been admitted as the inspiration of overzealous campaign workers. What had to be concealed were "the other things," in Nixon's parlance, the collection of dirty tricks and illegalities he sponsored through Ehrlichman, Colson and Hunt.

Tapes of Himself Condemned Nixon

Memory telescopes the events of what Kutler calls the Age of Watergate. The roots were in the divisive dramas of the sixties. The cover-up itself lasted more than two years—from June 1972 to Nixon's resignation under fire on August 9, 1974. It might have worked. By July 1973 a great deal of damaging information had come out. But the dirty water seemed to be receding from the White House. Senator Sam Ervin's committee was running out of steam. Haldeman, Mitchell, Ehrlichman had gone. Nixon had a bushy-tailed new chief of staff in General Alexander Haig. Dean's testimony implicating Nixon in the cover-up for eight months had been damning, but it was the President's word against someone characterized by Senator Howard Baker as "a sleazy lying little sonofabitch," a stool pigeon trying to save his own skin. Nixon was in for censure from the Watergate committee, but once again he was going to survive, perhaps compensate with another dazzling coup in foreign policy. Only the chance exposure of the White House taping system by Alexander Butterfield on Monday, July 16, 1973, precipitated the President's downfall. And even then it was not assured. The hearsay case against Nixon could not have proceeded to the point of a bipartisan vote for three articles of impeachment, as it did the following summer, without the tapes themselves. He might have burned all the tapes between July 16 and July 24, 1974, when the Supreme Court rejected the argument of executive privilege and ordered him to surrender 64 conversations; and he did briefly contemplate defiance. He did not destroy the tapes, he told Monica Crowley 20 years later, because he believed there was enough on them to clear him. Knowing what he did now, would he have destroyed them? she asked. "He lowered his eyes and simply nodded his head, yes." He spared America the final act of obstruction of justice, and there was a poetic justice in the act; the wiretapper had fatally eavesdropped on himself.

No Coups...No Tanks...No Mobs

Bill Moyers

Sudden changes and unprecedented events are unsettling to everyone. In many nations, a change of leadership is often associated with riots, the army taking control of the government, or plots and assassinations. Historically, when Americans have suddenly lost a president, a certain uneasiness comes over the public atmosphere. In the following selection, Bill Moyers reflects on the peaceful process by which the Watergate crisis came to a conclusion. Despite divisions caused by party membership and ideology, the Constitution guided Americans to a solution and to a peaceful shift of power from one president to the next. Notice the sense of relief expressed by the author that Watergate was coming to a conclusion. Moyers writes this article from the context of having served on the staff of Lyndon B. Johnson, who became president after John F. Kennedy was assassinated in 1963. Since writing this article, Moyers has continued to be a well-respected author and television commentator on American culture and life.

A s Richard Nixon was saying farewell, I remembered something in my briefcase, something I had put into a folder of miscellany over a month ago, before the House Judiciary Committee hearings, before the President's admission of guilt with the release of the last tapes. It was a long excerpt from a speech by Secretary of Commerce Frederick Dent. Some headline writer had fixed on the article this echo of the White House's own (at least then) line of defense: THE WORLD CAN'T DO WITHOUT PRESIDENT NIXON.

Now the world was preparing to do just that; on the screen he was already a ghost of a President. Suddenly he was gone, and all we saw was something he couldn't take with him: the seal of the office of the President of the United States. It stays. The power is in the office, and no one takes it with him.

I found the clipping in my briefcase and read it again. Mr. Dent's argument went like this: The four-year term assures continued leadership by giving Presidents "the luxury of becoming unpopular while in office" when they feel the need to pursue a course the public temporarily disagrees with. Congress should follow the course prescribed in the Constitution, but the President should not resign, for that would "open our generation to the charge of having damaged, perhaps permanently, the government of this great nation."

Orderly Succession

Men delude themselves this way. President's men can be especially vulnerable, as if the whole history of this country were a blank to them. For nothing has proven so durable in our system as the orderly succession of the Presidency according to the constitutional process. In this century alone, it has persisted through Presidential assassination, incapacitation and incompetence; it has survived depression, wars and scandals, including now the revelation that an incumbent himself has been involved, by his own words, in obstructing justice.

All this, and no coups. No tanks surround the White House, no one gets arrested and spirited away overnight—neither the President's men nor their adversaries. No mobs take to the streets. Instead, at noon on a Friday, a man from Grand Rapids, Mich., a man rather like most of us, with no great pretensions, lifts his hand, repeats an oath now almost 200 years old and succeeds the man "the world can't do without."

Gerald Ford has never been elected to national office, but no one will go to court to say he doesn't belong there, no political faction will connive to claim his power illegitimate. Even before his swearing-in—at some incalculable moment when the people realized Richard Nixon was finished—national consensus prepared to accept his authority.

Automatic Shift

I remember the last time it happened. The circumstances were grimmer: John F. Kennedy had been murdered. I served in a junior position in his Administration, was in Texas when he was killed and hurried instinctively to the side of the man who would succeed him—a man for whom I had once worked: Lyndon Johnson. The new President had not been sworn in when I reached the plane, but as if by silent command the whole apparatus of government was already deferring to him. It was an automatic and mechanistic shift, as if an alternate generator had gone instantly into action when the main power source failed. "Where's Vice President Johnson?" I asked of a Secret Service agent at the ramp. "The President's in the middle compartment," he answered instinctively. There was no mystery to it. Oath or no oath, the agent accepted without challenge the mandate of an arrangement made two centuries earlier and contained in a document he probably hadn't read since high school.

So did the rest of the nation. Lyndon Johnson did, too, although he was shaken and uncertain about the protocol of the circumstances; when I walked into his quarters on Air Force One, he looked as Gerald Ford looked all through the day before Richard Nixon resigned. I started to greet him, "Mr. President—" only to be interrupted as he said quietly: "Not yet." But it was so, and he couldn't even wait for the oath to start making decisions.

"Kennedy is dead," he said, addressing his words to no one in particular. "The rest of the world will wonder if we're going to steer sharply off course. Those fellows in the Kremlin must be wondering. The Negroes at home, especially—they'll think a Southern President will just naturally be against 'em. And I'll bet Don Cook and his crowd are sitting up there wondering what the hell to expect now [Donald Cook, chief executive of American Electric Power Co., was a businessman whom the new President considered a good mirror of the enlightened business community]. I've got to show the whole bunch of 'em that a steady hand's on the wheel. And I don't know how to do that except to take up where Kennedy left off."

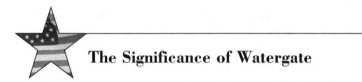

The Significance of Watergate

Sam J. Erwin Jr. served as the chair of the Senate committee which investigated the charges against President Nixon. He explains the seriousness of the Watergate crisis. The government should serve the people, not serve the private goals of the president and his staff.

Watergate has become a symbol for corruption in government. It has thus contributed to a growing cynicism in the American people about those in elected or other public office. I consider Watergate to be one of the great tragedies of our history, overshadowing Teapot Dome [a scandal involving Cabinet-level bribery in the 1920s] as well as scandals in the nineteenth century.

That the combination of events known as Watergate, events that far transcend what once was casually labelled a "third-rate burglary," could have occurred should result in the most sober reflection by all thoughtful Americans about the nature of their government. For it is *their* government that was involved; after all, the Constitution of the United States begins with the memorable words, *We, the people of the United States . . . do ordain and establish this Constitution. . . .* And it is the people who have suffered from the Watergate derelictions.

Sam J. Ervin Jr., "Foreword," in *Watergate: Implications for Responsible Government.* New York: Basic Books, 1974.

He did just that. "Let us continue," he said to a grieving people, and by just about everyone's account, the transition was among his finest hours.

All this comes back as I watch Gerald Ford on television. He is in front of his house in Alexandria, Va. Richard Nixon's speech is over. In my hand is Secretary Dent's speech, setting forth the argument that Richard Nixon's resignation would inspire efforts to repudiate the last election. It won't happen. I let the clipping fall into the waste basket. Ford is a man who voted against almost every piece of legislation I worked to enact in the '60s. We are poles apart politically and he will undoubtedly work to carry forward the policies Richard Nixon espoused in 1972, policies which were aborted not by liberal opposition but by the corruption of his own stewardship. But the Presidency is in Ford's hands now, legitimately, and that's the important thing. The long and unsettling process of watching one President destroy himself in public is over, and the foundations of the state, which seemed so often in jeopardy, have held. Somehow I think this man on the screen is a reminder that the guarantees of the founding covenant, when honored, do work.

It is late now. The screen is dark. I think of something George Washington wrote, when he warned against the disease of factionalism which gradually inclines the minds of men "to seek security and repose in the absolute power of an individual: and sooner or later, the chief of some prevailing faction, more able or more fortunate than his competitors, turns this disposition to the purposes of his own elevation on the ruins of public liberty." To dampen the spirit of factionalism and its effects on the continuity of our traditions: there is the seed of a mandate. It sounds simple and quaint for these modern times. Yet I wonder; watching people milling around, not wanting to go home, although there is nothing more to say, I sense they yearn for a season of first things.

1976: Bicentennial Reflections

Barbara Tuchman

Barbara Tuchman is a historian and Pulitzer Prize–winning author. In this selection she comments on the flaws and the ideals of America as the country celebrated its two-hundredth anniversary. Tuchman has a negative resignation toward America. She points out that America's emphasis on liberty and opportunity was damaged by the development of a "half-hearted imperialism," which started when America gained Spanish territories at the end of the Spanish-American War. The earlier optimism of Americans has, according to Tuchman, given way to self-doubt, disenchantment, and contempt for the law. Yet the author rallies in her conclusion to affirm that the United States is still the best, and most successful, social experiment in human history.

The United States is a nation consciously conceived, not one that evolved only out of an ancient past. It was a planned idea of democracy, of liberty of conscience and pursuit of happiness. It was the promise of equality of opportunity and individual freedom within a just social order, as opposed to the restrictions and repressions of the Old World. In contrast to the militarism of Europe, it would renounce standing armies and "sheathe the desolating sword of war." It was an experiment in Utopia to test the thesis that given

Reprinted from "On Our Birthday—America as Idea," by Barbara Tuchman, *Newsweek*, July 12, 1976. Copyright ©1976 by Barbara Tuchman. Reprinted with the permission of Russell & Volkening, as agents for the author.

freedom, independence and local self-government, people, in [Hungarian patriot and statesman Lajos] Kossuth's words, "will in due time ripen into all the excellence and all the dignity of humanity." It was a new life for the oppressed, it was enlightenment, it was optimism.

Regardless of hypocrisy and corruption, of greed, chicanery, brutality and all the other bad habits man carries with him whether in the New World or Old, the founding idea of the United States remained, on the whole, dominant through the first 100 years. With reservations, it was believed in by Americans, by visitors who came to aid our Revolution or later to observe our progress, by immigrants who came by the hundreds of thousands to escape an intolerable situation in their native lands.

Materialism and Drive

The idea shaped our politics, our institutions and to some extent our national character, but it was never the only influence at work. Material circumstances exerted an opposing force. The open frontier, the hardships of homesteading from scratch, the wealth of natural resources, the whole vast challenge of a continent waiting to be exploited, combined to produce a prevailing materialism and an American drive bent as much, if not more, on money, property, and power than was true of the Old World from which we had fled. The human resources we drew upon were significant: every wave of immigration brought here those people who had the extra energy, gumption or restlessness to uproot themselves and cross an unknown ocean to seek a better life. Two other factors entered the shaping process—the shadow of slavery and the destruction of the native Indian.

At its Centennial, the United States was a material success. Through its second century, the idea and the success have struggled in continuing conflict. The Statue of Liberty, erected in 1886, still symbolized the promise to those "yearning to breathe free." Hope, to them, as seen by a foreign visitor, was "domiciled in America as the Pope is in Rome." But slowly in the struggle the idea lost ground, and at a turning point around 1900, with American acceptance of a rather half-hearted imperialism, it lost dominance. Increasingly invaded since then by self-doubt and disillusion, it survives in the disenchantment of today, battered and crippled but not vanquished.

What has happened to the United States in the twentieth century is not a peculiarly American phenomenon but a part of the experience of the West. In the Middle Ages, plague, wars and social violence were seen as God's punishment upon man for his sins. If the concept of God can be taken as man's conscience, the same explanation may be applicable today. Our sins in the twentieth century—greed, violence, inhumanity—have been profound, with the result that the pride and self-confidence of the nineteenth century have turned to dismay and self-disgust.

In the United States we have a society pervaded from top to bottom by contempt for the law. Government—including the agencies of law enforcement—business, labor, students, the military, the poor no less than the rich, outdo each other in breaking the rules and violating the ethics that society has established for its protection. The average citizen, trying to hold a footing in standards of morality and conduct he once believed in, is daily knocked over by incoming waves of venality, vulgarity, irresponsibility, ignorance, ugliness, and trash in all senses of the word. Our government collaborates abroad with the worst enemies of humanity and liberty. It wastes our substance on useless proliferation of military hardware that can never buy security no matter how high the pile. It learns no lessons, employs no wisdom and corrupts all who succumb to Potomac fever.

Combating Faults

Yet the idea does not die. Americans are not passive under their faults. We expose them and combat them. Somewhere every day some group is fighting a public abuse—openly and, on the whole, notwithstanding the FBI, with confidence in the First Amendment. The U.S. has slid a long way from the original idea. Nevertheless, . . . it still offers a greater opportunity for social happiness, that is to say, for well-being combined with individual freedom and initiative, than is likely elsewhere. The ideal society for which mankind has been striving through the ages will remain forever beyond our grasp. But if the great question, whether it is still possible to reconcile democracy with social order and individual liberty, is to find a positive answer, it will be here.

When Ideals and Reality Clash: The Presidency of Jimmy Carter

Theodore H. White

Theodore H. White has written extensively about the American presidency and about presidential campaigns. In this selection, White gives an introduction into Jimmy Carter's values and personality. Carter's distance from the Washington establishment helped him win the election in 1976, but his distaste for politics weakened his ability to get things done. While Carter's idealism appealed to many people, he was criticized for seeming weak.

Jimmy Carter was the apotheosis of all the good will and liberal thinking that had made the Democratic party of the United States the majority party for forty-four years.

He had won his presidency as the "outsider," the country-style, small-town boy who had campaigned against Washington and its insiders.

He had proved himself a master of the mechanics of the new primary system and the most successful craftsman in the use of television until the appearance on scene of Ronald Reagan. Yet he arrived in Washington having won both his nomination and his election on personality alone, without an organized party behind him.

It was a combination of these qualities that dominated American imagination and public life for the first few months of his presidency.

Excerpted from *America in Search of Itself: The Making of the President, 1956–1980*, by Theodore H. White (New York: Harper & Row, 1982). Copyright ©1982 by Theodore H. White. Reprinted with permission from Harper-Collins Publishers, Inc.

Carter had promised, and promised again, and then again, to change the direction of American affairs. A memorandum of 111 pages listed all the promises he had made to the American people in his three-year-long campaign for the presidency. They were fair and decent promises; they embodied every hope of every group and institution that good-willed people had created in reeving the old system. There would be instant registration of any man or woman seeking permission to vote who appeared at any ballot box anywhere in the United States. Cabinet meetings would be open to the press; sunshine laws would purge secrecy from any crevice where sinister special interests did their work. The budget would be balanced by 1980. The income tax, "a disgrace to the human race," would be reorganized. "Big-shot crooks" would be punished. The nuclear arms race would be halted. American troops would come out of Korea. Welfare would be reorganized. The blacks, the poor, the underprivileged, would be comforted. The Third World would be recognized. The environment would be cleaned. The bureaucracy would be called to account and slimmed down to lean-muscled efficiency. No hope any liberal had expressed anywhere at any time would be ignored.

Jimmy Carter had come out of a campaign carrying a garment bag over his shoulder, using symbols on television to press his image home on America. His administration began, thus, as had so many administrations before his, with symbolic action. On his first day in office, by executive order, all draft evaders of the Vietnam War were pardoned. He followed in a few days by slashing to the bone the use of official limousines by White House personnel. The Marine Corps orchestra was silenced as he greeted his first audience in the East Room—no ceremonial ruffles and flourishes or "Hail to the Chief" when Jimmy Carter entered. There was to be no chief of staff; Carter would run his White House as he had governed Georgia. It was a frigid winter in which he took office, so, said the President, thermostats at the White House must be set at a patriotic low of 65 degrees to save energy. (Two and a half years later, in the next energy crisis, he turned off White House air conditioning and averred that people could work comfortably in the sweltering executive mansion at 80 degrees.) He had proclaimed, in accepting the Democratic nomination in 1976, "I have spoken a lot of times this year about love. But love must be aggressively translated into simple justice." So people were puzzled as they watched him move into operation—and would remain puzzled to the day he departed, four years later.

Jimmy Carter was always a mystery, this man with the straw-colored hair and clear blue eyes, whose enemies came to despise him while those who would be friends could not understand him. Carter fit no mold. . . .

The personality of Jimmy Carter was the same from the day he decided to run for the presidency until he lost it. And that personality, rather than changing from an "old" to a "new" Carter, had to be examined as a set of layers of faith, of action, even of unpleasantnesses. What made it most difficult was that the most important layer of the personality was a Christianity so devout and concerned that political writers found it awkward to write about.

Carter: The Christian

That layer—of true belief—was uppermost and undermost. I encountered it initially before he became President, when I had my first long talk with Carter in Plains, Georgia, in his pleasant middle-class home, surrounded by oak trees— a home comfortable by any standards but by no means the style of mansion so many presidential candidates had acquired. At that time, in 1976, I was pursuing the candidates with a single-track question that might possibly be useful if I was to write a book on that year's campaign. "Where did modern American history really begin?" I would ask, and all had different answers. Jimmy Carter began with civil rights, "the most profound sociological change that's taken place in the country." It was the law as well as Martin Luther King that brought the change in the South, he said. So long as civil rights had been something administered by

124

HEW [the Department of Health, Education, and Welfare], and while local and state laws contradicted federal laws, there was this question: "Whose laws do you obey?" But once the federal courts took over, everything changed. The South *wanted* to change, and the federal courts forced it along. Carter rambled on in answering my question and then got to family life. "When I grew up, the family was my community," he said. "I always knew where my mother and father were, they always knew where I was. I never had a problem where there was any doubt or fear except . . . disappointing my family . . . and there was a greater centering of the life in the community, for which our schools and church were the center." He has since been called a "dispassionate President," but when he talked quietly, he could be passionate. And on black rights he was most passionate of all. Sumter County is one of the most segregationist counties of the Old South; but he had led the fight there for integration, had refused flatly, publicly, to join the White Citizens Council or the "segs." To give the blacks their open and equal opportunity was a matter of faith—of Christianity. Somewhere Carter had crossed a line in his past; blacks as well as whites were the children of God.

Much could be said about the archaic fundamentalist underpinning of his Christianity. But it was real. He believed. No other candidate could write, as did Carter, an open letter to a newspaper declaring his belief in creationism. He taught Sunday school in Plains, held prayer breakfasts in the White House, began lunch, even with such amused big-city politicians as Ed Koch, mayor of New York, by asking permission to say grace. "Why not?" Koch, who had come to plead for aid for his city, is reported to have replied. "We can all use a little extra help."

It was impossible to ignore that motivation of love and mercy which Christianity brought to the administration of Jimmy Carter. He tried to make real all the promises that a generation of liberal programs had substituted for old faith. He ticked off to me the record of previous Presidents, their shortcomings, their lack of faith. Of Kennedy, he said, he "lacked boldness."

Then there was a second layer of the Carter personality—Jimmy Carter the engineer. He had answered my first question by talking of civil rights. Then he gave me an alternative beginning for his reflection on where modern American history began: Sputnik. "Sputnik shook people," he said, "the first dawning of the belief that the Soviets were actually able to challenge us in a world that we thought was uniquely ours from a scientific and technological [view]."

No journalist ever gets to know a President, unless he has known him years before on his way up. Presidents are too busy to spend time on any but those who are useful to them. So a writer must invent the outline of the man he fitfully glimpses. And it seemed to me that one could invent a Jimmy Carter on the model of Sir Isaac Newton. Newton was also a man of science and of God; Newton thought the universe was a

President Jimmy Carter

clockwork mechanism fashioned by God with some ultimate unfathomed design, and that by exploring the mechanics of things he could bare the larger design.

These two layers of Jimmy Carter's personality intersected. A pilot named Peterson had flown me down to Plains for my first visit. I sat beside him and we talked of Carter. Peterson was devoted to him. He had flown Carter from Atlanta to Plains several times. On their flights Carter would sit beside him, ask him how the plane worked, had learned to understand and operate the instruments in the cockpit. Then Peterson added a catching observation. He and Carter attended the same Baptist church in Plains and Carter would say occasionally, "Saw you in church on Sunday." But Mrs. Peterson did not go to services. Peterson recalled Carter asking whether he could call on her someday to talk about it. But he could not have been more surprised when Carter did indeed call (this in the midst of a presidential campaign), to talk with Mrs. Peterson about church, prayer, God, and the importance of Sunday services.

Carter: The Details Person

The engineer Carter was quite distinct from the Carter of faith. He would rise at five-thirty every morning at the White House and be at his desk before any of his staff. And he worked hard. He seemed to believe that if he could grasp all the facts and figures of a problem, he would understand its dynamics. A prominent New York Democrat, one of the major contributors to the party, visited Carter in midterm and was asked into the private study adjacent to the Oval Office. There sat Carter at his desk, with a pile of papers knee-high beside him. "Do you know what that is?" he asked the visitor. "That's the Air Force budget," said Carter. "I've read every page of it." The astonished executive talked briefly with the President, then made his exit through the office of Hamilton Jordan, who acted as chief of staff. There he sat down to enjoy a good conversation on politics and policy. It was as if, said the businessman later, Carter was the chief researcher, Jordan the chief policymaker. This appetite for swallowing detail went with Carter always. At his summit conference with Brezhnev in Vienna, both were invited to a performance of Mozart's *The Abduction from the Seraglio*. Brezhnev, in his box, tired and restless, would doze, nod, occasionally chat and joke with his attendants. But Carter in his box had brought with him the full libretto of the opera and, turning the pages, followed the score act by act, scene by scene, even making notes in the margins. "Carter," said one of those with the President, "is not exactly a bundle of laughs."

There were also all the other layers of Carter. Carter the yeoman, for example. He knew the name of every tree he

127

saw, and loved them all. I mentioned to him, on my first visit, that I had seen a stand of Southern cypress a few miles south of his home, near the town of Americus. The observation caught him. "That's a climatological line," he said. "North of that stand of cypress you won't find any more . . . all the way to the North Pole." He pulled the last phrase out with characteristic melancholy of tone, for he loved his Southern homeland. Then there was Carter of the primaries of 1976, a first-class mechanic of politics, aware of every county, city, voting bloc he must deal with, enjoying the adventure. Yet however much the public Carter on the stump, at the town meeting, in a student dormitory, seemed warm and outgoing, there was the other, prickly, private man—shy, soft-spoken, occasionally vindictive, withdrawn, unable to entertain give-and-take. . . . This was a wary, small-town Carter, peering at the world and the barons of Washington with the skepticism of a country visitor, fearful of being taken in by them as much as they, on his arrival, feared him.

Carter: The Nonpolitician

"You have to understand," said one of Carter's White House guard, "that Carter simply did not *like* politicians. He had set his mind on being governor of Georgia, and he got to be governor by politics; he set his mind on being President, and he got that job done using politicians. But he didn't *like* them. He asked Russell Long over to the White House once to ask for his help on a tax bill, gave Long half an hour, and when the half hour was over, he simply got up and said, 'Thank you.' He wasn't offering friendship. We tried to get him to see the older Democrats, the wise men, people like Clifford and Harriman. He tried that twice and then just stopped. We told him he had to make friends in Congress. Of course, he didn't drink, but he played tennis. So we made a list of congressmen and senators to be invited over for a game. He went through the names, played once with each of them, checked them off the list. And that was that."

Carter performed with serenity and grace at his press conferences, always well prepared. But his major speeches to the nation, in which a President must lift and inspire the people, were dry, rustling sermons. He had little sense of cadence, less humor, and his habit was to emphasize a point by lowering rather than raising his voice. Once the novelty of the style wore off, it sounded flat—provoking that biting wit Eugene McCarthy to remark that Carter's speeches had all the "eloquence of a mortician."

Few ever questioned Carter's high purpose or moral integrity. He was going to make the world better. Closest to his heart lay his large causes: to cleanse and purge the environment, to eliminate the threat of nuclear arms, to make civil rights and affirmative action not just the preaching of the righteous but a reality in American life. And above all, he was going to solve the energy crisis, free America from its dependence on the oil dictators of OPEC [Organization of Petroleum Exporting Countries].

Carter was going to make his programs work, as he had made them work in Georgia, by appealing to the people over the heads of Congress and the entrenched interests. . . .

An Example of Slow Progress

Energy, then, was the overriding thrust of Carter's public effort for his first two months, and by April he was ready to go public with a television blitz. He had begun to prepare the public for the program early in February with a "fireside chat," as he sat in a beige cardigan before a blazing hearth in the White House. On Monday, April 18, he was ready for a full-dress address to the nation, telling the people that: "With the exception of preventing war, this is the greatest challenge our country will face during our lifetimes." Two days later, he was up before a joint session of Congress, presenting his bill. Two days after that, a televised press conference drove the message home.

"The energy bill," said a White House member, "was the single greatest political mistake we made in our first six months. When we couldn't pass it, people got the impression that the President just couldn't manage the government. It came slowly, but we never recovered from that impression." The bill was one drafted in virtual secrecy by unnamed technicians; it had been put together at breakneck speed, much as Reagan's tax bill four years later, and was flawed with technical errors which Congress tried to unknot, in the process finding itself tangled with every lobby in the nation. It was eighteen full months before anything even resembling the original energy bill moved through Congress; and not until the spring of 1980 was a final, comprehensive, and reasonable program pushed through; but by that time it had stalled for so long that Carter won no political credit for his major achievement. . . .

An Example of Uncontrollable Events

Carter's last major triumph in foreign policy had come in January of 1979 with the celebration of America's new and vital relationship with China. But that month had also seen the collapse of the Shah Pahlevi regime in Teheran, and the Shah's flight from Iran. Only a year before, the President and his wife had celebrated New Year's Eve with the same Shah in Teheran, and there, despite the Shah's abominations in the domain of human rights, Carter publicly praised Iran as an "island of stability" in the Middle East. Months of riot, demonstration, and bloodshed had followed, providing television's evening news shows with their magnificent color pictures of total chaos. It was obvious that the Shah would have to go; the President was urged to encourage or unleash the Iranian army in a military coup. But Carter preferred to believe that the Ayatollah Khomeini, in some strange way, represented the will of his people and that the Islamic republic's revolution would lead to an Iranian expression of democracy and human rights in its own tradition.

The events of the Iranian upheaval would soon ricochet around the world. There would come, first, the choking off of Iranian oil from the world flow of trade; world oil prices would soon rocket—and so would gasoline and fuel oil prices in America, as in Europe. Next, the Japanese trade offensive against the American automobile industry would go into high gear as Americans switched from Detroit's old-fashioned "gas guzzlers" to the neat, fuel-efficient Japanese cars. Gold prices around the world would start their crazy gyrations. The compounding of rising energy prices with the panic flight from the dollar to gold would give the steadily rising inflation at home an afterburst that would crack through all American traditions of saving and thrift. . . .

Ideals Versus Realities

Yet, through it all, he remained the same decent man, the same peace seeker. After the 1980 election, I visited him again. I was talking with him this time in another context, about the campaign just ended, and went to one of the journalistic stock-in-trade questions: What did he think were his most lasting achievements? Carter, a very proud man, was at this point melancholy, but firm. He thought a moment, mentioned deregulation and the Camp David accords, and then came back to the center of his personality. "Emphasis on human rights," he said. "[I] printed that commitment on worldwide consciousness. It may have permanent results. . . ."

That remains to me the essential Jimmy Carter statement. He loved humankind—but he gave his love and affection to very few individual members of humankind. He was always remote and distant, and all those who had expected to find in him an effective, avenging saint were disappointed. He was poor-mouthed by those who sought to get close to him—from the stuffy Helmut Schmidt of Germany, to the taunting President López Portillo of Mexico; from his loyal supporter, Tip O'Neill of the House, to his loyal opposition, Howard Baker, Republican leader of the Senate. It is better for a sovereign to be feared than loved. Carter achieved neither.

It was with this record of the presidency that Jimmy Carter entered on his campaign for reelection in the summer of 1979.

What the American people seek when they vote for the presidency is someone they trust, someone who is better and abler than themselves. The President must control matters—must control the Congress, the economy, bread and butter, war and peace, must persuade the people, through the filter of the hostile press, that he is doing their will.

Carter had done his best to do the people's will, to give them, as he had promised, a government as good and decent and compassionate as the American people themselves. His motives were pure; but his thinking was muddled. He was for a government of charity and a government of austerity at the same time. His problem, in essence, was that he could not quite understand the world in which he lived. Nor his party, which he took over in shambles and left in shambles. Nor the Congress, whose partnership he sought yet disdained. Nor the grime and fear of the big cities, whose decay could not be turned about by any call to brotherhood. Nor, most of all, the world of wicked and paranoid men, who were changing the globe beyond the seas. He was a man caught and gripped, then squeezed and crushed, by those stupendous forces of history rising from a world America had once freed and dominated—where now Jimmy Carter's moralities were irrelevant.

A revolution of goodwill had run its course; and now as the graduate of that revolution Carter was about to face judgment on how he had managed the nation's affairs. Goodwill had not restrained the inflation which terrified all citizens, high and low alike. Goodwill had not mollified America's adversaries in the Third World of the newly freed, or in the Second World of the Communist bureaucracies. Americans were still seeking for something undefined in politics—who they were, where they were going, and whether the nation they had created over the years could still be governed reasonably by the old ideas.

CHAPTER 3

Environment, Energy, and Automobiles in the 1970s

Structures to Protect the Environment

Philip Shabecoff

Philip Shabecoff is a journalist who documents some of the structural changes (laws, agencies, and programs) which followed Earth Day in 1970. Before the '70s, state and federal governments did not focus on environmental concerns. In the early '70s, however, laws and government agencies were quickly established to address a wide range of concerns: air pollution, water pollution, hazardous conditions in the work place, noise control, etc.

The federal government, which frequently moves at a glacial pace in dealing with social problems, responded in the 1960s and 1970s with surprising speed to the rising concern over the deterioration of the environment. In the 1970s, Congress churned out a series of environmental laws that, taken together, must be regarded as one of the great legislative achievements of the nation's history.

On January 1, 1970, President Nixon signed the National Environmental Policy Act, which requires the federal government to analyze and report on the environmental implications of its activities. A Council on Environmental Quality was created later that year to oversee compliance with the law by federal agencies. The council also was assigned the job of preparing an annual report on the state of the environment and, at least in theory, of advising the

Excerpted from "The Environmental Revolution," by Philip Shabecoff, in *A Fierce Green Fire: The American Environmental Movement.* Copyright ©1993 by Philip Shabecoff. Reprinted with the permission of Hill and Wang, a division of Farrar, Straus & Giroux, Inc.

President on it. Under Russell Train, its first chairman, and two of his successors, Russell Peterson, former governor of Delaware, and Gus Speth, the council played a significant role in prodding the government to take an active role in protecting the nation's resources and fighting pollution.

Another agency created by act of Congress in the seminal year 1970 was the Occupational Safety and Health Administration, or OSHA as it is commonly called. The new agency was given authority to ensure that the workplace was safe and healthy and that employers did not subject workers to toxic chemicals or other dangerous substances such as asbestos and cotton dust or to unsafe machinery and equipment. The new agency gave workers and their unions a potentially powerful new tool for protecting themselves from careless or unscrupulous employers. The same law that created OSHA established the National Institute of Occupational Safety and Health to do research into the causes of workplace accidents and illness and to design criteria for lowering risks. While the Labor Department sometimes administered the law in ways that seemed more inclined to placate employers than to protect workers, that was not the fault of the statute.

The Environmental Protection Agency, the most powerful and controversial environmental institution in the federal government, was a product of congressional inaction. In December 1970, President Nixon, responding to the rising political winds, submitted a reorganization plan to Congress, lumping a number of federal public health and regulatory bureaus and programs into a new patchwork organization called the EPA. Neither house of Congress voted against the reorganization, which would have killed the new agency. The EPA, which was to be the federal government's watchdog, police officer, and chief weapon against all forms of pollution, was thus created without benefit of any statute enacted by Congress. It quickly became the lightning rod for the nation's hopes for cleaning up pollution and its fears about intrusive federal regulation.

William D. Ruckelshaus, appointed by President Nixon

as the agency's first administrator, later recalled, "From a management point of view, the task was daunting: how to form a cohesive, integrated, functioning entity out of fifteen different agencies and parts of agencies throughout the federal government." Ruckelshaus said during an interview in 1989 that the normal condition of the EPA was to be ground "between two irresistible forces. Here was one

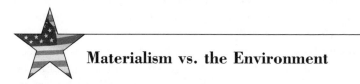

Materialism vs. the Environment

Do American lifestyles contribute to environmental problems? If the primary goal of life is consumption, then a great deal of waste results.

The American people are materialistic, intent on consuming as many economic goods as possible. The goal of the society is success in terms of money and the goods and services it will secure. The most important barometer of the nation's wealth is the Gross National Product. The whole society—families, religions, industries, schools, advertising agencies, government—train the young and support adults in the pursuit of consumption. Be a good American: exploit, consume! could be our national anthem. This way of life cannot continue if our environment is to survive.

Today our air is contaminated; the streams, the lakes and even the oceans are polluted. Man's refuse is piling up in great heaps in the forms of car bodies, garbage, aluminum cans, bottles, and so on. The number of Americans is 204 million-plus and increasing one every fourteen seconds—well over two million per year. Man's powerful and destructive intervention into nature has already eliminated a number of different plants and animals. Many other varieties of birds, fish, and animals are now threatened with extinction. Will man soon have to place himself on a list of "endangered species?"

Rex R. Campbell and Jerry L. Wade, *Society and Environment: The Coming Collision*. Boston: Allyn and Bacon, 1972.

group, the environmental movement, pushing very hard to get [pollution] emissions down no matter where they were—air, water, no matter what—almost regardless of the seriousness of the emissions. There was another group on the other side [industry] pushing just as hard in the other direction and trying to stop all of that stuff, again almost regardless of the seriousness of the problem."

The EPA had no choice but to hit the ground running. To carry out the Clean Air Act of 1970, it was required to come up with rules for reducing air pollution 120 days after it opened its doors. Congress passed one law after another that added to the agency's mandate. Ruckelshaus soon banned the use of DDT by administrative order, something that Congress had been unable to do by legislation. The agency established regional offices and research and testing facilities in a number of states. Its presence was soon felt—and usually resented—by a wide swath of industry, municipal governments, and even other federal agencies. The role of the EPA is not only to force polluters to obey the laws but also to explain the laws, to provide information and technical assistance to help polluters comply with the laws, to identify the sources of danger within the environment, and to inform, educate, and assist the public on how to protect themselves and the environment.

Although political pressure by industry—all too frequently supported by the White House and members of Congress—and the EPA's often excessively bureaucratic approach to its task have tended to blunt the agency's sword, it is today still the single most effective guardian of the nation's air, water, and soil.

A cascade of environmental legislation flowed from Capitol Hill during the Nixon, Ford, and Carter administrations. The Federal Water Pollution Control Act was adopted in 1972. Also enacted in 1972 were the Federal Insecticide, Rodenticide, and Fungicide Act (the nation's basic pesticide control law), the Noise Control Act, the Coastal Zone Management Act, and the Marine Mammals Protection Act. The Endangered Species Act was passed in

1973 and the Safe Drinking Water Act in 1974. Pausing for a deep breath in 1975, Congress produced in 1976 the Toxic Substances Control Act and the Resource Conservation and Recovery Act (both dealing with the control of dangerous materials), the Federal Land Management Act, and the National Forest Management Act the following year. In 1977 the Clean Air and Water laws were expanded and strengthened.

In 1980, after an epic legislative battle between environmentalists, who wanted to preserve as much as possible of our last wild and primitive state in a pristine condition, and those who wanted to exploit the land and resources for economic purposes, Congress enacted the Alaska National Interest Lands Act, setting aside over 100 million acres in perpetuity for the enjoyment of the American people. Millions of acres were also designated by Congress in the lower forty-eight states during the 1970s and 1980s as protected wilderness areas, wildlife refuges, and parks. In a lame-duck session in 1980, Congress passed the Comprehensive Environmental Response, Compensation, and Liability Act, or Superfund as it is commonly known, more or less successfully establishing a well-financed program for cleaning up the thousands of dangerous abandoned toxic waste sites around the country. Many other environmental laws of somewhat lesser significance also emerged from Congress in those years.

Trouble at Love Canal

Samuel S. Epstein, Lester O. Brown, and Carl Pope

Love Canal, an area within the city of Niagara Falls, New York, was many things. It was a place where children played, it was a place where an elementary school was built, it was a place where average people bought homes, and it was a very dangerous dumping ground of toxic chemicals. The chemicals had been buried in steel barrels between 1947 and 1952. By the 1970s, those chemicals were leaking into the soil, into the houses, and into the air. After years of painfully slow investigations and lobbying, the area was vacated. Epstein, the lead author, is a medical doctor who has written widely about environmental issues. He teaches environmental health and human ecology at Case Western Reserve University Medical School. Brown has worked as an agricultural economist for the U.S. government and has been involved in many overseas agricultural development projects. Pope is a writer and activist concerned with environmental issues and population control.

The Love Canal was originally excavated in the 1880s by entrepreneur William T. Love as part of his grandiose scheme to create a sprawling industrial complex between the two branches of the Niagara River. This "model city," he boasted, would take advantage of the massive electric power that could be generated by the water's steep drop

Excerpted from *Hazardous Waste in America,* by Samuel S. Epstein, Lester O. Brown, and Carl Pope. Copyright ©1982 by Samuel S. Epstein, M.D., Lester O. Brown, and Carl Pope. Reprinted with permission from Sierra Club Books.

from the canal's entrance just above the falls to its terminus at the Niagara River, several miles away and several hundred feet below. At the time Love conceived his model city, use of electricity, then only in direct current (DC) form, was severely restricted, since it could only be transported for short distances. In Love's new city, industries located on the shores of the canal would be able to take full advantage of the abundant hydroelectric power.

Love's plan received enthusiastic support. The state of New York granted him uniquely broad authority to develop his planned city for two hundred thousand people and gave him "authority to condemn properties and to divert as much water from the upper Niagara River as he saw fit, even to the extent of turning off Niagara Falls!"

Unfortunately for Love, just as his plans were reaching fruition, alternating current (AC) was developed, making it feasible to transmit electricity over long distances. The canal's major selling point immediately vanished, and, over the next two decades, Love's model-city plan collapsed. All that remains today is a small segment of the unfinished canal between Frontier Avenue and Colvin Boulevard, some eight miles north of the falls.

During the twenties and thirties, the abandoned canal filled with water and was used as a swimming hole. Art Tracy, a local resident for forty years, remembers, "When we first moved there, the Love Canal was there and it was a beautiful body of water. We used to go and get on cardboard or something else on top of the hill of dirt and slide right down into the water."

Creating a Dump

The Hooker Electrochemical Corporation (later Hooker Chemical and Plastics Corporation) began operations in Niagara Falls in 1905. As one of the first industries in the area, it took full advantage of the Niagara's hydroelectric power. Over the years, the Hooker operation expanded to include the manufacture of industrial chemicals, fertilizers, and plastics.

In 1942, Hooker signed an agreement with the Niagara Power and Development Corporation, the owners of the canal, to dump chemical wastes in the canal. About the same time, the city of Niagara Falls started dumping garbage in the canal. Tracy well remembers those days. There were few people living in the area, and there was little or no opposition to the dumping. But Tracy wasn't happy. He wanted to see the canal area turned into a picnic ground. Instead, the canal became an offensive nuisance. Soon he and his neighbors were "overrun by rats" and constantly overwhelmed by the odors.

In 1946, Hooker purchased the Love Canal from the Niagara Power and Development Corporation and turned it into a chemical dump site. From 1947 to 1952, Hooker dumped over 43 million pounds of industrial chemical wastes into the canal. These wastes included over 13 million pounds of lindane (benzene hexachloride), a highly toxic and carcinogenic chlorinated hydrocarbon pesticide; over 4 million pounds of chlorobenzenes, chlorinated derivatives of the highly toxic industrial solvent benzene, which is known to induce aplastic anemia and leukemia; and about half a million pounds of trichlorophenol (TCP), used in the manufacture of herbicides, such as 2, 4, 5-trichlorophenoxyacetic acid, also known as 2, 4, 5-T, and of cosmetic ingredients, such as hexachlorophene (HCP).

The TCP was heavily contaminated with several hundred pounds of TCDD, formed as an accidental by-product of overheating TCP during the manufacturing process. Less than three ounces of TCDD could kill the entire population of New York City. At parts-per-billion (ppb) levels, exposure to TCDD can result in chloracne, an intractable and disabling chronic skin disease, and a wide range of other diseases and disturbances in metabolic functions. TCDD is also the most potent known carcinogen and teratogen, producing these effects in experimental animals at concentrations as low as 10 to 100 parts per trillion (ppt).

While Hooker was turning the canal into a chemical-waste dump, the city of Niagara Falls was expanding rapidly. By the early 1950s, the Board of Education and the city of Niagara Falls became eager for the canal and the land around it. The board wanted to build a school on the banks of the canal, and the city and private developers wanted to use the rest of the land for residential development. In 1952, the school board and the city instituted condemnation proceedings on the property adjacent to the canal and, according to Hooker, threatened to condemn the canal itself.

Hooker knew that it had buried millions of pounds of highly toxic wastes in the dump, that the area should not be used for construction of a school or homes, and that it might be held responsible for any of the canal's problems if the property was condemned. Hooker then decided to take action that it thought would insulate the company from all future responsibility. In April, 1953, Hooker sold the land to the school board for $1 in exchange for the board's signature on a deed with a provision intended to absolve Hooker from all future liability for injury or property damage caused by the dump's contents. Hooker insists that it warned the school board against "any construction activity of any kind going on at that disposal site." However, the deed clause failed to explain that the Love Canal waste dump site contained many chemicals known at the time to be highly toxic.

In January, 1954, while attempting to lay the foundation for the Ninety-Ninth Street Elementary School, the construction company struck "a pit filled with chemicals." Charles Thiele, the school board's architect, expressed grave concern. "It is poor policy to attempt to build over this soil, as it will be a continuous source of odors, and until more information is available regarding the materials dumped in this area, we must assume that it might be a detriment to the concrete foundations," he wrote. The board nevertheless decided to go ahead with its plans. In an attempt to avoid the "chemical pit," the foundation was shifted eighty-five feet north of the originally planned site. Efforts were also made to "clean up and bury as much of the [chemical] debris as possible." Thiele directed his contractors to "fill up the two chemical pits towards the north end of the southerly section of the property." However, he warned that placing fill in these pits would probably cause the chemicals inside to "overflow and cover adjacent areas," and for this reason decided to eliminate the school's planned basement.

The Ninety-Ninth Street School opened in the fall of 1955. About five hundred children enrolled. The canal fascinated and frightened them, and they told each other tales of a monster that lived there, a monster that emerged from the depths of the canal with each full moon.

Barbara Quimby grew up on Ninety-Ninth Street. She attended the Ninety-Ninth Street School and, like her future husband and other local children, spent many years playing in the school yard. In the late fifties, Barbara remembers, she and her friends used to go down to an area behind a house on Ninety-Seventh Street that they called the "quicksand lagoon." There, she and her playmates poked sticks into the surfacing drums of chemicals and skipped rocks over the black sludge that accumulated there. The rocks popped and smoked as they bounced.

The canal, which was mostly a large, swampy field of unkept grasses and gullies, was also a favorite play area for Barbara and the local school children. However, playing there became more and more unpleasant. Barbara explains, "We had special shoes which we kept in our garages to wear over there, because once you wore something, a pair of sneakers or whatever, you couldn't get them clean again." Barbara remembers how children were often burned by liquids oozing from the canal. Neighborhood dogs that spent a lot of time at the canal also seemed affected. Their hair fell out in clumps, some developed severe skin diseases, and others became sickly and died.

Hooker soon found itself involved in these problems, as local parents started calling the company dispensary to inquire about the proper treatment of an increasing number of chemical burns suffered by their children. In June, 1958,

Jerome Wilkenfeld, assistant technical superintendent of the Niagara Falls plant, informed the management that several children playing near the dump had been burned by chemicals that had "surfaced" in several areas of subsidence in the northern section of the canal and that "the entire area, [although not] officially designated for that purpose, was being used as a playground."

Although Hooker insists that it warned the school board that children should be kept from playing in areas where chemicals had surfaced, they did not warn local residents about the danger. . . .

Homes on the Dump

Many prospective residents were attracted to buy houses surrounding the canal by realtors who promised that the canal area would soon be turned into a big park and that owning a home there was an investment in the future. In 1965, the Bulkas were among the couples hooked by this sales pitch. They quickly shed their illusions. The Bulkas' single-story, three-bedroom ranch-style house was on Ninety-Seventh Street. A large, empty lot, an extension of the canal grounds, lay just to the north. This favorite playground of the local children, "the lagoon," was almost always filled with a muddy, black liquid. But the lagoon was a dangerous place to play. Soon after the Bulkas moved in, their son Joey fell into one of the pits. "He was covered with thick, black, sooty stuff," Peter Bulka recalled. A small amount of the sooty material got into Joey's ear. Shortly after, his eardrum was perforated.

The Bulkas complained to the school board and the Niagara city and county health departments about the lagoon. "We called every day. They did absolutely nothing," Peter Bulka said. The children's injuries were not the only reason for the Bulkas' concern. "We called one time because [the fumes from the dump] were taking the bark and everything right off the trees [and] turned the white paint on our house pink." A private developer finally solved the immediate problem. He filled in much of the lagoon and built a house on it, into which Debbie and Norman Cerrillo moved.

"I was one of the suckers," Norman says. The Cerrillos were told the developer was going to "build a beautiful park" on the old canal site. The realtor promised "swings and a ball diamond and things like that. That's what sold us."

The Cerrillos, like their neighbors, soon found that living by the canal was a continuing nightmare. Their problems began when Debbie tried to cultivate the barren expanse of their backyard. "In the last sixty feet of the yard we planted grass; then we planted grass; then we planted grass. We even went so far as putting sod there. Nothing would grow. We tried one year to grow a garden. We planted tomato plants, and they stayed their original size all summer. I also tried my hand at growing summer squash—they never got any bigger than a large tomato. Usually you'd get them sometimes a foot long. The summer squash was as hard as a gourd right from the beginning. You couldn't cut them with a knife." Debbie, known for her green thumb, refused to give in and tried growing other vegetables. "I planted three packages of beets. I should have had hundreds of beets. I ended up with one. It was the size of a pumpkin and hard as wood." Their neighbors, the Bulkas, had worse luck. All they could grow were dandelions. . . .

Major Problems in the '70s

A new problem developed in the early seventies. After each heavy rainfall, homes with basements closest to the canal, on Ninety-Ninth and Ninety-Seventh Streets, began to flood with black sludge. Since the Niagara Falls area gets an average of thirty-six inches of rain a year, flooding became a constant problem. The Bulkas tried to cope by installing a sump pump in their basement. The liquid sludge rapidly corroded it. The Bulkas would ultimately replace their new sump pump many times. "We had sump pumps lined up against the basement wall," Peter remembers. "The stuff would eat out the bottom of the pump. One time I had a stainless-steel pump, and it ruined that one too." The worst problems occurred in the spring, when the ground thawed and the rain was heavy. Peter recalls the smell being so strong "you couldn't stand on the basement stairs—your eyes would water."...

A barrage of complaints from neighbors about the flooding of their basements, destruction of their sump pumps, and the appearance of offensive black liquid in holes throughout the area finally prompted the city of Niagara Falls to seek help from Calspan, a prestigious Buffalo-based engineering consulting firm. At this stage, Hooker Chemical also offered to help.

The Calspan investigation went into full swing in June, 1977. As soon as the engineers arrived on the scene, they noted that very strong "fume odors from the site are evident at all times," particularly on warm summer days. They also found that water from several monitoring wells sunk around the canal had "an organic-type odor," suggesting that the groundwater had become heavily contaminated.

Calspan, in its final report of August, 1977, concluded that, over the years, the drums nearest the surface of the canal had become increasingly corroded and exposed, and that there had been massive leakage of contaminated liquid from the canal into the sumps and storm sewers of adjacent homes, particularly on the Ninety-Seventh Street side of the landfill. Several samples of groundwater and surface water were found to be heavily contaminated with highly toxic chemicals, including hexachlorocyclopentadiene (C-56), (HEX), a precursor of the pesticide mirex; hexachlorobenzene, a fungicide; and a wide range of other carcinogenic chlorinated hydrocarbons.

At first the Calspan report seemed to interest the local media more than the area residents, with one major exception—Lois Gibbs, who lived several blocks from the canal. Lois was typical of Love Canal mothers. She had no interest in politics and spent most of her time washing, cooking, and cleaning. Her son Mike had had a long history of illness since enrolling at the Ninety-Ninth Street School, including asthma, nephritis, and hepatitis. The press accounts of the Calspan findings convinced Lois that her son's problems were caused by the toxic chemicals in the dump, and she decided it was high time to get him out of the Ninety-Ninth Street School.

In May, 1978, armed with a note from her doctor, Lois petitioned to get Mike transferred to another school. The Board of Education refused. "If they had allowed Mike to transfer, they would have had to let the other kids go too," Lois observed. "They didn't want to set a precedent."

When Lois was turned down, she decided her only remaining course of action was to close the school. As she began an effort to do just that, she soon found that many other parents were equally concerned about their children sitting in classrooms on top of the oozing, toxic wastes. They were also concerned about the children playing in the adjacent fields, where barrels of chemicals were now surfacing more frequently, particularly since the heavy rains and snowfall of 1977 and 1978.

As Lois went from door to door with her petition, neighbor after neighbor expressed concerns about the canal. And much to her surprise, almost everyone had a health problem they couldn't explain. They all wondered if the canal had been poisoning their families over these years. "I finished my half of Ninety-Ninth Street, where I first started, and I decided it was more than the school. It was the immediate area too," Lois recalls. The "parents' movement" now became a residents' movement.

Debbie Cerrillo worked with Lois on the petition drive. Debbie had not previously realized that there were so many sick people in her neighborhood. What she soon learned frightened her. Karen Schroeder had given birth to a daughter with multiple birth defects, including a double row of teeth in her lower jaw and a cleft palate. In one family, three children had all been born with incomplete skull closures, each requiring multiple surgery. In the next house, a young child had to be kept on oxygen most of the time because of severe asthma. Two children in another family had been born with congenital heart defects. Directly across the street, a neighbor recently had a stillborn baby. Between

Debbie's house and one corner of Ninety-Ninth Street, she found several hyperactive children. In the first nine houses on her block, five women had had miscarriages. There had also been two crib deaths on the same block.

As the petitioning continued, families several blocks from the canal also began to speak up about health problems. Seventeen-year-old Laurie Nowak, who lived on 101st Street, reported that, when she was thirteen, her hair had begun to fall out, and she had to wear a wig for six months. Laurie married and had three miscarriages while living at Love Canal and a fourth while temporarily relocated in the autumn of 1979. Her only child has a birth defect. . . .

While Lois Gibbs and other residents were collecting signatures to close the school, the state Department of Health started a survey of local residents, and the state Department of Environmental Conservation initiated tests to determine the extent of the groundwater, soil, and air contamination.

The results of these surveys alarmed state experts. In the southern section of the canal, women between the ages of thirty and thirty-four had a miscarriage rate nearly four times higher than normal. The air, water, and soil of the entire canal area were found to be heavily contaminated with a wide range of toxic and carcinogenic chemicals coming from the former Hooker dump; particularly high levels were found in the air of basements in houses near the canal. Sediment samples from Black Creek, which ran behind the Kennys' house, were found to be contaminated with 31 ppb of TCDD, a level about 700 million times greater than that calculated by the EPA to produce one cancer death per million population. Chloroform was found in the air of one Love Canal home at a level more than one hundred times that considered by the EPA to cause a significant excess of cancer risk.

The state then tried to get the county to close the school and to declare a general emergency in the area. The county medical officer, Francis Clifford, known as "Cancer Clifford" to Love Canal residents, refused to act. Worried by the increasing evidence of danger and angered by Clifford's refusal, state health commissioner Robert Whalen stepped in. In August, 1978, on the day that Lois Gibbs and Debbie Cerrillo arrived in Albany to present their petition, Whalen announced that the Ninety-Ninth Street School would be closed, dozens of families would be evacuated, and their homes would be purchased by the state. The state believed that this decisive action would satisfy all concerned. Instead, the announcement caused general panic.

As eligible families packed to leave, neighbors watched in silence. The Cerrillos, Bulkas, and Schroeders were moved out, while the Kennys, Quimbys, Nowaks, Hillises, Grenzys, Gibbses, and hundreds of others remained behind, frightened and angry. It just didn't seem to make sense. If it was unsafe for someone living just a dozen yards from their home, why was it safe for them to stay? Moreover, health surveys in areas outside the evacuation zone had strongly suggested that there was an excess of miscarriages, birth defects, and chronic disease among the remaining residents. . . .

While the scientific community battled over the Picciano data [a study suggesting changes in the residents' chromosomes], the Love Canal residents became more militant with each passing hour. On the afternoon of May 19, two federal experts, after discussing the situation with area leaders at the Love Canal Home Owners' Association headquarters, were temporarily trapped inside as a large, angry group of residents blocked the exits from the building. The local police surrounded the area, and the FBI was called in. After several tense hours, the "hostages" were allowed to leave. No one was arrested, and no charges were filed.

The EPA kept its word and on Wednesday, May 21, announced that all remaining residents would be temporarily evacuated pending further tests. For Lois Gibbs, Barbara Quimby, and Art Tracy, the fight seemed over. They had won. And although they knew the announcement only discussed "temporary" relocation, behind the scenes, the White House had already committed itself to a more permanent arrangement, including funds for "temporary permanent" relocation. . . .

The Love Canal residents have now been "temporarily permanently" removed. Many have new homes, with the help of federal and state tax credits and low-interest loans. In the fall of 1980, a $15-million fund was established to purchase 550 homes within a thirty-square block area surrounding the dump at "fair market value," usually in the range of $30,000 to $35,000, which is claimed by some residents to be an underestimate.

Several additional reviews of the Picciano data have since been made. Most independent reviewers agree with Picciano that some abnormalities had been found, but differ on their precise significance. The canal residents, exhausted after years of fighting, have resisted any further government attempts to study their health. No one really knows what impact the chemicals in the canal have had or, more importantly, will have on the residents.

Accident at Three Mile Island

Peter Stoler

During the 1960s the costs of building nuclear power plants hindered the growth of this new source of power. When oil prices began to climb in the 1970s, some people felt the time was right to begin a major program of building more nuclear plants. However, environmentalists were worried about accidental releases of radiation, and they worried about the disposal of radioactive wastes from such plants. In 1979, the accidental release of radioactive steam at Three Mile Island forced all Americans to consider the safety of nuclear power. Peter Stoler is a journalist who specializes in scientific topics. The following selection gives some of his findings related to the accident at Three Mile Island.

It is one of the best-known of all physical laws. It is known as Murphy's Law, and it is nothing if not simple. It says: "If anything can go wrong, it will.". . .

Few events illustrate the applicability of Murphy's Law better than the one that occurred on the morning of March 28, 1979, at Three Mile island, a narrow strip of scrub-covered soil a stone's throw from the east bank of the Susquehanna River a few miles downstream from the Pennsylvania state capital at Harrisburg. In the hours before dawn, the engineers operating Metropolitan Edison Company's 900-megawatt TMI Unit 2 were shocked out of somnolence by the ringing of alarm bells as reactor pressures began to rise and the coolant level to fall. Before the

Excerpted from *Decline and Fail: The Ailing Nuclear Power Industry*, by Peter Stoler (New York: Dodd, Mead, and Company, 1985). Copyright ©1985 by Peter Stoler. Reprinted with permission from Betty Marks, literary agent for the author.

sun rose, their actions and the flaws in the plant's design and equipment brought the plant closer to a meltdown than anyone cared to contemplate and transformed what might—what should—have been a routine turbine trip into the worst nuclear power plant accident in history. For five full days, as NRC (Nuclear Regulatory Commission) officials and engineers scratched their heads and let their actions and contradictory statements attest to their bafflement, the plant, which had released at least some radioactive gases and materials into the atmosphere, teetered on the brink of disaster. For five days Pennsylvania's governor and civil defense officials pressed the NRC for advice on whether they should begin to evacuate people from the area. For five days the state of Pennsylvania, not to mention the rest of the U.S. and people elsewhere around the world, held their breath, watched, and waited until TMI-2 was brought under control.

The TMI accident killed no one, at least not outright. The plant did not blow up, melt down, or cause people to glow in the dark, though the accident did generate a certain amount of mordant humor, some of which could be seen in some souvenir T-shirts put on sale shortly after the accident. The shirts showed a sketch of the island's familiar' hourglass-shaped cooling towers and bore the legend: "I survived TMI—I think." The accident was not anywhere near as bad as it could have been. But it did an enormous amount of damage nonetheless, for it showed people that, the assurances of the nuclear power industry and its regulators to the contrary notwithstanding, accidents—and potentially disastrous accidents at that—were more than just statistical possibilities. They could really happen. . . .

What Happened?

The reactor had been operating for about a year, and was up and running at 97 percent of capacity on the morning of March 28. People of the area had become accustomed to the way the plant's huge, hourglass-shaped cooling towers dominated the landscape. They had even become accustomed to hearing the alarm bells on the island as the plant experienced minor malfunctions or as the staff conducted safety drills. So no one off the island heard—or thought—anything amiss as the hands of the clock moved slowly toward the hour of 4:00 A.M.

But Fred Scheimann, one of the operators, did. Shortly before 4:00, he had descended eight flights into the bowels of the turbine building, hoping that he could figure out a way to clear up a problem in one of the steam generator's filter tanks, where the resin balls used to filter the water had become stuck together. He had just climbed atop a huge pipe to get a better look at a gauge when his ears detected, first, silence, which meant that a pump had shut down, and then a noise that sent chills down his spine. The noise was like that made by an express train. It was the sound made by a slug of steam rushing through a pipe. Scheimann heard it just in time. He leaped clear only a fraction of a second before the pipe on which he had been standing was ripped from its mounting, tearing out valves and releasing a spray of scalding water.

A second later things began to go crazy in the control room. Alarm bells began ringing. Alarm lights began flashing. Supervisor Bill Zewe, a veteran of the Navy's nuclear program, rushed from his office in time to grab the intercom and tell the sixty or so people at work on the island as much as he knew. He announced that TMI Unit 2 had tripped and was shutting itself down.

It took operators a while to figure out what had happened. But eventually, they managed to piece things together. What had happened was that a pump failed in the reactor's secondary loop, which carries nonradioactive water into the plant's steam generator, where it absorbs heat generated by the nuclear chain reaction in the reactor core from the plant's radioactive primary loop. Normally, this nonradioactive water is turned into steam that drives the turbine and generates electricity. With no steam to push it, though, the turbine had shut down.

Turbine trips are routine occurrences at nuclear—and

other—power plants. But they pose an extra problem at nuclear plants, for the steam does more than merely power the turbine. The steam also helps remove heat from the water that is cooling the reactor core. Without steam in its steam generators, the coolant in a nuclear plant can heat up, expand, and build up a dangerous level of pressure in the reactor core. When this happens, the plant's first safety system, a relief valve at the top of the core, is supposed to open automatically, releasing the excess pressure.

This is what happened at Three Mile Island. Unfortunately, it is not all that happened. For the relief valve on TMI-2 was small—too small, in fact, to release all the pressure necessary to prevent the reactor's coolant from overheating. So the plant's second automatic safety device, the SCRAM, dropped the control rods into the reactor core—or tried to. Propelled by small charges of nitrogen, the control rods were thrust into the core so fast that several of them bent and jammed. Those that were in place could not stop the reactor from producing heat. Because nuclear decay continues even after the main chain reaction has been stopped, the reactor continued to produce heat at the rate of about 6 percent of normal capacity.

In theory, the overheated coolant should have lost its heat, albeit slowly. But in fact, that is not what happened. The relief valve atop the core was supposed to have closed down again thirteen seconds into the accident, when the pressure in the reactor returned to normal. Had this happened, the closing would have prevented undue loss of core coolant. But it did not happen, and the plant's operators were unaware of the fact. A light on the control panel showed that the electric current that had opened the valve had been switched off, leading the operators to believe that the valve had closed. In fact, the valve had stuck in the open position. Worse, it would remain open for two hours and twenty minutes, draining the vital coolant from the reactor and causing plant operators to lose valuable time looking elsewhere for the cause of the coolant loss. Within five minutes of the initial turbine trip, some 32,000 gallons of coolant escaped. Before the problem was discovered, more than 250,000 gallons of radioactive water would flow out of the reactor and collect on the containment building floor.

The jammed relief valve, though, was only one of the problems confronting TMI-2's operators as they struggled to bring the reactor under control. Operator errors were compounding their mechanical problems. One of the errors was procedural. The plant's operating manual warned operators that a pipe temperature of 200 degrees or more indicated an open valve. But the operators either did not look or failed to take note of the temperatures in the pipes, which recorders show reached 285 degrees. Instead, they said later that temperatures at the plant routinely registered high because some valve was always leaking.

These errors and others caused the upper part of the reactor's core to become uncovered. The lack of covering caused the core to overheat. In fact, the core did more than just overheat. It began to overheat rapidly. Its temperature soared to the point where the fuel rods' zirconium-alloy cladding began to melt and deform, and that was high indeed. Zirconium is highly heat-resistant and does not begin to melt until its temperature exceeds 3,000 degrees. Zirconium has another peculiar property, too. It can react with steam to produce hydrogen. And hydrogen, as anyone who has read about the *Hindenburg* disaster knows, possesses an interesting property of its own. It can combine with oxygen to produce an explosion.

The possibility of a hydrogen explosion (and a minor one actually did occur in the reactor the afternoon of the accident) was not, however, the plant operators' primary concern during the early hours of March 28. Heat was. The core was heating up at a staggering rate. If it reached a temperature of 5,200 degrees, it would melt through the bottom of the reactor vessel and drop into the water-filled sump in the containment building. If it did that, several things could happen. The white-hot core could cause the water in the sump to flash off as steam, which could rupture the containment and release a radioactive cloud. Or it could cause the water to boil off more slowly, though without giving up much heat of its own, and melt its way through the floor of the reactor building and into the ground, causing another cloud of radioactive steam the moment it came into contact with groundwater.

Either way, the results would be disastrous. A cloud of radioactive materials would drift downwind, causing radiation sickness, latent cancers, and all the other problems about which scientists warned in WASH-740 and the later Rasmussen Report. The plant would not, to be sure, explode like a bomb. But the effects on people in the path of the radioactive cloud would be little different from those caused by a nuclear blast. . . .

Public Trust Is Broken

Meanwhile, the NRC, which had arrived on the scene, found itself contradicting the company by reporting that it had detected radioactivity as far as sixteen miles from the plant and revealing that radiation levels within the containment building had soared to a searing 1,000 rems. By Thursday NRC officials were describing the plant failure as "one of the most serious nuclear accidents to occur in the U.S." They were also trying to respond to questions from Pennsylvania Governor Richard Thornburgh, who had suggested that pregnant women and children leave an area within a five-mile radius of the plant, and who wanted to know whether he should order a general evacuation of the area.

The public was not reassured by the news coming from the crippled plant. On Thursday Creitz conceded that similar incidents had happened earlier at TMI's Unit 1, which had been shut down for routine refueling at the time of the accident, but that in these instances the tanks had not overflowed. At this time, too, company officials revealed that some of the reactor's fuel rods had been damaged when the core became uncovered early in the accident. Met Ed said that less than 1 percent of the reactor's 37,000 fuel rods had been damaged. After doing some checking of their own, however, NRC officials tipped the estimate to 60 percent.

By Friday the public's credulousness was stretched to the breaking point by the news that additional releases of radioactive steam were coming from the plant. The releases, like those that had taken place earlier, were accidental. According to NRC investigators, plant workers had been trying to remove some radioactive water from the pump building. But as the water flowed into a storage tank, the temperature and pressure both began to climb, causing a valve to open and allowing the gases to escape into the building. There, they were sucked up by the ventilation system and blown out a stack—just, as Met Ed's luck would have it, as a federal-state monitoring crew flew by in a small plane. . . .

On Sunday President Jimmy Carter, a one-time U.S. Navy nuclear engineer, helicoptered from Washington to Middletown, where he donned yellow plastic boots and toured the plant for a briefing on what had happened and what was being done to end TMI-2's excursion and bring it back under control. The NRC determined that the hydrogen bubble—if it had actually existed—was gone. Radiation monitors spotted around the area revealed that radiation levels had returned to normal. The reactor itself was stable and cooling down, though too slowly to make anyone involved with it feel completely at ease. Governor Thornburgh heaved a sigh of relief at the realization that an evacuation would be unnecessary, and the 100,000 or so of the area's 650,000 residents who had fled—many of them to cots set up in an auditorium at an amusement park in nearby Hershey—began to return to their homes. The crisis at Three Mile Island was over.

But much work remained to be done. The reactor still needed to be cooled to the point that officials could declare a "cold shutdown" and allow NRC engineers and plant workers to begin the monumental task of cleaning up the mess and decontaminating the reactor and auxiliary buildings. An investigation had to be launched to determine what had happened, to review the design and the mechanical and human failures that had caused and contributed to the accident, and to determine what could be done to see that they did not happen again. And the nuclear power industry, which had allowed its own handling of the accident to destroy in days such credibility as it had managed to build up over a period of years, had to take stock of itself and see what it could learn from its terrifying experience.

The week after the accident was spent in installing new plumbing so that a process of natural circulation could be used to cool down the reactor and get the temperature of its coolant down to a safe 200 degrees or less. It was also spent in assessing the damage to the plant, which was considerable. Robert M. Bernero, an NRC expert on nuclear plant decommissioning, estimated that the cost of cleaning up the plant could easily come to more than the $700 million GPU had spent to build TMI-2 in the first place. . . .

But it was NRC Commissioner Victor Gilinsky, a Carter appointee and a frequent critic of the nuclear power industry, who best summed up the effect of the accident at Three Mile Island. "What shook the public the most," he said, "was seeing the men in the white lab coats standing around and scratching their heads because they didn't know what to do. The result was that accidents got taken seriously in a way they never had before."

Gilinsky was right. Before Three Mile Island, nuclear accidents were only theoretical hazards, the stuff of movie plots or eventualities conjured up by people in the antinuclear movement to strengthen their philosophical arguments against nuclear power. Before Three Mile Island, nuclear accidents seemed less than real to most people, remote possibilities that might or could happen, but not something likely to happen soon or in the worst way possible.

The accident changed the public's perception about nuclear risks just as dramatically as a miracle changes the faith of those who witness it. It showed that major accidents, accidents that *could* endanger the lives of hundreds of thousands, that *could* meet all the conditions of the Rasmussen Report's worst-case scenario, could really happen. It showed, too, that neither utility company executives nor the NRC really knew how to deal with major mishaps at nuclear power plants. It showed, finally, that the public was not being well protected by the agency that licensed and monitored nuclear power plants, for one of the things that came out early in the period following the accident was that TMI-2 had been plagued with problems since it first went on-line and that neither the company nor the NRC had done much to solve them.

The accident at Three Mile Island did not kill or injure anyone immediately, as company officials were quick to note. But it did kill something. It killed public trust. Americans might have been willing to trust the industry and the NRC before the accident. Now they were suspicious of both.

The Romance with the Automobile Ends

Robert L. Shook

For years Americans loved American automobiles. Expensive cars pointed to a person's level of success. Cars with big gas-guzzling engines were statements of power. Large, heavy, chrome-laden sedans were expressions of luxury, comfort, and style. In the '70s these assumptions were suddenly attacked by the realities of limited and expensive gasoline. As the decade progressed, foreign cars were increasingly accepted for their quality and economy. Robert L. Shook is a writer who enjoys exploring the workings of large corporations. His earlier books have dealt with computer mogul IBM and the Honda Motor Company.

The automobile offered an extraordinary convenience, and by the 1950s, practically every family owned one. In the 1960s, two-car families were commonplace. In time, merely owning a car was no longer the status symbol; instead it was the kind of car that counted. It was a period when bigger meant better in America, and bigger cars provided more prestige. They were heavy and bulky. Many even came equipped with "fins" to add a few inches to their already excessive length. As car sizes increased, so did fuel consumption. But during the 1950s and 1960s it did not matter that Detroit produced gas-guzzlers—energy was cheap.

Excerpted from *Turnaround: The New Ford Motor Company,* by Robert L. Shook (New York: Prentice-Hall, 1990). Copyright ©1990 by Robert L. Shook. Reprinted with permission from the author.

By the early 1970s, Americans, an estimated 5 percent of the world's population, drove nearly 40 percent of the world's motor vehicles with 120 million cars on the road. There was practically a car for every licensed driver (140 million Americans possessed a driver's license). The car had become a necessity. Making one's car payment took priority over the mortgage payment.

As far as the public was concerned, there was a bottomless oil well beneath America's soil. The government artificially kept the price of energy low, so there was no reason for anyone to think differently. Washington had no real energy policy. The federal government spent $77.8 billion to construct an interstate highway system on which Americans could travel at 70 miles per hour (MPH) from coast to coast. The Big Three [automakers: General Motors, Ford, and Chrysler] continued to produce oversize behemoths that were purchased as quickly as they rolled off assembly lines.

Even when it became known that there was a limit to the American oil supply, it had no appreciable effect on the production of gas-guzzlers. Americans still wanted their big cars, and the domestic automakers delighted in accommodating them. There was an added incentive: Big cars generated big profits.

The First Oil Shortage

On October 6, 1973, on the eve of Yom Kippur, the most holy day in the Jewish religion, Egypt attacked Israel. Israel struck back, and, for the third time since World War II, the small Jewish state whipped an enemy who greatly outnumbered her. The defeat humiliated the entire Arab world, and it retaliated with its most powerful weapon: an oil boycott, aimed primarily at the United States, Israel's supporter. It took the Yom Kippur War to create an awareness in America that the well did indeed have a bottom. The boycott began in November 1973, and lasted until the following March. For many Americans, it was traumatic to learn that one out of every three gallons of fuel poured into their gas tanks came from faraway, volatile countries. For the first time in memory, Americans were forced to do with less. Some of our smugness vanished, particularly when, by early January 1974, we found ourselves bumper-to-bumper in long lines to purchase gasoline. Long lines also appeared at the showrooms of automobile dealerships selling sub-compacts and, in particular, fuel-efficient models equipped with stick shifts.

The gas shortages across America resulted in forecasts of small-car sales capturing 50 percent of the market by the end of the year. Big Three headquarters' predictions said this figure could reach 60 percent by 1980. Executives at American Motors, which only manufactured small cars, were patting themselves on the back for having anticipated the trend as they enjoyed an immediate 28 percent increase in sales by the end of 1973. In the meantime, Detroit was busy reducing the weight of its 1975 domestic models, which led to a 13.5 percent improvement in fuel economy. Automobile executives started gearing up to build small cars to accommodate the public demand.

Return to Normal?

Gas prices, however, leveled off at 60 cents a gallon by the spring of 1974, and a fickle America abruptly became disenchanted with little cars. By the end of the third quarter in 1974, huge inventories of small cars began to pile up. Ford had a 96-day supply of Pintos while the demand for Lincoln Mark IVs was so great that its employees were working two shifts to assemble them. General Motors (GM) was sitting on a 105-day supply of Vegas, yet its Cadillac plants were working overtime with an inventory down to 26 days. Chrysler accumulated a 105-day supply of Plymouth Valiants, and the inventory of its Japanese-made minicar, the Dodge Colt, was up to a 113-day supply.

The demand for small cars was suddenly so light that major rebate programs were implemented so automakers could rid themselves of their large inventories. Chrysler was the first to rebate, offering discounts on its entire line, the highest rebates offered on its small cars. GM and Ford gave rebates only on their subcompacts. Meanwhile, American Motors, which had enjoyed record sales on its hot-selling Gremlin only six months previously, was now forced to sell that model at a substantial discount.

Even with their bargain-basement prices, the huge inventories of small cars did not go away. Henry Ford II went to Washington to persuade the federal government to place a 10 percent tax on the price of gasoline, which would make small cars more appealing. President Gerald Ford's new energy czar, John Sawhill, went so far as to propose a $1 per gallon tax in an effort to induce the nation to conserve energy. By this time, a high percentage of the American public was seriously questioning whether there had ever been a gas shortage in 1973, calling the whole thing a hoax engineered by profit-hungry oil companies.

Confusion About Oil Supplies

There was good reason for the average American to reach such a conclusion. The profits the oil companies realized when the oil embargo ended were huge. When it was over, the price of crude oil had quadrupled from $2 to $8 a barrel, which doubled the price of gas at the pump in the United States from about 30 cents to 60 cents. With a barrel containing 42 gallons, each $1 increase amounted to 2.38 cents per gallon. So while the increase from 30 to 60 cents was a big one, it was quite modest in view of the frightening predictions of the $2 and $3 per gallon costs rumored only months before. At 60 cents a gallon, the fuel cost of running an American car in 1973 was less than 4 cents a mile, or about $1 a day, small potatoes for the average worker who put in less than five minutes at his job to pay for the gasoline consumed in a ten-mile trip.

Consumer advocate Ralph Nader was one of the first to insist that vast oil reserves existed throughout the world and there was no real need to worry about shortages. Before long, the media had convinced the public that greedy oil companies were exploiting the consumer for obscene profits. A Democratic Congress disregarded President

Ford's plea to abolish price controls on oil and actually voted to lower the price for the election year of 1976. Hence, in early December 1975, the Federal Energy Administration was ordered to roll back the price of oil by one dollar a barrel by February 1976. Although the legislation did permit the price of oil to increase with the rate of inflation, the increase was limited to no more than 10 percent annually. In effect, the government told its citizens loudly and clearly that cheap gas was here to stay. Energy analysts estimated that under the worst scenario, the price of a gallon of gasoline would remain below 70 cents through 1980.

There was no incentive for consumers to conserve oil, nor, for that matter, were domestic oil companies motivated to extract the precious substance from the ground. This prompted the government, under the auspices of the 1975 Energy Policy and Conservation Act, to establish Corporate Average Fuel Economy (CAFE). In doing so, the burden of energy conservation was placed on those manufacturers that built cars. Under CAFE, each automobile company's fleet of cars was required to be improved to achieve an average of 18 MPG by 1978, with this number increasing to 20 MPG by 1980 and to 27.5 MPG by 1985.

American Automakers Struggle

The year 1978 was selected as the first year for mandatory improvement in fuel efficiency, giving Detroit a three-year lead time to come up with the technology to meet CAFE requirements. However, imported cars, especially those made in Japan, were already small and had adequate fuel efficiency. The mandatory government regulations worked in their favor, providing them a strong competitive advantage over American automakers. This created a real dilemma in Detroit. The demand in America was for big cars, and while eager to offer what the public wanted, car manufacturers also had to comply with federal regulations.

The nation's two biggest automakers had the staying power to begin extensive retooling programs to "downsize," which appeared to be an adequate solution. GM announced that it would invest $15 billion by 1985 to downsize its entire line of cars. Following GM's lead, number two and much smaller Ford would make a more modest investment focusing on the immediate market. When Ford brought out its 1977 LTD, it was advertised as "big as a Cadillac, but priced like a Chevrolet," and it sold well. Both companies' full-size cars, such as the Mercury, Buick, and Oldsmobile, were built to give the appearance of being big, but actually were greatly reduced in length and weight. The public thought it was buying big cars and was satisfied.

Meanwhile American Motors, which had prospered during the oil embargo, had by the spring of 1975 begun the tailspin that eventually led to its demise. By 1978, American Motors had retained only about half the number of workers on its 1962 payroll. Only the sale of Jeeps kept the ailing company afloat. Chrysler was also in considerable trouble. It did not have the financial strength to keep up with Ford and GM. When the demand for big cars accelerated in 1976, the number three automaker began to flounder. Although 1978 was a big year for Ford and GM, Chrysler was operating in the red. In spite of having the best corporate average fuel economy of the Big Three, the company could not weather the demands of a market that teetered back and forth between small cars and big cars.

More Government Regulations

In addition to fuel efficiency regulations, the government saddled the domestic carmakers with another burden. The growing concern with the nation's environment created a public awareness of air pollution. Shortly after the publication of Rachel Carson's provocative book, *The Silent Spring*, April 22, 1970, was declared Earth Day, a symbolic event with millions of Americans demonstrating their sentiments for a cleaner environment. Public opinion placed the blame on those companies that made certain products, among which the automobile manufacturers were denounced as the most flagrant villains. It was the same year that the Clean Air Act was passed. Under the jurisdiction of the U.S. Environmental Protection Agency, the law declared that by 1975 federal standards would require hydrocarbon emissions to be no greater than 0.41 gram per mile. Carbon monoxide was limited to 3.4 grams per mile, and nitrogen oxide emission had a ceiling of 3.1 grams per mile. Meeting these standards would reduce by 96 percent the pollutants in the air caused by automobiles. To achieve this objective, all cars with a conventional internal combustion engine that did not meet these standards would be required to have a catalytic converter to suppress the production of the unwanted pollutants. The catalytic converter and other add-ons increased the cost of a car by an estimated $350.

Views of American-Made Automobiles

In the 1970s cars built in the United States were attacked for their lack of quality. As a result, imported automobiles grew in popularity.

The situation reached ludicrous heights in 1978, the last boom year for Detroit (9.3 million car sales). The Big Two and the Little Two (Chrysler and AMC) pumped out automobiles at a furious rate, with negligible regard for quality. At the same time, the companies were making a major effort to meet stringent government emission control and safety regulations and to launch a new generation of down-sized automobiles. With the best engineering talent focused on the future, little attention was paid to the briskly-selling machinery that was pouring off the assembly lines. The result? Some of the shabbiest automobiles in the history of the industry.

Such popular cars as the Oldsmobile Cutlass and the Ford Thunderbird were officially recalled no less than nine times during 1977 and 1981 to correct defects in the steering, suspension,

There is no doubt that the needs for improved fuel efficiency and air free of automobile engine pollutants were crucial to the well-being of the nation. From the automobile industry's viewpoint, however, the government had taken the wrong approach. As Ford's Helen Petrauskas, vice-president of environmental and safety engineering and the company's highest-ranking woman, explains, "The government insisted that nonexisting technology be invented according to a specific schedule it had legislated. The industry was forced to develop technology by 1975 that had never before been done. To make matters worse, we were asked to meet certain requirements piecemeal—do this by this date, so much by this year, and then do this, and so on, meaning that every year, we had to regroup and

fuel and electrical systems. The GM X-cars that were thrown onto the market to meet the imported front-wheel drive threat were recalled no less than *four* times in 1980 alone to repair factory-built brake, suspension, fuel system and transmission flaws. Hardly a day passed without an announcement issuing from Detroit that one or more of its products was being summoned back to the dealerships to make special repairs. . . .

The result has been a public perception of domestic car quality as inferior to that of foreign makes. This has long been a source of bafflement to American automakers, who have pointed out that domestic power plants are the most trouble-free in the world and that American-made automatic transmissions have unprecedented durability. Many executives, principally Lee Iacocca of Chrysler, have reminded us that because of their products' greater vulnerability to rust, no Japanese manufacturer will offer a five-year/50,000 mile warranty. But the public is insistent; poll after poll indicates that Americans believe Japanese and European cars are better built.

Brock Yates, *The Decline and Fall of the American Automobile Industry*. New York: Empire, 1983.

come up with more changes. It would have been more reasonable if each specific requirement was set with a long-term goal for which the industry was responsible. To do so would have been more reasonable and certainly more efficient. It's unfortunate but the government bureaucrats who didn't understand automotive technology had the power to set unattainable standards."

Henry Nichol, general manager of Ford's Powertrain Operations, puts it more bluntly, "It simply was not in the cards for the industry to meet the emission control regulations set by the government in the allotted time frame."

Thus the late 1970s were frustrating years for automobile executives. Ford's chairman, Henry Ford II, had good reason to declare, "They [the government] took the fun out of the business."

To make matters worse, Washington's goals were conflicting. The improvement of engines that would result in less air pollution would also result in less fuel efficiency. Frustrated automotive executives stated their position at a series of Washington hearings, but for the most part government officials turned a deaf ear, frequently accusing the industry of dragging its feet. The public was unsympathetic to the industry's problems.

Japanese Technology and Quality

Honda's 1973 introduction of the compound vortex controlled combustion (CVCC) engine made the formerly minor automaker one of the major players in the U.S. market. Prior to the CVCC, Honda was considered a motorcycle manufacturer that also happened to sell cars. With its breakthrough technology, Honda was the only car company that eliminated the need for a catalytic converter, and by 1975, Honda was selling 10,000 Civics a month. When an article appeared in the December 1975 issue of *Reader's Digest,* titled "From Japan—A 'Clean Car' That Saves Gas," Honda quickly gained credibility. The following year, Honda brought out its larger Accord, which was named *Motor Trend* magazine's Import Car of the Year. This was a major turning point for Honda, Japan's third largest automobile manufacturer. By the 1980s, Honda became the fourth largest seller of cars in the United States, right on the heels of Chrysler.

So while the American automakers were concentrating on meeting government regulations, Honda and other Japanese automakers were able to gain a competitive edge. Although every manufacturer selling cars in the United States was governed by the same regulations, the Japanese companies sold mainly small cars, and were already capable of meeting CAFE standards. The Big Three sold a broad range of cars that included large sedans and station wagons, and this forced them to come up with improved technology so that their entire product line would *average* those required standards, as established by the 1975 Energy Policy and Conservation Act.

The Japanese automakers took full advantage of their opportunity to gain ground. While Detroit executives were racking their brains to come up with the new technology, the Japanese were engaged in an all-out effort to improve the overall quality of their cars. In particular, they focused on adding deluxe features generally earmarked for big cars, such as automatic transmission and power steering. They also intensified their efforts to include extras as standard equipment.

In spite of the difficulties facing the domestic automobile industry, Ford and General Motors continued to sell their big, expensive cars and enjoyed big profits. It was as though the 1973 oil embargo had never happened. The U.S. automobile industry realized $3 billion in profits during 1978, having its third best year in history (although this was when Chrysler started losing money). Ironically, it was a year in which Detroit was fearful that it would be unable to fulfill the strong consumer demand for big V-8-powered sedans. Not only did the domestic automakers produce more V-8-powered, full-sized cars, they also built longer and heavier compacts, many loaded to the hilt with options.

The Second Oil Shortage

In 1978, when the American economy appeared to have fully recovered from the 1973 oil embargo, more troubles in the Middle East were brewing. The Ayatollah Khomeini's eventual overthrow of the Iranian government was underway, and the Shah of Iran, who had ruled since 1953, was about to lose power. Since the 1950s, the United States had centered its Middle East economic policy around its support of the Shah. Billions of U.S. dollars in military and economic aid had gone his way. But in the end, the Shah could not appease the mullahs, the holy men. Knowing he could not win what had become a holy war, the Shah and his family escaped from Tehran on January 16, 1979, taking a sizable fortune with them. The handwriting was now plainly on the wall; the world must brace itself for another energy crunch.

Once the Ayatollah seized control of Iran, he showed his contempt for the United States by denouncing anything connected with the Western world. Khomeini turned off the spigot and created a second oil crisis. In a matter of weeks the price of gasoline doubled. Once again, America was caught off guard. As Allan Gilmour, who then served as Ford's executive director of Corporate North American Analysis, explains, "On the surface, the business of Ford Motor Company was going very well. The company was enjoying a series of consecutive record quarterly profits. Then, along comes a second oil embargo, and the critics started to shout, 'But you damn fools, why didn't the company anticipate another oil crisis?' To them, my stock reply is we didn't hear anyone on the outside saying that the Shah of Iran was going to be thrown out." A valid point for the public to remember is that the U.S. government, even with its vast network of intelligence, was not aware of what was happening in Iran. So why should the nation's business community be expected to have been prepared for a second oil crisis?

In 1974, Henry Ford II vetoed a decision to spend $2 billion to build a U.S.-made, front-wheel-drive subcompact, instead opting to downsize the LTD and other models, and save money. In 1978, it was obvious that the Ford chief executive officer (CEO) had made the wrong decision. The redone LTD had weak sales when it came out in the fall, and Ford had no new domestically built subcompacts in its inventory. "We misread where the market would be today," Henry Ford confessed. "We were not as well prepared for it as we should have been. It was a big mistake."

At the time of the Shah's fall there had been waiting lists for the Big Three's full-size cars, so much so that Ford was actually rationing V-8 engines. By the spring of 1979, however, Americans across the country were waiting in long lines for gas. A few weeks later, service stations were working banker's hours and drivers were hard pressed to find gas on the weekends. Americans began forming car pools, and in some areas, most notably Los Angeles, cars on the freeways with no passengers were confined to nonpassing lanes. Not only was gasoline hard to buy but the price continued to rise. Once again the general consensus was that the cost of a gallon of gasoline would hit the $2.50 mark within a few years.

The End of the Gas-Guzzler

History repeated itself. There was an overnight demand for small cars, and once again, the domestic automobile industry did not have them. As early as January 1979, Datsuns, Toyotas, and Hondas were packed into dealers' showrooms and lots. Suddenly, there was enormous demand for Japanese fuel-efficient cars and there were plenty of them to meet the demand. According to *Ward's Automotive Reports*, by March 1, a total of 529,703 unsold Japanese cars and light trucks had accumulated at the docks and dealer lots and showrooms across the country. Thousands more were sitting on idle ships anchored in bays, waiting for somewhere to unload their cargo. The Japanese had made practically nothing but small cars for three decades, so whenever the demand changed, they were ready.

Lines of customers formed at Japanese automobile dealer

showrooms throughout America. Suddenly, the American consumer was sickened by the thought of purchasing a U.S.-made gas-guzzler. Japanese cars offered excellent fuel efficiency and improved quality, and they now contained many of the features of the big cars. At the same time, the quality of American automobiles had actually slipped a few notches in the late 1970s as domestic manufacturers struggled to meet new fuel economy and emission standards.

It was no contest. The Japanese cars sold like hotcakes, and, to the delightful surprise of their purchasers, *they were good cars,* with far fewer problems than those made in the United States. *Made in Japan* was no longer synonymous with shoddy merchandise. The American public quickly forgot that, as recently as 1970, imported cars accounted for only 15 percent of the market but amounted to 45 percent of the total recalls that year. By May 1979, there were waiting lists of up to a year for some Japanese models.

CHAPTER 4

Popular Culture in the 1970s

Pop Music in the '70s

David P. Szatmary

David P. Szatmary holds a Ph.D. in American history and has extensively studied the history of rock music. In the selection below, Szatmary discusses the fragmentation of rock music in the 1970s. He discusses not only the new directions which popular music was developing, but also new forces in popular music. In contrast to the radical, change-the-world idealism of the 1960s, rock in the '70s became more conservative, more private, and less concerned with social reform.

"We know that people and movements are fallible," one college senior from American University told *Time* magazine in the early 1970s. "We're afraid to believe too much in anything or anyone."

In the aftermath of Kent State, most youths in the Woodstock generation agreed with the jaded, critical sentiments expressed by the college senior from American University. Sent to a war in a faraway land and attacked by National Guardsmen at home, they abandoned the hope for a revolution in values and began to turn inward.

Economic conditions caused further concern. From 1969 to 1970 unemployment in the United States increased from 3.5 percent to 6.2 percent. In the same year, the buying power of the dollar declined by nearly 6 percent and the government cut public spending and imposed credit re-

Excerpted from *Rockin' in Time: A Social History of Rock-and-Roll*, 2nd ed., by David P. Szatmary. Copyright ©1995. Adapted by permission of Prentice-Hall, Inc., Upper Saddle River, N.J.

strictions. Throughout the country, fears of a major recession racked most Americans.

The music reflected a sober, conservative mood as many deserted a hard-driving rock. "The fading out of ear-numbing, mind blowing acid rock," *Time* contended in early 1971, "is related to the softening of the youth revolution. Its decline is variously viewed as a symptom of either progress toward harmony and thoughtfulness or a tragic slide from activist rage to a mode of 'enlightened apathy.'"

Rather than the pounding, loud sounds of psychedelia or the wrenching, angry urban blues, rock became soft, serious, and introspective. Built upon the yen for experimentation fostered during the hippie era, it was fused with more respectable, established musical forms such as jazz, classical, country and folk. From 1970 to 1973, rock-and-roll became an apolitical, intensely personal experience.

A New Fusion of Styles

Rock-and-roll had always been a union of diverse types of music. At its inception, it had been an amalgam of electric R & B [rhythm and blues] and country, first joined together by Chuck Berry, Elvis and the rockabillies. During the mid-1960s, when Bob Dylan plugged an electric guitar cord into an amplifier, rock merged with folk for what critics called folk rock. Later in the decade, the Beatles and others introduced Indian musical instruments such as the sitar to their music.

Performers during the early 1970s continued to fuse rock with other musical forms such as jazz. Jazz great Miles Davis, who had been present at the inception of bop during the mid-forties, spearheaded the trend. In 1970, Davis blended a raw-edged, slightly dissonant sixties jazz with the electric sound of rock, emerging with *Bitches Brew*. Wrote Ralph Gleason in the liner notes on the album: "This music is new. This music is new music and it hits me like an electric shock and the word 'electric' is interesting because the music is to some degree electric music. . . . Electric music is the music of this culture and in the breaking away (not the breaking down) from previously assumed forms a new kind of music is emerging."

The album included the innovators of the fusion movement: John McLaughlin on guitar, Joe Zawinul's electric piano on some cuts, Chick Corea's electric keyboard on others, and the soprano sax of Wayne Shorter. John McLaughlin, playing with the Graham Bond Organization in the early sixties and later with the Tony Williams Lifetime jazz outfit, went on to form the jazz-rock Mahavishnu Orchestra. Zawinul and Wayne Shorter continued the fusion experiment in Weather Report, and Chick Corea in 1972 brought together Stanley Clarke, Joe Farrell, and Airto Moreira in Return to Forever. These musicians, along with a number of mainstream jazz performers who hoped to make some money with the new style, defined and shaped the sound of the jazz-rock fusion.

Some rock bands grafted a horn section onto their music in the fusion experiment. Organized by Al Kooper, a former member of the Blues Project, Blood, Sweat and Tears played a blues-based music complimented by the horns of such New York jazzmen as trumpeter Randy Brecker on their first LP, the 1968 *Child Is the Father to the Man*. When Kooper quit in 1969 after the album failed to sell, the band recruited vocalist David Clayton-Thomas who added a pop element to the jazz rock for the top-selling *Blood, Sweat and Tears*, which included the music of jazz great Billie Holiday.

The band Chicago also featured a horn section. Formed in 1967 as Big Thing by school friends, guitarist Terry Kath and hornman Walter Parazaider, the band changed its name to Chicago Transit Authority and in 1969 released a political jazz-rock album that included protest chants from the 1968 Democratic National convention. Under the guidance of manager James William Guernico during the early 1970s, the band shortened its name to Chicago, dispensed with radical politics, and fused its sound with pop for a string of hits such as "Saturday in the Park." "These days nobody wants to hear songs that have a message," asserted

Robert Lamm by the early 1970s.

Pink Floyd, a sixties British psychedelic band, changed course in the seventies to expand upon fusion's flirtation with electronics. Formed in 1965, the band began by playing R & B music, named after country-blues duo Pink Anderson and Floyd Council. By 1967 Pink Floyd had developed a psychedelic sound, releasing two records in the genre. When vocalist-guitarist Syd Barrett became incapacitated because of an LSD experiment, the group hired guitarist David Gilmore who led the band to a subtle, electronic sound evidenced on a number of soundtracks. By their 1973 masterpiece, *Dark Side of the Moon,* which took nine painstaking months to produce, Pink Floyd had perfected a Wagnerian, electronic sound that provided a backdrop for tales of alienation and paranoia. . . .

Back to the Country

Confronted by the harsh, complicated realities of an unwanted war in Vietnam and events at Kent State, some folk rockers began to move toward a storytelling country music which extolled simple living and rural traditions. "Country rock," observed *Time* in 1970, was a "turning back toward easy-rhythmed blues, folk songs and the twangy, lonely lamentations known as country music." The new musical blend, continued *Time,* was a "symptom of a general cultural reaction to the most unsettling decade that the U.S. has yet endured. The yen to escape the corrupt present by returning to the virtuous past—real or imagined—has haunted Americans, never more so than today."

Bob Dylan, the most visible protest singer of the 1960s, led the movement back to the country. In May 1969, Dylan released the country-influenced LP, *Nashville Skyline,* recorded in the country music capitol, which on "Girl From North Country" featured a duet with former rockabilly and country music giant, Johnny Cash. In the same month, Dylan appeared with Cash on a television special filmed at the Grand Ole Opry.

The Band, Dylan's sometime backing group, began to

achieve popularity with its country-based rock. Joining rockabilly singer Ronnie Hawkins in the early sixties, guitarist James Robbie Robertson, pianist Richard Manuel, drummer Levon Helm, bassist Rick Danko and organist Garth Hudson by 1964 had formed their own group. Robertson and Helm backed Dylan when he first plugged in an electric guitar and after Dylan's 1965 motorcycle accident the group moved near the reclusive singer in Woodstock, New York.

The Band, as they were now called, recorded their debut at Woodstock in their large, pink-colored house and in 1968 released *Music From Big Pink* which included a number of Dylan songs. The next year, they hit the Top 10 with the heavily country-influenced, self-named LP which included the hit, "Up on Cripple Creek." By late 1970 the group reached the Top 5 with their third album, *Stage Fright*. The Band, wrote *Time,* perfected a rock hybrid that "comes on mainly as country music full of straight lines and sentiment."

Poco offered a similar brand of country rock. In late 1968 when the folk-rock group Buffalo Springfield splintered into the trio Crosby, Stills and Nash and a solo career for Neil Young, Springfield guitarist Riches Furay decided to form a country-rock outfit with his friend Jim Messina. "Richie and I were riding in a cab in Nashville," remembered Messina. "We talked about forming a new band that would be an extension of what we'd been doing with the Springfield, but more country and rock than folk and rock." The duo invited guitarist Rusty Young, bassist Randy Meisner and drummer George Grantham to join Pogo, renamed Poco when the owners of the Pogo comic strip threatened legal action over the use of the name. After two moderately successful efforts, in 1971 the group neared the Top 20 with the LP *Deliverin'* which relied heavily on such traditional country instruments as steel guitars, mandolins and dobros. . . .

The disintegration of the American family, coupled with the decline of political activism, gave rise to a less countrified version of folk music that dealt with the loneliness of the single adult. In the 1970s, as the number of women in the work force doubled, many Americans, especially the baby boomers, began to divorce their partners at an increasing rate. In 1969, only three Americans in 1,000 filed for divorce. Five years later, 4.5 per 1,000 divorced their mates. By the end of the decade, 5.3 Americans in 1,000 ended their marriages, and for every five Americans who married, three divorced.

Many baby boomers began to question the institution of matrimony. In one study conducted during 1971 among college students, more than 34 percent of the respondents believed that marriage was obsolete. Two years later, according to a Rutgers University student survey, 30 percent of the seniors felt that marriage was no longer a viable option.

Getting divorced or no longer entering wedlock, many baby boomers lived the sometimes lonely life of the unmarried adult. By 1978, more than 1.1 million Americans lived in single households, an increase of 117 percent in a decade. To find companionship, they populated singles bars, singles resorts, and singles housing complexes.

James Taylor

In the early 1970s, singer-songwriters sang ballads about the emotional traumas of divorce, lost love, and loneliness in a plaintive, confessional music that had its roots in sixties folk. James Taylor, the prototype of the easygoing seventies folkster, grew up in North Carolina and spent his summers on the exclusive Martha's Vineyard near Boston listening to the records of the Weavers, Woody Guthrie, and Pete Seeger. He began playing with friend Danny Kortchmar as a folk duo, James & Kootch, which won a local hootenanny contest. In 1966, he joined Kortchmar's band, The Flying Machine, which performed in such Greenwich Village coffeehouses as the Night Owl before disbanding a year later. Taylor, exhausted and suffering from a heroin addiction, in 1968 traveled to England, where he recorded his first LP for the Beatles-owned Apple

Records. When his vinyl debut failed to chart despite background work by Paul McCartney and George Harrison, the singer returned to the United States.

Taylor rebounded from his setback in 1970. After appearing at the Newport Folk Festival, he landed a contract with Warner Brothers through manager Peter Asher. In early 1970, he recorded the album *Sweet Baby James,* which reached the Top 5 and remained on the charts for more than two years. The singer followed with *Mud Slide Slim and the Blue Horizon,* which neared the top of the charts in the United States and Britain and included the Carole King–written chart-topper, "You've Got a Friend," a soft, reassuring ballad appropriate for the millions of divorced and unmarried baby boomers.

Taylor, as with most of the seventies singer-songwriters, wrote and performed a collection of acoustic confessions. "I wish I weren't so self-centered or self-referred all the time with the stuff I write," he later complained, "but for some reason that's the window I utilize, hopefully in an open-ended way."

Carole King and Carly Simon

Other seventies folk artists, congregating around James Taylor, penned self-revelatory paeans of loneliness and confusion. Carole King, the Brill Building sensation of the early 1960s, became intrigued by the New York folk scene after she divorced her husband-collaborator Gerry Goffin. She backed The Flying Machine in Greenwich Village and in 1968 with Danny Kortchmar formed the short-lived band City.

In 1970, through the help of James Taylor, King again hit the top of the charts. That year she played piano on *Sweet Baby James* and with the encouragement of Taylor released the LP *Writer.* At mid-year, she toured with Taylor to promote the album. In October, with drummer Russ Kunkel, Kortchmar, and Taylor, Carole King began to record the album *Tapestry* which sold more than 15 million copies and included her own version of "You've Got a

Friend" which, as with the Taylor rendition, climbed to the top of the charts. She also composed such tales of lost love as "So Far Away" and "It's Too Late."

Carly Simon had an even more intimate relationship with James Taylor. Daughter of Richard L. Simon, co-founder of Simon & Schuster publishers, Carly left the exclusive Sarah Lawrence College to perform and record as a folk duo with her sister, Lucy. In 1967, after the Simon Sisters disbanded, she signed with Bob Dylan's manager Albert Grossman, who hoped to promote her as a female Dylan and recorded four unreleased tracks. Two years later, Carly met Jac Holzman, owner of Elektra Records, who signed her to his label and in 1971 released the singer's solo debut, which reached number 30 on the charts. She recorded her second LP, *Anticipation,* which included the top-selling single of the same name. In 1972, Carly Simon topped the charts with the single "You're So Vain," and the LP *No Secrets,* and on November 3 married James Taylor in her Manhattan apartment. In 1974, the husband-wife team dueted in the Top 5 single "Mockingbird."

Joni Mitchell and Others

Joni Mitchell, collaborating with a number of sixties folksters, strummed to the top of seventies folk. Born Roberta Joan Anderson, she began to play an acoustic folk in her native Calgary, Canada. In 1964, she performed at the Mariposa Folk Festival and the next year, after moving to Toronto, she met and married Chuck Mitchell, who played with her as a folk duo in local coffeehouses. In 1966 Mitchell moved to Detroit, where she became a sensation on the folk scene and began to make appearances in New York City. While in Greenwich Village, Mitchell met such folk artists as Judy Collins, who hit in 1967 with Mitchell's "Both Sides Now."

Mitchell, signed to Reprise Records in 1967, released her debut album, which was produced by ex-Byrd David Crosby and included on guitar Stephen Stills, formerly of the folk-rock band Buffalo Springfield. The next year, she recorded her second LP, *Clouds,* which reached the Top 30 and earned her a Best Folk Performer award.

Mitchell, as with other singer-songwriters of the era, sang about the loneliness of broken relationships. In 1971, enlisting the support of Stephen Stills on bass and James Taylor on guitar, who had asked Mitchell to sing background vocals on "You've Got A Friend," she recorded the album *Blue* which featured such tales of lost love as "The Last Time I Saw Richard," "This Flight Tonight," and the title song. "When I think of Vietnam or Berkeley, I feel so helpless," Mitchell told *Time.* "I just write about what happens to me."

Joni Mitchell helped propel to stardom Crosby, Stills and Nash, two of whom had aided Mitchell on her debut LP. In mid-1968 after the breakup of the folk-rock group, Buffalo Springfield, Stephen Stills began to practice with ex-Byrd David Crosby (a.k.a. David Van Courtland) and Graham Nash, formerly of the Hollies. A year later the folk rockers released a self-titled album which featured a blend of floating harmonies and acoustic guitars. As their album slowly scaled the charts, the group asked ex-Buffalo Springfield guitarist Neil Young to join and in May 1970 released *Deja Vu* which topped the charts and included their best-selling single, Joni Mitchell's "Woodstock." Unlike most other seventies folksters, in 1970 Crosby, Stills, Nash and Young directly confronted the tragedy at Kent State, recording the blistering, electric "Ohio." In late 1970 amid a tour, the foursome disbanded due to internal tensions and splintered into four successful solo acts. With the help of Joni Mitchell, David Crosby neared the Top 10 with the album *If I Could Only Remember My Name.* Stephen Stills, studying guitar with Jimi Hendrix, released a blues-drenched solo LP which almost topped the charts, and in 1971 Graham Nash recorded his solo debut. In late 1970, Neil Young released the Top 10 LP *After the Goldrush* and two years later followed with the chart-topper *Harvest,* which featured James Taylor and Linda Ronstadt.

The Arizona-born Linda Ronstadt provided the focal point for several other folksters. In 1964, she moved to Los Angeles to join the folk trio the Stone Poneys. Though selling few copies of their debut, the group scored in 1968 with "A Different Drum" before disbanding.

After a series of unsuccessful solo albums, Ronstadt recruited from the Troubadour folk club in Los Angeles a tour band including Glenn Frey, Bernie Leadon, Randy Meisner, and Don Henley. In 1973, she hired as manager Peter Asher who had advanced the career of James Taylor.

With a new band and manager, the singer released the LP *Don't Cry Now*, which remained on the charts for fifty-six weeks. During the next five years, Ronstadt recorded a number of top-selling albums that combined the sensitive ballads of seventies folk with new renditions of country-based oldies such as the Everly Brothers' "When Will I Be Loved," "I Can't Help It If I'm Still in Love with You" by Hank Williams, and Buddy Holly's "It's So Easy" and "That'll Be the Day."

Linda Ronstadt professed jaded, conservative beliefs so prevalent during the early 1970s. She hoped for a "real resurgence of patriotism in this country." After campaigning for liberal candidates, the singer felt that "I really didn't know what I was talking about. Who knows who should be President and if anybody should have an interest in determining those things, shouldn't Standard Oil? I mean, they have more to gain and more to lose. If something terrible happens to Standard Oil, a lot of people will be out of jobs. You can say what you want about big multi-nationals running the country and stuff, but the fact remains that we need that, we need their services, we need jobs from them and they are in a better position to decide what's going to be good for the economic climate of the country and for the rest of the world.". . .

Rock of the Absurd

Rock music during the mid- and late-1970s reflected the excessive preoccupation with the individual, which became apparent in a theatrical, glittery, sometimes androgynous heavy-metal rock epitomized by David Bowie. Born David Jones, a teenaged Bowie joined a number of rock outfits, including the King Bees, the Mannish Boys, and The Lower Third, which released unsuccessful singles. In 1966 he changed his name to avoid confusion with Davy Jones of the Monkees and the next year took mime dance lessons. In 1969, amid the furor of the first moon landing, Bowie released "Space Oddity," which hit the Top 5 in Britain.

Bowie began to change his image at the turn of the decade. After backing Marc Bolan, who had begun a

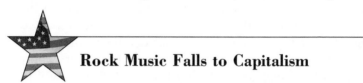

Rock Music Falls to Capitalism

In the 1960s, rock music rebelled against the established cultural values of America. In the 1970s, rock music came to represent and reflect American culture.

In the previous decade, rock was the stuff of the counterculture; in the 1970s and on into the 1980s, this music *was* the culture. In the 1960s, the music's authenticity was measured by the distance it placed between its rebellious, unkempt, adversarial point of view and the acquiescent, mannerly, tame world of professional entertainment. In the 1970s, this notion gradually came to be viewed as unrealistic and immature. For some longtime rock fans, this was proof positive that rock was no longer any good, that it had sold out and become family entertainment only slightly more daring than Buddy Hackett's nightclub act. For others, though, it suggested the enormous outreach and ambition of the music. For the first time in its history, large numbers of people began to think that maybe rock and roll really *was* here to stay; that it could grow and become an artistic medium that could adapt to its aging audience as well as continue to attract the young fans who would remain the lifeblood of the music. What some saw as the death of rock as a challenging, creative glitter-rock craze in England as T-Rex, the singer began to affect an androgynous image, appearing in a dress in public and on the album cover of the LP *The Man Who Sold the World*. In January 1972, Bowie declared his bisexuality to the British music paper the *New Musical Express*.

Expanding on his image, Bowie created the bisexual, space-age, glittery persona of Ziggy Stardust. On August 16, 1972, at the Rainbow Theater in London, he materialized from a cloud of dry ice adorned by a tight-fitting, glimmering jumpsuit, high-topped, sequined hunting boots, and orange-tinted hair. "His eyebrows have vanished, replaced

---

medium, others recognized as an opportunity to spread the music's diverse messages to an unprecedented number of people. And, in some cases, to get rich while doing it.

Let's not underestimate that last part. The first half of the 1970s enjoyed an economy that could support an industry growing at the steady rate of 25 percent each year. The economic drain of the Vietnam War hadn't hit the average music consumer, and with the fall of Saigon in 1975, it was assumed that more able-bodied citizens would be out there roaming the shopping malls with ready discretionary income. Which is to say, the audience for rock was exploding, fueled by enough money to transform the music into big business.

It's significant that at the start of the 1970s, the cant term for music within the industry was *product:* The music had become merchandise to be packaged and sold. Following good capitalist theory, the music industry began to approach its product as a series of alternatives, of choices for the consumer. This was the neatest way to package the growing sprawl of 1970s popular music, and thus the profusion of products lining the record store shelves arranged by neat labels: *singer-songwriters, heavy metal, soft rock, art rock, country rock, disco, reggae,* and *punk.*

Ed Ward, Geoffrey Stokes, and Ken Tucker, *Rock of Ages: The Rolling Stone History of Rock and Roll,* 1986.

by finely sketched red lines. He's wearing red eyeshadow which makes him look faintly insect-like," added the *New Musical Express*. "The only thing that shocks now is an extreme," explained the singer about his space-age character. "Unless you do that, nobody will pay attention to you. Not for long. You have to hit them on the head."

The shocking image of Ziggy Stardust began to sell. After having only limited success with his previous albums, Bowie sold more than a million copies of *The Rise and Fall of Ziggy Stardust and The Spiders from Mars*, which featured a hard-rocking band anchored by guitarist Mick Ronson. The next year, he hit the Top 10 with the album *Aladdin Sane* and began to chart with such previous LPs as *Hunky Dory*.

The heavy-metal androgyny of Ziggy Stardust gave direction to the careers of other bands such as Mott the Hoople. Begun in 1969 as a hard-rock outfit led by singer Ian Hunter, Mott the Hoople initially released four poor-selling albums, which convinced the group to disband. On the eve of their dissolution in March 1972, they met David Bowie, a longtime fan of the group, who offered them one of his songs, "All The Young Dudes." The band, agreeing to wear nine-inch platform shoes, heavy mascara, and sequined costumes, recorded the song, which hit the charts in both Britain and the United States and became a gay-liberation anthem. "We were considered instant fags," remembered the heterosexual Hunter. "A lot of gays followed us around, especially in America.". . .

The New York Dolls adopted the Bowie-defined image of heavy-metal androgyny. Formed in 1971 and fronted by guitarist Johnny Thunders and singer David Johansen, the group began playing locally at such clubs as the Mercer Arts Center. In 1973 they released their first album, which included such thrashing, driving, proto-punk anthems as "Personality Crisis." On the cover, done in gray and shocking pink with the band's name written in lipstick, the group posed with heavy makeup, jewelry, and ruby lipstick. Johansen, a shoulder thrust forward, stared wistfully into the mirror of his powder box. The other group members looked straight ahead, attired in six-inch-heeled boots, skin-tight leather or spandex pants, and provocative blouses.

Kiss tried to outdo the New York Dolls, their cross-town rivals. "In 1972 there was only one impressive band in New York and that was the New York Dolls," remembered Gene Simmons, the former schoolteacher who started Kiss. "I was impressed mostly by their stage presence, and the fact that they didn't look like other American bands." "In the beginning," he added, "we were extremely jealous of the New York Dolls and we were going to do them one better."

To grab attention, the band, according to Simmons, "decided to put on bizarre makeup. I was the bat, without the black lips, wearing a sailor suit. I had no clue. Paul [Stanley] had the rouge and the whiteface, very much like a pretty boy." Like cartoon characters, the face-painted group began to dress in skin-hugging, bejeweled, spandex pants, platform shoes, and black, glittering, leather shirts. Coached by ex-television producer Bill Aucion, Kiss assaulted their audiences with rockets, police lights, snow-machines, smoke bombs, and levitating drum kits. By 1975, when they released the million-selling albums *Dressed to Kill* and *Alive!* the hard-rock band had become one of America's hottest acts. . . .

Disco

Disco epitomized the excesses of the 1970s. It began in New York City at black, Latin, and gay all-night clubs where disc jockeys played nonstop dance music with an insistent, thumping beat. Gradually disco incorporated the antiseptic, rock-steady, electronic beat of such European synthesizer groups as Kraftwerk which, according to Ralf Hutter who started the group with Florian Schneider, consisted of "industrial music; not so much mental or meditative music, but rhythmically more primitive."

By the mid-1970s, disco began to appeal to self-obsessed baby boomers who yearned for center stage. "A few years ago, I went into clubs, and I realized people needed mood music," remarked Neil Bogart, then president of Casablanca Records. "They were tired of guitarists playing to their amplifiers. *They* wanted to be the stars."

Disco, unlike most rock-and-roll, allowed the participants to assume primary importance. Not involving musicians standing on stage, it centered upon the audience. "It's like an adult Disney World. We really give people a chance to get off on their fantasies," explained Steve Rubell, co-owner of one of the premier discos, Studio 54 in New York. "I think the theater atmosphere has a lot to do with it. Everybody secretly likes to be on stage and here we give them a huge space to do it all on." Discos should let "everyone feel like a star," echoed Mark Hugo, manager of a Boston disco.

The various elements of the disco culture embodied the narcissistic extravagance of the mid- and late-seventies. Discotheques, *Time* told its readers in 1977, offered "a space-age world of mesmeric lighting and Neroian decor." Studio 54, once the baroque Fortune Gallo Opera House, featured theatrical lighting, flashing strobes, and more than 450 special effects, including plastic snowfalls and eighty-five-foot backdrops. Zorine's in Chicago offered members rooms of mirrors, twisting staircases, balconies, and secret nooks. In Los Angeles, Dillion's boasted four floors, which were monitored on closed-circuit television. Pisces, in Washington, D.C., was distinguished by old movie sets, 1,000-gallon, shark-filled aquariums, and exotic flora.

The dancers reflected glittery opulence and freewheeling sex through their clothing. Men sported gold chains, gold rings, patent leather platform shoes, tight Italian-style pants, and unbuttoned shiny satin shirts. Women wore low-cut, backless, sequined gowns, spiked heels, long gold necklaces, and gold lamé gloves. "The new boogie bunch dress up for the occasion—with shoulders, backs, breasts and midriffs tending to be nearly bare," observed *Time*. In a disco, where the participants became the stars, remarked photographer Francesco Scavullo, "the dress becomes your dancing partner.". . .

The star-studded disco became a craze near the end of

the decade. In late 1977, Robert Stigwood, owner of RSO records, filmed the movie *Saturday Night Fever,* which showed the transformation of a poor, trouble-ridden, Italian teenager, played by John Travolta, into a white-suited disco star. He constructed the score of the film around songs written and performed by one of his groups, the Bee Gees. By 1978, the record executive had scored a major success with the movie and had sold more than 30 million copies worldwide of the soundtrack.

Discomania spread across the country in the wake of *Saturday Night Fever.* In New York more than 1,000 discos opened their doors for business. The Holiday Inn motel chain added more than thirty-five discos on its premises. A $100,000 disco even opened in the small town of Fennimore, Wisconsin (population: 1,900). High schoolers went to disco proms and disco roller-skating rinks. One disco in Dubuque, Iowa, provided a disco wedding service complete with smoke-machine effects. Throughout the country in 1978, more than 36 million Americans danced on the floors of 20,000 discos. . . .

Many disco owners, such as Steve Rubell, strove to capitalize upon the music. "When you want to win, you want to win," stated Rubell, a former stockbroker. "And that's how it shows—the score—by the financial success."

Other artists, as with the baby boomers for whom they played, performed for money. To Alice Cooper, "the idea all along was to make $1 million. Otherwise the struggle wouldn't have been worth it. . . . I am the most American rock act. I have American ideals. I love money."

To make money, many musicians eagerly embraced the rock business establishment. Gene Simmons of Kiss equated a "successful rock and roll band" with "a well-oiled machine. It's a good business." As Greg Geller, talent scout for Columbia, noted in the mid-1970s: "Now artists are more upfront about admitting that they are interested in selling some records. This is not an ivory tower age: there's some recognition that we're involved in commerce."

For some, the record business paid off. Don McLean,

who scored a hit with the song "American Pie," which described the decline of the sixties' consciousness, sold 4.5 million singles and 1.8 million albums of "American Pie," netting around $1.1 million in royalties. Along with $460,000 in publishing and writing royalties and $200,000 in foreign sales, the singer-songwriter earned nearly $1.6 million. After giving his manager 10 percent, McLean took to the bank more than $1 million. Peter Frampton, a former Humble Pie guitarist who became one of the most publicized artists of the decade with *Frampton Comes Alive!* grossed $67 million in 1978 on album sales and tours.

Many seventies stars invested their earnings. The Bee Gees, one of the biggest draws of the 1970s, established their own merchandising company, which sold—as Barry Gibb told it—"things like nice T-shirts. We deal in jewelry but only real gold plate. We're doing a little electronic piano with Mattel Toys that'll be available soon." They also marketed "a cute Andy Gibb doll." Alice Cooper financed such films as *Funny Lady* and *Shampoo* for tax shelters and invested in art, antiques, and tax-free municipal bonds. Ted Nugent, the guitarist who scaled the charts during the seventies with a heavy metal sound and neanderthal costumes, owned a mink farm and a trout operation. Said Bob Weed, the Nuge's financial manager, "all of this fits in with Ted's plan for acquiring land. Sure, we're involved in some oil and gas-lease tax shelters, but when I tell him about property, that's something he understands." Rod Stewart, the blues croaker turned disco star, had a similar investment strategy. "I've always said that Rod isn't a rock star. He's a growth industry," remarked Billy Gaff, Stewart's manager. "Rod is essentially very conservative. He doesn't invest in football clubs or crazy movie- or record-financing schemes. The tax shelter scams are all a little scary, so we stick to art and real estate." All told, in 1973 *Forbes* estimated that at least fifty rock superstars earned and invested between $2 and $6 million a year, each musician accumulating from three to seven times more than the highest-paid executive in the United States.

A Sample of '70s Television

Harry Castleman and Walter J. Podrazik

Harry Castleman and Walter J. Podrazik's book *Watching TV* is an encyclopedia of television history and facts. The following selection is a mere sampling of some of the programming found on television in the '70s. As the authors point out, the *Happy Days* series symbolized an escape from the problems facing Americans at the time. The evolution of *Saturday Night Live* showed that some audiences wanted to see current issues discussed in sometimes playful and sometimes sarcastic ways. The development of *60 Minutes* into a top-rated program demonstrated that people were interested in current issues, if the issues were presented in a fast-paced, entertaining way.

The 1973–74 mid-season [television lineup] shakeup ... resulted in another welcome hit for ABC, the nostalgic *Happy Days* (produced by Garry Marshall, who had adapted *The Odd Couple* for television). As its name implied, *Happy Days* turned from the grim reality of the turbulent early Seventies to the simple rituals of teenage life in the already legendary Fifties. *Andy Griffith Show* veteran Ron Howard played cute-but-shy Richie Cunningham, a very average, very bland teenager living in the very bland city of Milwaukee with his nondescript family: a kind and bumbling father (Tom Bosley), a cardboard mother (Marion Ross), and a cute-but-devilish younger

Excerpted from *Watching TV: Four Decades of American Television,* by Harry Castleman and Walter J. Podrazik (New York: McGraw-Hill, 1982). Reprinted with permission from the authors.

sister, Joanie (Erin Moran). The sitcom usually focused on the escapades of Richie and his bosom buddy, Potsie Weber (Anson Williams), two struggling high school innocents who shared teenage fantasies about sock hops, girls, and hot rods. The *Happy Days* pilot episode had run on *Love, American Style* in February, 1972, and the show's premise was far removed from the new wave of comedy of CBS. . . . Nonetheless, *Happy Days* immediately entered the top twenty, right behind *The Six Million Dollar Man* in the ratings.

Happy Days owed much of its initial success to momentum from the theatrical film "American Graffiti" (the surprise blockbuster of 1973), in which Howard (the only cast member carried over to the TV series) had played Steve Bolander, a character very similar to Richie Cunningham. Unlike the film, though, the TV series initially lacked a strong central character (such as Richard Dreyfuss's Curt Henderson) to carry the plots. Howard's Richie was made far too weak and Potsie was a klutz. There was a token hood, Fonzie (Henry Winkler), similar to the John Milner character of the film (played by Paul LeMat), but unlike LeMat, Winkler had only a minor role in the stories at first. It was only when Winkler's character became a central figure in the stories that the entire series jelled.

In its first unveiling, though, *Happy Days* was content to present itself as an entertaining relic of the less troubled Fifties. In reality, though, the program failed to rise above the simplistic humor of its nondescript setting, settling into the mold of the Archie and Jughead comic strip or the Aldrich Family radio show. Just as ABC's *Roaring Twenties* had relied completely on the outward trappings of period topicality to carry the entire series, *Happy Days* settled for the increasingly popular revisionist interpretation of the Fifties as an era filled with jive-talking pseudo-juvenile delinquents, mindless adults, and prophetic rock'n'rollers. Viewers found the revamped image easy to comprehend and a convenient substitute for the rapidly fading memories of the bygone era. . . .

Saturday Night Live

In the fall of 1974, NBC slotted a monthly news and public affairs program, *Weekend,* in the Saturday night slot of 11:30 p.m. Its slightly tongue-in-cheek style catered toward [the] young adult crowd. For the fall of 1975, NBC's new Saturday night comedy-variety show was to fill in the remaining three weekends of each month.

In setting up the new program, [producer Lorne] Michaels was determined to develop *Saturday Night Live* as a special entity, different from standard prime time network variety. Like NBC's *Your Show of Shows* from the early 1950s, there would be guest stars, but they would be generally limited to a guest host that would work with a continuing company of writers and supporting players. Like the late night rock shows, the musical guests (rock, jazz, and folk-oriented) would be presented straight, performing one or two songs without engaging in banal "transition" patter. Like *Laugh-In* and the original *Smothers Brothers Comedy Hour,* there would be topical references and satirical jabs, as well as parodies of television, movies, and commercials. And, like the fondly remembered golden age of television, the program would be presented *live,* from New York City, before a real studio audience.

The decision to do the program as a live New York production immediately gave the project a distinct flavor and generated high expectations, while the late night weekend slot provided the much needed time to work out the rough spots. The first broadcast of NBC's *Saturday Night Live* took place on October 11, 1975, with veteran comic George Carlin as host and Billy Preston and Janis Ian as the musical guests. It was very uneven. Singer-songwriter Paul Simon hosted the second show and, in effect, turned it into a Paul Simon musical special. (He had three guest singers and together they performed nearly a dozen numbers.) Yet in just a few months, working with subsequent hosts such as Rob Reiner, Lily Tomlin, Candice Bergen, Richard Pryor, Buck Henry, and Dick Cavett, the program's crew jelled

193

and the show began to develop its style, a reputation, and a following.

High school and college students were among the first to latch on to the show, partially because the program was deliberately outrageous, sometimes even tasteless, in the style of the increasingly popular BBC import, *Monty Python's Flying Circus,* and the homegrown radio, stage, and magazine efforts of the *National Lampoon.* The opening joke on the very first show involved the Python-ish premise of two men dying of heart attacks, capped with the punchline: *"Live,* from New York, it's *Saturday Night!"*

"The Not Ready for Prime Time Players"

As with *Your Shows of Shows,* the company of regular performers evolved into the real stars of the series. Dubbed "The Not Ready for Prime Time Players," Dan Aykroyd, John Belushi, Chevy Chase, Jane Curtin, Garrett Morris, Laraine Newman, and Gilda Radner each developed their own distinctive character types and caricatures. Chase was the first to attract a following, based chiefly on his mock newscasts ("Weekend Update") and his portrayal of a bumbling, dull-witted President Gerald Ford.

Aykroyd, Belushi, and Chase also served as program writers, joining *National Lampoon* co-founder Michael O'Donoghue, Lorne Michaels himself, and nearly a dozen others. They produced the expected excellent movie and television parodies, including a remake of "Citizen Kane" (revealing Kane's last words to be: "Roast Beef on Rye with Mustard"), *Star Trek's* final voyage, and a "Jaws"-like urban killer, the "Land Shark." Political and topical subjects ranged from President Richard Nixon's final days in office to Claudine Longet's "accidental" shooting of a number of helpless skiers on the slopes. (The latter prompted an on-the-air apology.) Yet there were also very effective mood pieces such as a chance coffee shop encounter between a young man and a woman he had admired from afar years before, in high school. By the spring of 1976, *Saturday Night Live* had gained such a following that even Gerald Ford's press secretary, Ron Nessen (a former NBC news correspondent), agreed to serve as host, bringing along film inserts of President Ford himself.

For the next four years, *Saturday Night Live* grew in popularity and quality. Though the very nature of a live weekly show meant that any particular episode might be weak, overall the series emerged as the most daring and innovative television program of the late Seventies. Hosts such as consumer advocate Ralph Nader, football star O.J. Simpson, and rock star Frank Zappa, as well as more traditional Hollywood actors such as Cecily Tyson, Richard Benjamin, and Elliott Gould, turned in excellent performances as headliners. Though Chevy Chase left the cast in the program's second season to pursue a solo career in films (he was replaced by another of the show's writers, Bill Murray), the rest of the players remained, further developing their stock of characters and routines. Skits became increasingly complex and sophisticated with such presentations as "The Pepsi-Syndrome" (based on the nuclear accident at Three Mile Island and the film "The China Syndrome") running nearly twenty minutes.

After five seasons, all the players as well as Lorne Michaels himself left the show. (A completely new cast took over in the fall of 1980.) Most attempted solo film projects, with Chevy Chase and John Belushi scoring the biggest successes (Chase in "Foul Play" and Belushi in "National Lampoon's Animal House" and—with Dan Aykroyd—in "The Blues Brothers"). One of the biggest stars to emerge from *Saturday Night Live,* though, was comic Steve Martin. He hosted the show a half dozen times (beginning in the second season), launching a fabulously successful concert, film, and writing career in the process. . . .

From *The Iran Crisis* to *Nightline*

All three networks did their best to report every available detail on the hostage crisis and, on November 18, each one broadcast its own filmed interview with Iran's religious and secular leader, Ayatollah Ruhollah Khomeini (conducted by

Mike Wallace for CBS, John Hart for NBC, and Peter Jennings for ABC—all of whom had to submit questions in advance). After a flurry of late night reports following the embassy seizure, though, both CBS and NBC pulled back, scheduling a late night wrapup only if there were some dramatic developments that day. ABC, however, committed itself to a broadcast at least fifteen minutes long each weeknight "for the duration" (beginning November 8), under the title *The Iran Crisis: America Held Hostage* (anchored first by Frank Reynolds, then by Ted Koppel). In the process, the network not only attracted a huge audience (sometimes outdrawing the entertainment offerings on both CBS and NBC), but also found itself in a position to deal with the story in much greater depth. Instead of merely repeating what had been reported on the nightly news, *The Iran Crisis* featured longer and more detailed presentations on all aspects of the story. At first, the reports covered the obvious questions: What happened today? What do Americans think about it? What can the United States do now? These soon led to a far more difficult question: Why did it happen? In trying to answer that, each evening's report became, in effect, a minilesson in basic foreign policy and Mideast history.

The *Iran Crisis* reports served as an all-around unexpected bonus for . . . ABC News. The show attracted a large, steady audience and helped viewers to become accustomed to a late night news program. It also established ABC as *the* network with complete coverage of the situation. This boost in credibility and viewership spilled over into other programs. *Good Morning America,* which had been gaining on *Today* for a while, at last pulled ahead with the bonus carryover audience of people who had gone to bed watching ABC and who then woke up with the TV dial still set there. *World News Tonight* also rose in the ratings, moving into a virtual deadlock with NBC for the number two position behind CBS.

The hostage situation lasted far longer than anyone first imagined. Through November, December, and early January, reporters filed hundreds of stories on virtually every movement, rumor, and protest in and around the captured embassy. Media coverage, in fact, became an issue itself both in the States and in Iran. American correspondents complained that many of the "spontaneous" demonstrations against "Western imperialism" probably took place because the Western camera crews stationed outside the embassy were ready and eager to film. Officials in Iran, on the other hand, grew increasingly frustrated at their inability to control the image of their own country sent back by the journalists. In mid-January, Iran ordered all American reporters out of the country, so subsequent stories had to be filed from "listening posts" in nearby countries or through other foreign reporters allowed to remain.

By March, though there was still no end to the hostage situation at hand, ABC decided to change its late night *Iran Crisis* "special reports" into a permanent nightly news show that would cover other stories as well. The show was extended to twenty minutes each night and retitled *Nightline*. The revamped program followed the *Iran Crisis* format, though, concentrating on in-depth coverage of a few items rather than a recap of the earlier nightly news (much like PBS's *MacNeil-Lehrer Report*). While *Nightline* was not as big a draw as the Iran wrapups, four months of late night reports had built a solid base audience for ABC, and the show was able to compete successfully in the slot. ABC News emerged from the crisis with stronger news credibility, an expanded news schedule, and higher ratings overall for its *World News Tonight* program. . . . Even the nightly news lead would be up for grabs soon because Walter Cronkite was nearing retirement.

60 Minutes

Despite ABC's improved news performance, CBS was still considered the leader in news, based on the tremendous public respect for Cronkite as a credible source, the quality of CBS's own special reports, and its increasingly successful news magazine, *60 Minutes,* which had actually become a top ten show.

60 Minutes had been around since 1968, attracting little attention at first with its deft mix of hard-hitting investigative reporting and softer, entertaining feature pieces. It ran for three seasons in prime time, but was exiled in 1972 to the fringe period of very early Sunday evening where it was preempted every fall by professional football. During the summer of 1975, the show ran in a Sunday prime time slot and managed to land in the top thirty. When it returned in December, following the football season, *60 Minutes* was placed at the beginning of prime time against *The Wonderful World of Disney*. At the same time, correspondent Dan Rather joined Mike Wallace and Morley Safer as one of the program's co-anchors.

Through 1976 and 1977, the program's ratings rose steadily, benefiting from the hefty audience of its fall sports lead-in, NFL football. In April 1977, the CBS news division announced an unheard-of development: Due to the success of *60 Minutes*, it was showing a profit. This was a dramatic change from the long-standing image of news programs as prestigious loss leaders, and for the 1977–78 season CBS made every effort not to have its Sunday afternoon football coverage run overtime and thereby shorten *60 Minutes*.

Going into the fall of 1979, *60 Minutes* was an established top ten show and, by October, it ranked as the number one network show overall. This was no fall ratings fluke as *60 Minutes* hung on through the winter and spring, eventually finishing as the number one program for the 1979–80 season—the first television news show ever to reach those rarefied heights. Such ratings success sent a clear message to all the networks' programming departments: *60 Minutes* was the biggest bargain in television. Not only did it now offer both prestige and high ratings, but, as a news show, its budget was only a small fraction of most entertainment series, thus allowing a tremendous profit margin. Both NBC and ABC joined the bandwagon and reinstituted prime time news shows, with mixed results.

Television Families and Reality

Ella Taylor

The following selection is excerpted from a book that surveys the ways in which families have been presented in television programming. Ella Taylor points out that, in the early '70s, the major networks shifted from stereotypical family situations with no social agenda to shows that examined social problems and change in lighthearted but meaningful ways. As the nation faced unsettling changes in its views of what defined normal family life, television comedies reflected the uncertainties already felt by the audience. Taylor teaches communications, focusing on cultural issues on television, at the University of Washington. She has also written newspaper reviews of television programming.

I n 1970 Bob Wood, the incoming president of entertainment at CBS, undertook an extensive overhaul of his network's programming strategy. Wood realized that although CBS was the number one network in raw ratings, its most successful shows (*Gunsmoke, The Beverly Hillbillies, Hee Haw*) appealed primarily to older, rural viewers and rated less well among younger, more upscale audiences in the cities. Wood also saw that from the point of view of advertising sponsors what mattered was less *how many* people tuned in than *how much* they earned and were willing to spend on consumer products. These insights, together with his perception that younger, more affluent, urban social groups were fast be-

Excerpted from *Prime-Time Families: Television Culture in Postwar America,* by Ella Taylor. Copyright ©1989 by The Regents of the University of California. Reprinted with permission from the University of California Press.

coming if not numerical then cultural leaders, prompted Wood to revise his ideas about targeted audiences and shop around for program ideas that would "fit" the new markets. The name of the new ratings game was "demographics," which meant breaking down the mass audience by age, sex, income, and other sociological variables that would isolate the most profitable sources of revenue—namely, urban viewers between the ages of eighteen and forty-nine, especially women, who remained the chief buyers of consumer goods for themselves and for others in their families. Accordingly, scheduling became an elaborate strategic exercise whose purpose was no longer merely to reach the widest possible audience with any given show but to group programs and commercials in time slots by the type of audience likely to watch (and spend). The purpose was not to dismantle the mass audience but to fine-tune it, focusing on its most lucrative segments. Thus it was that the themes of youth, in television if not in everyday life, were played out within and reconciled with the theme of family. Throughout the 1970s and 1980s television advertising has reflected the same trend toward specialization of markets within the mass audience, with commercials carefully orchestrated to draw specific demographic groups in appropriate time slots while retaining advertising geared to the whole family.

These shifts of perspective on audiences awakened Wood and CBS chairman William Paley to innovative programming suggestions that departed from existing formulas and led the network entertainment division into a fruitful alliance with several independent production companies, notably Norman Lear's Tandem and Grant Tinker's MTM Productions, and with veteran comedy writer Larry Gelbart. Their work for CBS, together with the refinement and sophistication of television programming and marketing, would quickly establish a new style of comedy, modifying and extending the genre, articulating with particular shifts in public consciousness while producing commercially successful products, and setting the tone for prime-time entertainment throughout the 1970s and early 1980s.

That tone was influenced primarily by three comedy series that formed the backbone of CBS's highly successful Saturday night lineup. The first, MTM's *The Mary Tyler Moore Show*, a comedy about a single woman in her thirties taking up a career at a minor Minneapolis television station, picked up a substantial and loyal following among viewers for the next seven years (not to mention its long and continuing life in syndication). Among them, perhaps, were the same fans who had so adored Moore in her role as Laura Petrie in *The Dick Van Dyke Show*. In January 1971, thanks again to Bob Wood, the new series was joined by Norman Lear's *All in the Family*, a comedy whose pilots had twice been rejected as too controversial by ABC. The show, based on the enormously successful British television comedy *Till Death Us Do Part*, depicted a white working-class bigot, Archie Bunker, angrily confronting a new era of liberal pluralism through a ceaseless war of words with its youthful advocates, his "progressive" daughter and son-in-law (the latter was, all too appropriately, a sociology student). The program was a slow starter in the ratings, taking a full sixteen weeks to get off the ground, but Wood was patient and stuck it out, protecting Lear from the censoring hand of network executives fearful of alienating both viewers and sponsors. His tenacity was rewarded when *All in the Family* climbed into first place in the ratings and remained there for five years. In 1973 these two hits helped nurse along another CBS hopeful, *M*A*S*H*, which, when sandwiched between the other two in the Saturday night lineup, leaped into the top ten and remained there until its demise in the early 1980s. Based on the 1970 Robert Altman movie about an army medical unit surviving the Korean War, *M*A*S*H* combined a moderately antiwar position with a "war-is-fun" wackiness that was likely to draw in younger viewers with widely varying political perspectives in the aftermath of the Vietnam War.

New Shows Reflect Social Issues

A woman, single and attractive but no longer in the first flush of youth, struggles to forge a career and a new personal life in a corporate world dominated by men. A working-class conservative nurtured on blind patriotism, xenophobia, and respect for hard work, family, and paternal authority finds his most cherished beliefs challenged first by his offspring, then by his wife; eventually he suffers unemployment, impotence, his daughter's divorce, and a host of other social problems that erode his domestic haven. An army medical unit stumbles through a war whose purpose is far from clear and whose military leadership commands at best an ambivalent allegiance. What set these shows apart from most of their predecessors was their topicality for audiences in the 1970s, a topicality refracted through the defining lens of the news media. All three were centrally concerned with rapid social change and its attendant normative dislocations, the daily confu-

Changes in Top-Rated Prime-Time Programs, 1968–1974, Ranked by Audience Size

Nielsen Averages through 4/2/69		Nielsen Averages through 5/8/74	
1968–1969	**% TV homes**	**1973–1974**	**% TV homes**
Laugh-In (NBC)	31.1	*All in the Family* (CBS Tandem)	31.2
Gomer Pyle, U.S.M.C. (CBS)	27.1	*The Waltons* (CBS Lorimar)	27.9
Bonanza (NBC)	27.0	*Sanford and Son* (NBC Tandem)	27.6
Mayberry R.F.D. (CBS)	25.8	*M*A*S*H* (CBS Gelbart)	25.8
Family Affair (CBS)	25.2	*Hawaii Five-O* (CBS)	23.7
Julia (NBC)	25.1	*Sonny and Cher* (CBS)	23.4
Gunsmoke (CBS)	24.8	*Maude* (CBS Tandem)	23.3
Dean Martin (NBC)	24.1	*Kojak* (CBS)	23.3
Here's Lucy (CBS)	23.7	*The Mary Tyler Moore Show* (CBS MTM)	23.2
Red Skelton (CBS)	23.6	*Cannon* (CBS)	23.0

Erik Barnouw, *Tube of Plenty: The Evolution of American Television.* New York: Oxford University Press, 1975.

sion thrust on ordinary people (as opposed to the glamorous undercover agents and streamlined advocates of *Mod Squad* and *Storefront Lawyers*) facing puzzling and often painful new conditions without adequate rules to guide their actions. Each dealt in its own way with the crisis of styles of authority—personal, occupational, political—grown arbitrary and irrelevant, whose legitimacy was constantly called into question; and each worked out the "newer" concerns of younger generations within the more traditional frame of family. The concerns expressed by cultural critics—the crisis of authority in both private and public life, the divisions of gender, age, race, and class—were finding their way into the discourses of television, mediated by the commercial exigencies of the industry as well as by broader changes in consciousness, in which, of course, the media had a shaping hand.

Balancing the Old and the New

For viewers there were both old and new satisfactions. In many ways the new shows were firmly rooted in the conventions of traditional situation comedy, relying on absurd escapades or misunderstandings uncovered or resolved by the end of each episode. *M*A*S*H's* bouncing repartee recalled the rapid-fire banter of standup comedy and of earlier army comedies like *The Phil Silvers Show* and *Hogan's Heroes*. Archie Bunker's blustering pratfalls and malapropisms echoed those of Ralph Kramden [of the *Honeymooners*]. . . . Sweet, accommodating Mary Richards [of the *Mary Tyler Moore Show*] stepped out of the chrysalis that had contained Laura Petrie. The familial structure of the sitcom, whether at home or in the workplace, remained as fundamental as ever; with or without a central star, the force of the shows came from the interactions between the group members. But there were also significant changes of style and mood. Humor in the new shows was more verbal and less dependent on action than that of previous sitcoms. No longer were these comedies filled with the happy mirth that resounded through the houses of the Cleavers and Nelsons, those advertisements for the American Dream. If mirth and solidarity were anywhere to be found, it was more likely to be in the growing numbers of series with workplace settings. What viewers could see in story after story was individuals negotiating, in a muddled, haphazard sort of way, increasingly familiar troubles and surviving them with a cheerful, if bemused, resignation. Resolution came less from a misunderstanding revealed, a situational asymmetry set to rights, than from a continuing process of social learning, a wobbly accommodation to new conditions of living without clear-cut rules or figures of authority.

It would be rash to infer the cultural temper of a decade of television from three comedies, but by 1973 the innovations pioneered by CBS were fast becoming a formula. Copying successful programs and scheduling strategies had long been routine in television entertainment. Now a new technique, the spinoff, speeded up the crystallization of new generic forms. Characters thought to have won audience affection were "spun off" into their own series. *All in the Family* generated its own family of similar shows: *The Jeffersons, Maude,* and *Good Times* in the 1970s, *Archie Bunker's Place* and *Gloria* in the early 1980s. From *The Mary Tyler Moore Show* came *Rhoda, Phyllis, The Nancy Walker Show,* and eventually *Lou Grant.* Trapper John of *M*A*S*H* was spun off into his own hour-long medical drama, and when *M*A*S*H* ended its final run in 1982, it produced the short-lived *Aftermash.* Not only characters but also occupations, themes, or relationships perceived as having "taken" among audiences were reproduced by the same production companies and then swallowed up by others, with the networks' blessings.

The Changing Image of the Cowboy

Richard Slotkin

Images of the frontier have played a major role in the American experience. In the following selection, Richard Slotkin shows that even though the genre of cowboy/Western movies was weak in the '70s, the images of the lone vigilante, the climactic gunfight, and exploring a wild, unknown frontier continued in American films. Slotkin has written a number of books on the myths that have guided American thought and culture.

B etween 1971 and 1977 urban crime dramas, featuring as heroes detectives, policemen, and "urban vigilantes," were the predominant type of American-location action film. The success of *Star Wars* in 1977 led to a boom in fantasy and science-fiction epics that were closely related in theme and visual style to the imperial epics of the 1930s. Toward the end of the decade the combat film reappeared, as Hollywood belatedly addressed Vietnam. And throughout the decade, horror and "slasher" films enjoyed consistent box-office success.

Urban Gunslinger Films

The French Connection and Clint Eastwood's *Dirty Harry* series typify the police-centered crime dramas of the period; Charles Bronson's *Death Wish* series inaugurated the "urban vigilante" genre. The heroes in these films are clearly the heirs of the hard-boiled detective, the gunfighter, and the Indian-hater. Eastwood and Bronson made their reputations in Westerns, and their urban gunslingers are steely-eyed, cynical, fast on the draw, and likely to resolve the plot with a climactic gunfight. *Taxi Driver* (1976)—the most artful version of this story-type—uses the captivity/rescue narrative plan of *The Searchers* to give a perversely mythic resonance to its portrait of the violent urban loner. . . . The

Films of the 1970s glorified the "urban vigilante." Among them was the film Taxi Driver.

police film *Fort Apache, The Bronx* (1981) treats the violence of contemporary racial ghettos in terms of the standard cavalry/Indian paradigm.

What makes the urban vigilante genre different from the Westerns is its "post-Frontier" setting. Its world is urbanized, and its possibilities for progress and redemption are constricted by vastly ramified corporate conspiracies and by monstrous accumulations of wealth, power, and corruption. Its heroes draw energy from the same rage that drives the paranoids, psychopaths, mass murderers, and terrorists of the mean streets, and their victories are almost never socially redemptive in the Western mode. In these respects, the world of the urban gunslinger film is cognate to that of the horror and "slasher" film, typified by *The Omen* and *Texas Chainsaw Massacre*. These films carry to an extreme the premise of *Dirty Harry* and *Death Wish*, that our world is out of control, pervaded by an evil against which we feel helpless, an evil that affronts us from without in the form of disfigured, bloodthirsty strangers and from within in the form of perverse dreams and desires or nightmare versions of the generation gap—our own children suddenly revealed as alien monstrosities, Rosemary's babies. Although horror/slasher movies have their own generic history, they are very much in the captivity-rescue tradition. Many of them invoke bogeys whose ancestors appear in the literature of the Puritan witch trials, like the Indian or voodoo spirits *(Manitou, Cujo)* or murderous backwoodsmen *(Texas Chainsaw Massacre, Friday the Thirteenth)* whose literary ancestors are the Harpes and Simon Girtys of early frontier romances.

However, both the urban vigilante and the horror/slasher genres *invert* the Myth of the Frontier that had informed the Western. The borders their heroes confront are impermeable to the forces of progress and civilized enlightenment; if anything, the flow of aggressive power runs in the opposite direction, with the civilized world threatened with subjugation to or colonization by the forces of darkness.

Space as Frontier

Although nominally offering an escape from real-world history, the science-fiction and fantasy films of the 1970s and 1980s owe a great and (in the case of the Lucas/Spielberg *Star Wars* trilogy) acknowledged debt to the Western. TV's *Star Trek* was always introduced with the incantation, "Space—the Final Frontier" (which became the subtitle of *Star Trek V*). *Outland* (1981) and *Battle Beyond the Stars* (1982) were science-fiction remakes of classic Westerns *(High Noon* and *The Magnificent Seven)*. Beyond such literal imitations, and the *hommages* to John Ford's *The Searchers* in *Star Wars,* both the *Star Wars* trilogy and the *Star Trek* series project a myth of historical progress similar to that in the progressive Westerns and "empire" movies of the 30s and 40s. The tale of individual action (typically a captivity/rescue) is presented as the key to a world-historical (or cosmic-historical) struggle between darkness and light, with perpetual happiness and limitless power for the heroes and all humankind (or "sentient-kind") as the prize of victory. Despite its futuristic setting, *Star Trek II: The Wrath of Khan* (1982) uses a vocabulary that seems drawn from films like *The Charge of the Light Brigade, Gunga Din,* and *Santa Fe Trail:* as villain, a despotic chieftain who is half-savage and half-aristocrat; as setting, a desert frontier world, which can also become a colonial paradise through the technical power of the soldier-colonists of the *Enterprise* and the Genesis project; as motive for violence, a massacre with tortures and murder that must be avenged; and as resolution, a suicidal "charge" by the *Enterprise* on Khan's ship.

The worlds of *Star Wars,* and of films similarly set either in fantasy-worlds or galaxies "far far away," are presented to us as alternatives to the historicized spaces of the Western and the pseudo-documentary or "journalistic" space of the crime film. Like fairy tales, they allegorize the condition and etiology of the present world, but they purchase imaginative freedom—the power to imagine the most magical or utopian possibilities—by keeping real historical referents at a distance. It would be inaccurate to describe the genre as entirely anti-historical, however. The *Star Trek* series continually undertakes explanations of how human society developed from its past of war, racism, and ecological crisis to its future of peace, tolerance, and balance under the Federation. In both the TV and the movie series, the crew of the *Enterprise* often go back in time to correct some historical flaw that might abort the utopian future. . . .

Vietnam Movies

Since 1976 Vietnam has also become a major subject for movie mythography. Cultural crisis is the mother of myth/ideological invention, and the Vietnam War is a particularly appropriate symbol of the catastrophe that overtook the liberal consensus and the New Frontier. It marked the moment when the failure of our latest "Indian war" coincided with the collapse of our expectation of perpetual and universal affluence, as the disappearance of hostile Indians and wilderness or virgin land had marked the end of the agrarian frontier for [historian Frederick Jackson] Turner and Roosevelt. [Writer] Michael Herr expresses the idea eloquently and concisely: "[M]ight as well say that Vietnam was where the Trail of Tears was headed all along, the turnaround point where it would touch and come back to form a containing perimeter."

The period of suppression and denial, during which the war was treated only indirectly, ended in 1977–78, with the first major Vietnam combat films, and in the 1980s Vietnam war stories became a significant element in commercial popular culture. Print media have produced a steadily increasing number of novels, memoirs, unit histories, even a multivolume Time/Life Books series titled *The Vietnam Experience*. The number, scale, and prominence of film treatments have grown from the modest success of *The Boys in Company C* (1977), through the epics *The Deerhunter* (1977) and *Apocalypse Now* (1979), to the more recent celebrity of *Rumor of War* (made for TV), *Platoon, Hamburger Hill,* and *Casualties of War.* Major documentaries have been produced for television and for distribution as videocassettes, and two television series have been set in the war (*Tour of Duty* and *China Beach*).

Fictional treatments of Vietnam have developed their own distinctive narrative conventions, centering on a characteristic set of ideological contradictions and concerns. Among the important recurring motifs are: the reality gap between "grunts" and rear-echelon commanders (or soldiers and politicians); racial conflict within the American forces; the power of the domestic anti-war movement to affect combat morale; the alienation of troops from people "back in the World"; the breakdown of normal language in a war where words are deliberately used to obscure reality rather than to define it. Nearly every fictional treatment uses a Mylai-like incident to symbolize the central moral/ideological problem of the war story. Those that do not, usually build narrative crises around some other symptom of "cross-over": the murder of a suspected VC [Vietcong] agent, the depredations of rogue counterguerrillas, or the betrayal of troops in the field by their officers, by the home front, or even by each other.

Star Wars, Raiders, and *Close Encounters*

Peter Biskind

Peter Biskind has written many articles evaluating movies and their themes. This selection looks at hidden themes in the blockbuster films (those that made enormous profits) of the '70s. Some of the themes examined in this selection include: rebels are good, empires are bad; ecology is good, pollution is bad; culture and reason are corrupting, sensitivity to one's spirit is enriching. Biskind, and other movie critics, challenge audiences to notice and evaluate such themes.

There's a dramatic moment at the end of the "origins" sequence of *Indiana Jones and the Last Crusade* where the young Indy, having seized the coveted Cross of Coronado from the bad guys, turns it over to the sheriff for safekeeping; the sheriff, however, is in cahoots with the bad guys and gives it back to them—much to Indy's astonishment. Indy, here played by River Phoenix, a child of the sixties (his parents were hippies), learns the *echt* lesson of the sixties: don't trust adults, particularly those in authority.

Real Life and the Movies

George Lucas and Steven Spielberg, who between them conceived, produced, and directed *The Last Crusade,* were also children of the sixties; their movies, despite their slick, formulaic sheen, are surprisingly personal (it's no accident

Excerpted from "Blockbuster: The Last Crusade," by Peter Biskind, in *Seeing Through Movies,* edited by Mark Crispin Miller (New York: Pantheon, 1990). Reprinted with permission from the author.

that Lucas's hero is named Luke) and so are permeated by countercultural values. *Star Wars,* for example, was a generation gap drama that sided with the kids. With its conflict between the weak rebels and the powerful Empire, it couldn't help evoking Vietnam and the attendant moral and political crises amid which Lucas and his generation came of age. Lucas has said that the Emperor was modeled on President Richard Nixon, which makes the Empire equivalent to the United States, Darth Vader to, say, Henry Kissinger, and the rebels to the Vietcong. Or, on an even more personal note, as Dale Pollock pointed out in *Skywalking,* his book on Lucas, the Empire is the monolithic studio system that thwarted him at every turn, while the Emperor and Vader stood in for appropriate studio executives.

With the appearance of Yoda in *The Empire Strikes Back,* the Vietnam analogy, which functioned as a subtext for the first film, became more intrusive. The gnomic jedi master is wrinkled, old, and wise and lives in the jungle. When E.T., Gandhi, and Mr. Miyagi (*The Karate Kid*) made their movie debuts a few years later, the resemblance among them was striking, leaving little doubt who Yoda was: a closet Asian. After all, he was colored, small (underdeveloped), "ugly" (non-Western), and mysterious ("inscrutable"). If the Emperor was Nixon and Vader was Kissinger, Yoda had to be Mao or Ho Chi Minh, the Spirit of the Third World. (In a review of William Kotzwinkle's novelization of *E.T.,* social critic Ariel Dorfman described the pint-sized alien as "more like a small savage from the third world . . . than a Milky Way wizard. There is no [other] reason why . . . he should get drunk, why he never proceeds beyond pidgin English ["E.T. phone home"] such as . . . countless Indians have stuttered. . . .")

Lucas's idea of the Third World, however, was patterned on Northern California, where he lived, not Vietnam, where the war was fought; Yoda's cryptic Zen-speak recalls its dreamy, druggy, ecologically correct counterculture the same way Princess Leia's Guinevere hairdo and Pre-Raphaelite white gown suggests such quaint Northern California institutions as the Renaissance Faire, not to mention the ornate art nouveau concert posters of the sixties. It was these values Lucas was trying to pass on to the next generation of teen-agers, in the guise of Luke.

This Northern California ambience was most pronounced in the Moon of Endor sequence that concluded *Return of the Jedi*. With its dense forests of sequoias and its feisty, fuzzy-wuzzy Ewoks who defeat the Empire's technology with slingshots, crossbows, rocks, and homemade booby traps, Lucas gives us his most vivid picture of Vietcong guerrilla warfare, Marin County–style. The authorized novelization describes the Ewoks as "cadres" attacking in "human waves" and criticizes the Empire (the First World) for wrecking (aka defoliating) the greenery of Endor's moon, described as "dying from refuse disposal, trampling feet, chemical exhaust fumes." With the members of the Alliance and their teddy bear Ewoks gathered around a campfire at the end of *Return of the Jedi,* the Vietcong in the sky became Boy Scouts on the ground. The Empire is defeated by a children's crusade, an alliance of teen-agers and teddy bears—in other words, the sixties. Nature, in the sixties equated with communes in the woods, Native Americans, and untrammeled innocence, defeats culture and civilization, which were widely regarded as both corrupt and corrupting. *Return of the Jedi,* where these themes are most pronounced, represents the greening of *Star Wars*.

However, this Luddite, anti-technological strain was present in Lucas's films from the start. Apropos of his 1971 proto–*Star Wars, THX-1138*, Lucas once said, "I was fascinated by the . . . idea of rocket ships and lasers up against somebody with a stick. The little guys were winning and technology was losing—I liked that." Therefore, the trilogy pits the battered Millenium Falcon and the rebels' one-man fighters against massive Imperial Star Destroyers, Imperial Walkers, and the like, and, more important, the mysticism of the Force against the arid rationalism of the Empire, whose officers even sneer at Darth Vader's old-time "religion." When Luke is zeroing in on the vulnerable reactor core of the Death Star at the end of *Star Wars*, Obi Wan Kenobi's ghostly voice advises him to turn off his guidance system, close his eyes, and rely on the Force, which he does. These films prefer the heart to the head, feeling to thinking. . . .

New Movie Styles

The next generation of directors, the "movie brats," were predominantly products of Los Angeles film schools. Lucas, Spielberg, and their young colleagues set out to restore or gentrify the genres they had learned to love in school. In the case of the *Star Wars* trilogy, this meant combat, sword and sorcery, Western, and, most important, sci-fi. Beyond specific genres, movie brat directors sought to revive the idea of genre itself. But to breathe new life into exhausted action formulas, it wasn't enough to put out the occasional sci-fi flick or Western (they invariably flopped); it was necessary to renovate the whole system that made genre possible, to restore, as Lucas put it, the naïve sense of romance, "awe," "wonder" that had accompanied the birth of the silents. If in *2001*, at least in its first half, Kubrick had demystified space travel by picturing space ships tricked out in humdrum HoJo [Howard Johnson] decor, a drab extension of the friendly skies of United [Airlines], Lucas not only wanted to remystify it, he wanted to remystify film itself.

Lucas achieved this goal by harnessing the dazzling, high-tech mega-effects pioneered by *2001* to the old action genres—really, the kids' matinee serials of the thirties—with their simple, functional narratives. He skipped at least a generation, turning his back on the anti-genre (and anti-war) films of the seventies, to old World War II films, with their unambiguous attitude toward combat. With what has often been called its "machine esthetic," *Star Wars* was both a product and a celebration of the technology that had made the Vietnam War possible. Its spectacular depiction of bloodless dogfighting in deep space sanitized and estheticized combat, in a manner all too reminiscent of the air war over North Vietnam.

The magic of the trilogy's effects lies precisely in their verisimilitude [having the appearance of truth], and their success depends largely on creating the illusion that we are entering a futuristic world that actually exists. Whereas for many of the anti-genre directors of the late sixties and early seventies the screen was a mirror that reflected moving images back on themselves, in the *Star Wars* films the screen was a window on a world of spectacular "realism." According to effects wizard Richard Edlund, speaking of the all-important opening shot of the monumentally large and immaculately detailed Imperial Star Destroyer drifting into the frame from above, "If somebody sat down in the theater and saw this monstrous thing come over the screen and keep coming and coming, and they were awed by that, then we had our audience just where we wanted 'em. But if they laughed, we were dead." According to Pollock, "Edlund shot the opening sequence five times until he was sure nobody would laugh." Despite Edlund's success in achieving what appears to be photographic verisimilitude, however, the effects are rarely naturalized. Because of the dynamic play of scale and speed, they never appear commonplace or overly familiar.

Star Wars looked back to the golden age of movies in other ways as well. It rolled back the sixties by employing actors with square-jawed, Waspy good looks like Mark Hamill and Harrison Ford who had been relegated to the unemployment lines in the Nixon era by "ethnics" like Dustin Hoffman, Al Pacino, and Elliott Gould. In employing a new generation of relatively unfamiliar nonstars like Hamill, Ford, and Carrie Fisher, Lucas succeeded in creating the perception that the films were newly minted, that he had started over, reinvented the movies.

Old-Fashioned Themes

At the same time, the *Star Wars* films embraced the simple values of heroism and old-fashioned individualism and revived a kind of Manichean [syncretistic religious or philosophical dualism], back-to-basics moral fundamentalism

215

suggestive of the Reagan era yet to come. "I wanted to make a kid's film that would strengthen contemporary mythology and introduce a kind of basic morality," said Lucas. "Everybody's forgetting to tell the kids, 'Hey, this is right and this is wrong.'" It's no accident that Lucas referred to the Empire's foot soldiers as "storm troopers," invoking a time [World War II] when it seemed easier to tell good from bad. *Raiders of the Lost Ark* and *Indiana Jones and the Last Crusade* carried this further, portraying the bad guys as literal Nazis. The immediate past of the Vietnam War was presumably too complicated to deal with directly.

The Indiana Jones films were always to the right of the *Star Wars* trilogy. They shamelessly revived and relegitimated the figure of the dashing colonialist adventurer who plunders and pillages antiquities from Third World countries for First World collectors. The end of the title sequence of *Raiders,* with a white man (Indy) being flown out of the jungle a hairsbreadth ahead of a bunch of spear-chucking natives, not only brings to mind the myriad of naïvely racist jungle movies of the thirties but also evokes the "fall" of Saigon; this light-hearted, veiled allusion to what, after all, was the most painful and humiliating episode in recent American history was the screen equivalent of Reagan's soon-to-be-notorious flippancy about life-and-death world issues. . . .

In borrowing, combining, and recombining elements from both right and left, then, the *Star Wars* trilogy breathed new life into the ideological consensus of the center on which their conventions depended, and succeeded in doing in the realm of culture what the Carter Restoration had, with only partial success, attempted in the realm of politics. It was crafted (intentionality aside) to appeal to members of the disaffected Vietnam generation and draw them back into the fold. It created a new consensus that included both proto-preppies (Luke et al.) and, as junior partners, an assortment of outsiders and loyal "minorities": Chewbacca, R2D2, and C-3PO, and, in *Return of the Jedi,* an astonishing array of weird-looking aliens, as well as Lando, an actual (nonmetaphoric) black man who becomes a general in the rebel army, in the same way that the actor who played him, Billy Dee Williams, became one of the few black entertainment figures to play a role in the Reagan campaign during the 1980 presidential elections.

Close Encounters

At the end of *Close Encounters of the Third Kind,* Spielberg's second blockbuster, the blessed and much anticipated event finally occurs: the alien ship gently touches down in a panoply of colored lights, accompanied by a crescendo of orchestral music, as a bunch of dumbstruck Earthlings watch in silent amazement. Since this film, itself a much anticipated marvel of techno-movie magic, is on one level as much about its own construction and reception as about its ostensible subject—visitors from other worlds—it's not hard to equate the space ship with *Close Encounters*–the movie, and the enthralled mortals with the blissed-out audiences who greeted the movie with similar awe.

For Lucas and Spielberg, those spectators in *Close Encounters* were the model audience. Although the agenda of *Star Wars* was nothing if not ambitious—to refurbish consensus for the seventies and after—the trilogy had other, bigger fish to fry, and its influence was vastly more profound. It attempted nothing less than to reconstitute the audience as children. Lucas said he wanted to make a film for "the kids in all of us." As Alan Ladd, Jr., put it, when he was head of Twentieth Century–Fox (which produced *Star Wars),* Lucas "showed people it was alright to become totally involved in a movie again; to yell and scream and applaud and really roll with it."

Blue Jeans as Self-Expression

Beverly Gordon

Throughout history humans have expressed themselves via their clothing. Kings and queens, soldiers and priests, police officers and chefs have all used their clothing to make statements about themselves. Beverly Gordon examines some of the statements associated with blue jeans. Though jeans are not unique to the 1970s, they became a dominant form of dress and self-expression for rich and poor Americans alike during this decade. Gordon is associate professor in the Department of Environment, Textiles and Design at the University of Wisconsin-Madison and serves as director of the Helen Allen Textile Collection.

B lue jeans, the now-ubiquitous denim garments that almost constitute a uniform on high school and college campuses, have been an integral part of the American scene for about 130 years. In that time they have embodied many different messages, and functioned in different ways—as symbols of rebellion; outlets for personal creativity; emblems of up-to-date, fashionable awareness; and as evidence of generational longing and insecurity. Changes in jeans styling, embellishment, and marketing are closely tied to changes in the society as a whole, and these changes serve as a subtle but accurate barometer of trends in contemporary popular culture. . . .

Excerpted from "American Denim: Blue Jeans and Their Multiple Layers of Meaning," by Beverly Gordon, in *Dress and Popular Culture,* edited by Patricia A. Cunningham and Susan Voso (Bowling Green, OH: Popular Press, 1991). Reprinted with the permission of Bowling Green State University.

The Wild West and the Farmer

Jeans first appeared in their now-familiar form in California in the second half of the 19th century. Levi Strauss, a Bavarian immigrant, came to San Francisco in 1850 with a supply of strong canvas cloth that he hoped to sell to people making tents and wagon covers, but when he saw the kind of hard wear the gold prospectors gave their clothes, he had it made into sturdy pants. "Levi's" were really born when Strauss switched to a heavy denim fabric a few years later. Copper rivets were added at the stress points in 1873. Jeans first evolved, then, as practical rather than fashionable clothing, and were associated with hardworking physical laborers, especially those from the rough and rugged West. By the early twentieth century, when Levis competed with other brands such as Wrangler and Lee, jeans and related denimwear such as protective overalls were the modal garments for farmers. By 1902 the Sears and Roebuck catalogue offered five different denimwear styles. Again, individuals who wore these garments were not "fashionable," they were not making a statement of any kind; they were simply choosing serviceable, affordable clothing. . . .

Making a Statement with Jeans

It was in the 1960s that the "jeaning of America" occurred, and jeans took on a new role. The first signs of the shift really began in the late 1950s, when another type of rebel, the bohemian or "beatnik," began to adopt them with black sweaters for everyday wear. Unlike the Brando/Dean "bad boy" rebel, this was a dissenter, an urban intellectual who came to an anti-fashion statement of this sort from a thought-out position about the materialistic, conformist society of the day. To wear plain jeans and dark colors was to reject the more-is-better, new-is-better mentality of the Organization Man world. 1962, according to Levi Strauss executive Alfred Sanguinetti, marked the "breakout" point in jeans sales, with sales figures doubling in just three years. They further quintupled between 1965 and 1970. By 1967 the anti-fashion statement was screaming across the land, for jeans were one of the most visible symbols of the rapidly increasing numbers of disenfranchised youth. The late 1960s were, of course, the turbulent period in which there was a marked escalation of the undeclared war in Vietnam, a war that polarized the society and led to a widespread rejection of mainstream social norms on the part of the younger generation. The youth-dominated counterculture, which was made up of the same baby-boomers who had worn jeans as play clothes and had grown up with James Dean and other such cultural icons, turned to jeans very naturally. Jeans were practical, long-lasting, and unchanging; they were the very antitheses of the mainstream "straight" world where fashion was by its very nature ever-changing and quickly obsolescent. They were cheap, comfortable, and associated with physicality; they represented freedom from dutifulness, and because they were simultaneously associated with work and play, came to stand for a society where there really was no distinction between the two. As Valerie Carnes put it in a 1977 article entitled "Icons of Popular Fashion,"

> Denim jeans became [in the 1960s] the ultimate no-fashion put-down style—a classless, cheap, unisex look that stood for, variously, frontier values, democracy, plain living, ecology and health, rebellion *a la* Brando, or Dean, a new interest in the erotic import of the pelvis, or, as Charles Reich suggests in *The Greening of America,* a deliberate rejection of the "artificial plastic-coated look" of the affluent consumer society.

Jeans may have been the common anti-fashion denominator among the young, but all jeans were not alike. Jeans wearers avoided the plastic veneer and the sameness and artificiality it represented by the very act of wearing their jeans. Jeans conformed more and more to their own particular body shapes as they were worn and washed (cotton denim shrinks and stretches each time it is washed and reworn). Over time jeans came to carry particular "scars"—

stains, rips, frayed areas, patches—that could be associated with remembered events and experiences. A pair of jeans became intensely personal. If a small hole developed it might be left alone as a "badge" of experience, or great deliberation might go into the choice of an appropriate fabric with which to cover it. Soon, counterculture youth were *glorifying* their jeans—decorating and embellishing them, making them colorful and celebratory, and making them into visible, vocal personal statements. Silk, velvet, leather, feathers, bells, beads, rivets, sequins, paint—anything that could be applied to denim fabric was applied to someone's jeans, jean jackets, and related accessories. Men who had never learned to sew and who under most circumstances would think of embroidery as unmanly learned the necessary stitches to work on their own clothes. The unisex garment that symbolized the alternative youth culture was an appropriate vehicle for the breakdown of gender roles, and besides, one's jeans were too personal to trust to anyone else. By 1974 imaginatively adorned jeans were such a pervasive and interesting phenomenon that the Levi Strauss company sponsored a national "denim art" contest and was deluged with entries. Entrants repeatedly stated that they found it difficult to part with the garments long enough for them to be displayed in the exhibition; they felt they were giving up a part of themselves. "I feel most myself when I have my jeans on" was a typical comment from an entrant. "My jeans are an extension of me"; "my shorts [are] my autobiography on denim."

Jeans in the '70s Culture

In some ways it had by this time become almost necessary to dramatically personalize one's jeans in order to still make an anti-fashion statement. Many of the outward signs and even some of the underlying ideas of the counterculture had been adopted (some might say usurped) by the mainstream culture at large. Blue jeans in and of themselves were so well accepted in the establishment that even such political figures as New York City mayor John Lindsay and presidential candidate Jimmy Carter were happy to be photographed wearing them. Anti-fashion had not only been absorbed by fashion, but had become part of its very

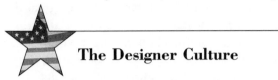

The Designer Culture

In the 1970s each person wanted to be unique, while also buying mass-produced clothing. The solution was designer clothing that carried a label and which was associated with a clearly promoted life-style image.

Once the whole of Western society had begun to participate in consumer culture, lifestyle became not only a phenomenon that affected subcultures but a commodity available to all. A range of manufactured lifestyles, each advertising its unique qualities, dominated the market-place and dictated consumption choices in the 1970s and 1980s. The boutique idea provided a basis on which countless retail set-ups were subsequently established. In Britain the success of the Laura Ashley and Next retail chains consolidated the role that the promotion of a complete lifestyle—clothing, furniture and interior decoration—played in selling goods to a particular group of customers. Whether nostalgic or modern, each consumer style functioned on the level of its visual and symbolic identity.

In the second half of the 1970s one option emerged which emphasized the role of the designer in creating style. The "designer-jeans" phenomenon, launched in the United States as a marketing ploy to help individualize and put added value into otherwise anonymous, mass-produced artefacts, quickly spread. Hairdressers became hair-designers, and designer-shops appeared selling ranges of "designed" products, from paper-clip holders to chairs. The goods were united less by their function than by the claim to individuality in the esthetic sensibility which had created them and which would, by implication, consume them.

Richard Maltby, *Passing Parade: A History of Popular Culture in the Twentieth Century*. New York: Oxford, 1989.

essence. John Brooks, writing in *The New Yorker* in 1979, attributed the fashionable usurpation of the jeans phenomenon to the early 1970s "search for the fountain of youth," but it may have been as much a sign of an underlying widespread hunger for life-affirming values in what was a confused and dark time.

Jeans and other denim garments were also seen in the early 1970s as quintessentially *American*. Jeans had been developed in the United States, of course, and had long carried associations of the American West, but once they had filtered into the international fashion scene, they came to stand for the country as a whole. In 1973 the American Fashion Critics presented a special award to Levi Strauss for "a fundamental American fashion that . . . now influences the world." Nieman Marcus also gave Levi Strauss its Distinguished Service in Fashion Award that same year. The popular press began to print rhetorical questions like, "after all, what's more American than denim?" and in 1974 American Motors Corporation contracted with Levi Strauss to provide blue denim fabric for upholstery for its Gremlin and Hornet cars. The Gremlin, which was promoted as America's answer to the Volkswagen beetle, was meant to be both upbeat and patriotic, and denim furnishings were thought to communicate both qualities.

Jeans sales continued to climb. By 1977 over 500 million pairs were sold in this country alone—more than twice the number of the total population. . . .

Fashion and anti-fashion came exceedingly close during this period, but there were continually two thrusts to the jeans craze. The counterculture continued to thrive and maintained and fostered a do-your-own, personalize-your-clothing vision. Numerous instruction books were published between 1973 and 1977 that carried a power-to-the-people message and told people how to fashion and re-fashion their own denim clothing. Publications with such titles as *Clothing Liberation* and *Make It in Denim, The Jeans Scene, The Jeans Book,* and *Native Funk and Flash* continued to advocate inexpensive and comfortable clothing that made use of worn garments and other available materials. Cast-offs and odds and ends could not only be salvaged, but creatively used.

At the same time, there was a high-fashion version of this democratic, anti-fashion trend. Couturiers who saw these creative outfits on the streets and in such legitimizing exhibitions as Wesleyan University's "Smart Ass Art" and Levi Strauss' "Denim Art" at the Museum of Contemporary Crafts (1974) moved in and produced their own high-style versions of counter-culture styles. Givenchy designed an entire denim wardrobe for film star Audrey Hepburn, for example, and Giorgio outfitted Dyan Cannon and Ava Gardner. A $2,325 denim-lined mink jacket and mink-cuffed jeans were shown on the fashion runways in Paris in 1974, and professionally designed embroidered, sequinned and nail-studded ensembles were going for about $500 in New York boutiques. Recycled and well-worn fabrics—hallmarks of the counter-culture look—were part of this style. Giorgio's jeans outfits that sold for $250 were made from already-used denim, for example, and designer shops in department stores like Lord and Taylor sold recycled jeans for three times the price of new ones.

By the late 1970s, when the baby-boomer generation had been largely absorbed into the work force and the responsibilities of parenting, and the counter-culture vision had become diffused, the high-style fashion forces won out over the anti-fashion style. Couture denim filtered down into the ready-to-wear market. Designer labels became an obsession; "designer jeans" were "*the* pants in America," according to a Saks Fifth Avenue retailer. Calvin Klein, who drew attention to jeans sporting his label with an erotic advertising campaign, sold 125,000 pairs a week in 1979. Designer jeans were in such demand that there was a thriving counterfeit trade, and by 1981 *Good Housekeeping* magazine ran a feature advising consumers how to make sure they were buying the "real thing.". . .

Blue jeans and related denim garments have, in sum, come to stand not just for the Wild West or the rugged laborer or the hardworking farmer—they have become an integral part of the whole American (and perhaps the world-wide) scene. They have been bleached, ripped, washed with acid, washed with stones, patched, cut up, decorated, distressed, and "worn to death," but they are resilient, and seem to always be able to return in yet another guise and take on yet another layer of meaning. They have at different times seemed matter-of-fact and part of the scenery, and at other times have called out for notice and attention. They have served both as symbols of the culture at large and of subsets of that culture, and of rebellious, outspoken counter-culture groups; they have been fashionable, unfashionable, and hallmarks of anti-fashion. They have embodied many of the longings, beliefs and realities of the generations that have worn them.

The Search for Self-Fulfillment

Daniel Yankelovich

Daniel Yankelovich is a social observer, author, and leader of a polling organization. He discusses two social changes that tore at the lives of individual Americans in the '70s. First, many people decided to seek self-fulfillment and risk the securities offered by traditional lifestyles. Many were willing to give up the safety offered by staying in one's existing location, by staying in one's existing marriage, and/or by staying in one's existing job. Experiments are always risky, but another factor confused the issues further in the '70s—a sluggish economy. Inflation reduced the value of the dollar that Americans needed to use to find self-fulfillment. The energy crisis limited the feeling of freedom once associated with cars and traveling to new opportunities. With fewer jobs available, career changes were difficult or impossible. Yankelovich concludes that at the moment when Americans were most interested in experimenting with their lives, the socioeconomic situation was creating greater limitations.

L et us start with the most obvious flaw in people's self-fulfillment strategies: the desires of most Americans to move toward expanded choice, pluralism of life styles and greater freedom, while the economy, besieged by inflation and recession, moves relentlessly in the opposite direction—toward restriction of choice. This creates many dilemmas for Americans.

The Muller Family

Consider, for example, one case from the several hundred life histories I gathered for this study, that of David and Cynthia Muller. David Muller,* a thirty-four-year-old photographer who is a lobster fisherman by avocation, explained his situation this way: "When my wife told me she was going back to work full-time, even though we have a three-year-old girl who needs a lot of care, I said, 'Sure. That's great.' What the hell, I get pleasure out of my work. Why should she be stuck in the house all day? She has a right to her own fulfillment. Well, it didn't work out as well as we thought it would. The first thing we did when she went back to work was to buy a more expensive house because we had two incomes to count on. But inflation gobbled up the extra money we had from her earnings. Now we're stuck with mortgage payments at 15 percent interest. The bloom is off the rose with her job—she likes it all right but not as much as at first. We take turns caring for our little girl, so we hardly see one another: when she's home, I'm working, and vice versa. Now she can't quit the damn job even if she wants to; we can't afford it. Both of us still think we did the right things, I'll tell you, but we're not as sure as we once were."

The Mullers' plight is typical of the predicaments that entangle people's lives as they break away from old patterns of behavior in search of self-fulfillment. In the interviews almost everyone concerned with self-fulfillment stressed how directly their plans hinged on their economic prospects. For many years Americans in the middle and upper income ranges had grown accustomed to steady increases in income and had taken for granted that in a flexible economy they could enjoy flexibility in their lives. In

* Place names and people's names and occupations have been changed in order to safeguard the identity of the subjects who consented to be interviewed only under this condition.

today's more stringent economy they find themselves saddled with the consequences of choices made in easier times.

Working to Support the House

My interview with Cynthia Muller, David's wife, confirmed her husband's story. She had had a job before they were married and kept it until she gave birth to their daughter. Then she quit to take care of the baby. At first she unreservedly enjoyed being a housewife and mother. But when the novelty wore off she began to worry about being "just a housewife." Her husband had shared in caring for the baby as an infant: he would get up at night to give the baby her bottle, and he even helped with the laundry. But gradually his help diminished without either of them talking about it much. It was understood that since she was home all day, and he worked, she would carry the main burden of child care.

Cynthia said she returned to her job "mainly for my self-fulfillment, but also because the money came in handy." She had assumed she could quit her job any time she wanted, especially if her daughter needed her. Now, she says, she feels she has been tricked. Her mother told Cynthia that because discrimination against women was so widespread in the past, when she was first married and also working her bank had refused to count her income in calculating how large a mortgage she and Cynthia's father could manage. Cynthia commented wistfully that she wished her bank had done the same; then she and David wouldn't both be working to support their house. But she quickly added she thought the house an excellent investment, and since they were not managing to save any money despite their two incomes, the house represented their future security.

The worst feature of their present life, she said, is that she and David seem almost to lead separate lives. "It's as if we have this business partnership in the house and in our child and in our jobs. It's all right, I guess. But somehow there's a difference between a business partnership and marriage. There's definitely something wrong with this arrangement but I can't put my finger on what it is."

Self-Fulfillment and the Economy

Economic growth helped to create an extraordinary cohesiveness in postwar America. From the late forties well into the sixties most Americans shared a vision of what they wanted for their lives, their families and their country. Under the impetus of the vision an entire nation devoted itself single-mindedly to the task of achieving a perpetual-motion machine of economic growth, and then used the machine to satisfy the national hunger for homes, cars, beefsteak and gadgets. The growth machine accomplished something the world had never seen before: the combination of human striving, technology, organization and cheap energy moved a mass population from want and scarcity into proud middle-class status.

For almost three decades the U.S. economy was marked by dynamism, rapid growth and expanding opportunities. A growing economy encouraged upward mobility: year after year, people improved their lot and came to take for granted ever-increasing levels of material well-being. Between 1950 and 1973 average family income doubled—from $5,600 to $12,000 in constant dollars—moving the mass of Americans from the edge of poverty to modest material comfort.

Americans quickly came to cherish the new freedom their affluence secured for them and to depend on the benefits of an expanding income. Middle-class Americans may find it hard to achieve psychological fulfillment, but in the sixties and seventies the practical aspect of the search was made easier than it had ever been before. If you didn't want the responsibility of caring for your aging parents, there were Social Security benefits, pensions, retirement villages, old-age homes and state-provided medical programs to do this for you. If you wished to supplement your income there were jobs. If you wanted training, there were training facilities. If you needed to acquire more education, schools and universities existed in abundance for doing so. If you thought moving to the Sunbelt would make you happier, the Sunbelt welcomed you and offered you an affordable place to live, cheap gasoline to get to work, and rambling schools for your children.

What Happened in the '70s?

Then, abruptly, came a stunning turnabout—a great reversal of the economy and the culture. Without warning or adequate preparation, in the late nineteen-seventies we suddenly found ourselves plunged into an unfamiliar world. Unaccountably, the culture and the economy seemed to have traded places with each other. As the culture has expanded, the economy has grown more restrictive. Economic opportunities have become less abundant. The tempo of growth has decelerated. Inflation is consuming our savings. The cost of living is outstripping disposable income; it is more difficult to save for the future, own a home, pay for college, and meet one's tax, food and medical bills. Inflation is forcing many people who planned to retire early to abandon their plans. Women like Cynthia Muller who originally chose to work outside the home for self-expressive reasons, are now obliged to continue working to pay the mortgage. People struggling to hold on to earlier gains find themselves working harder just to keep from falling behind. Suddenly, to the psychological difficulty of making the right choices is now added the haunting fear that the choices may be futile, and that new self-fulfillment goals may be unattainable because of economic reasons.

Starting in the seventies one economic trouble has followed another. Our annual rate of productivity increase began to falter; some of our key industries, such as steel, textiles and automobiles, grew less competitive with those of other industrialized nations, notably Japan. New floating exchange rates for the dollar saw the value of currency decline steadily as the price of gold moved ever upward, reflecting a world-wide inflation that has left in its wake severe structural problems.

The Reversal

In a matter of a few years we have moved from an uptight culture set in a dynamic economy to a dynamic culture set in an uptight economy. The search for self-fulfillment was conceived in the America of jet vacations to Europe because "your dollar goes so much further there." It has survived, somewhat battered, into the era of chronic stagflation, the dual-earner family that still cannot make ends meet, the decline of U.S. technological innovation, the rise of Soviet military power, the ninety-billion-dollar-a-year bill for OPEC [Organization of Petroleum Exporting Countries] oil and the influx of European tourists into New York City, some of whom come "because it is cheap to live there." The world we live in has been turned upside down.

Such a reversal in the relationship of culture to the economy is profoundly disorienting, especially when there are no warning signals. Nowhere did we find signs telling us: CAUTION: CULTURAL EXPANSION AHEAD, OR LOOK OUT FOR SLIDING ECONOMY.

The economic reverses of [the late '70s] have disoriented Americans because the shifts were so unanticipated and so seemingly arbitrary. People do not know what these bleak economic changes signify for their freedom to choose among life styles. What happens to choice when economic growth slows? What does the future hold for those who conceived their self-fulfillment in an economy of abundance and must now pursue their search under less promising economic conditions? How permanent are these new conditions? What does the future hold? These troubling questions are very much on people's minds, and for good reason.

The '60s Did Not Prepare Us

It is useful to remember that the search for self-fulfillment began in the economic climate of the 1960s and among a group—college students from affluent families—not notorious for their economic realism. Perhaps it made sense at one time to assume our economy was so well-heeled that everything was possible at once—high growth in a clean, safe environment, with social justice for all and a life replete with leisure, jet travel, second homes, glowing health and other "simple things" of life. But it does not make sense now and will not for the foreseeable future. Sad to say, hard choices are what now make sense.

But in the seventies, swept up in the psychology of the me-firstism and more-of-everythingism, we were not ready, psychologically, for hard choices. We took a vacation from our traditional American let's-be-realistic orientation. Americans in the past have been able to tighten their belts without growing panicky or gloom-ridden. But our [1970s-era] political leaders knew that Americans were in the mood to enjoy, not cut back. They made little effort to alert the nation to economic dangers and to keep it from getting

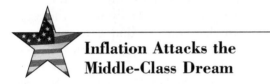

Inflation Attacks the Middle-Class Dream

In the 1970s, workers received minor pay raises, but the money lost its value faster than people received raises.

Ben and his wife Mary worked hard for what they have. Black, lower middle-class, they had grown up in Oakland, California, where their fathers worked for the city. They knew each other as kids, for their families were friends, and they both attended Oakland Technical High School, graduating in 1966. Ben then went to San Jose State for a degree in business administration, and landed a job with the Safeway grocery chain. Mary went to work as a secretary for Kaiser Steel right after high school, saving most of her salary so that she and Ben could get married when he finished college.

"It all worked out as we planned," Mary explains. "We were married in June 1970. Ben had a job as an assistant manager with the Safeway store off Grand Avenue, and we lived well."

"With both of us working we made $17,000," says Ben.

hooked on that most vicious of reality-avoiding addictions, the inflation habit. Of course, our political leadership is itself a cross section of American life: it reflects the public psychology, it does not create it. It, too, was caught up in the disorienting effects of a world turned upside down.

The new vulnerability of the American economy cannot be blamed on a public preoccupied with the search for self-fulfillment. Musings about sex, mid-life career changes and fulfilling one's potentials did not create OPEC, or the Japanese auto industry, or Third World demands for a new economic order, or a Soviet military build-up. There are many geopolitical explanations for the relative decline of U.S. economic strength in our quarrelsome world, a decline that contributes directly to inflation.

"That was a lot of money in 1970, so we were able to gradually build up our savings, buy some furniture, and start fixing up our apartment. We were looking forward to buying our first house."

It is now ten years later, and things look a lot different.

"I'm 33 years old, and this year our earnings will be about $27,000. Not bad, you say. Well, let me tell you about it," continues Ben.

"When we finish paying taxes, we are left with $18,000. We bought a condominium in Oakland last year for $58,000, and our monthly mortgage is $410. Our other monthly expenses include $40 for utilities, telephone $45, car payments of $150, food costs $300, gasoline is now up to $80 a month, insurance $100, medical expenses $50, child care costs $90, new clothes and shoes average $70 for the family, payments on furniture and appliances for our house run $50, and we have about $50 a month in miscellaneous expenses."

"Where does that leave us? It leaves us with about $50 extra each month for savings and fun!"

John Oliver Wilson, *After Affluence: Economics to Meet Human Needs.* New York: Harper & Row, 1980.

But the main problem we are now obliged to face in the 1980s is that we are living far beyond our means. The inflation that has plagued the country since the war in Vietnam is a symptom of a national failure to adapt to this reality. Between the mid-sixties and the early eighties the gap between the nation's assets (the market value of all listed shares of companies) and what we owe grew almost tenfold—from 366 billion to 3 trillion dollars. Henry Kaufman, the economist who made this calculation, interprets this trend as a dangerous erosion of the capital America needs to maintain economic growth. This massive build-up of debt reflects the demands Americans are making on the economy and government in their determination not to narrow their life choices. A society preoccupied with introspection is easily caught off-guard by an unanticipated shift in economic relationships. An era in which people are eager to enjoy the benefits of thirty years of unparalleled economic growth is a terrible time, psychologically speaking, to face disagreeable economic truths.

Lost Confidence

[In the early 1980s,] Americans are just beginning to realize that a change for the worse has taken place in the economy—and it disturbs them. We have an abundance of survey data to document public response to economic conditions. My review of this data, stretching back over the past three decades [1950s through 1970s], suggests that in the past ten years, a significant shift in American attitudes has taken place—from an optimistic faith in an open-ended future to a fear of economic instability. We now find a nation hovering midway between an older postwar faith in expanding horizons and a newer sense of lowered expectations, apprehension about the future, mistrust of institutions and a growing sense of limits.

Consider two survey statements posed by my firm, Yankelovich, Skelly and White. One states, "Our current standard of living may be the highest we can hope for." A recent cross section of 62 percent of Americans agreed. To the other statement, "Americans should get used to the fact that our wealth is limited and most of us are not likely to become better off than we are now," 62 percent also agreed. Moreover, agreement on both questions cuts across all demographic groupings, with virtually no differences between men and women, black and white, or urban and country dwellers. The largest differences relate to age and education, with older and less-educated people being somewhat more pessimistic, and younger people, especially well-educated ones, being less so. But there is one statistic that our surveys turned up that powerfully encapsulates how Americans are responding to the present economic climate. *Almost three out of four Americans (72 percent), shocked by the economic reverses the country has undergone since 1973, have concluded that, "We are fast coming to a turning point in our history. The land of plenty is becoming the land of want.".* . .

The great reversal in the relationship of culture to economy is a momentous event in American history, one we will be struggling with for years to come. It has rendered obsolete all self-fulfillment strategies based on the assumption that our standard of living will, of course, improve in the future as it has in the past.

Contradictions in Self-Fulfillment

Now let us look at another kind of flaw in the self-fulfillment strategy. It is true that a tighter economy has created difficulties for people who, like the Mullers, made their plans under one set of economic assumptions, only to find themselves saddled with burdensome commitments as conditions changed. But it would be a mistake to assume that all was well with people's self-fulfillment strategies when the economy functioned smoothly. A tighter economy has merely intensified strains and contradictions in the self-fulfillment search that have been present all along.

To illustrate, here are two more examples from life histories. The two people, one a man, the other a woman, are not "average Americans," but they are struggling with typical cross pressures arising from the search for self-fulfillment. The two people occupy roughly the same socioeconomic and age brackets. But one sees herself a winner in the self-fulfillment game, while the other sees himself a loser and a victim. Though their life styles are hardly typical, both share the epochal experience of our times: early conformity to traditional norms followed by a growing preoccupation with self-fulfillment projects that run counter to these norms.

Winners and Losers

Robert Agnoli, Ph.D., is Associate Professor of Political Science at one of those colleges in Boston that struggles for its identity under the shadow of Harvard and M.I.T.

In my interview with him, Professor Agnoli admitted that for the first time in his life he has come to think of himself as a loser, and he makes an impressive case to support his claim. In his early forties, he is married, with two children, ages twelve and fifteen. After some hesitation, he told me that his wife, Carole, whom he married when they were graduate students, had abandoned him and the children several months ago. . . .

"Both of us had reached a crisis in our lives and we knew we were not being fulfilled. I just don't feel like a middle-aged professor with tenure, two kids and a house in Lexington with a big mortgage. And she didn't feel like a typical housewife. We were living a stereotyped life but we didn't fit the stereotype. When we weren't arguing about who should do the dishes or the shopping, we'd sometimes talk about making a drastic change in our life style.". . . He and Carole talked often about moving to California. . . .

Unlike Robert Agnoli, Margaret Greenson considers herself one of life's winners, not a loser.

I interviewed her in her husband's office in the Indian Museum in Santa Fe where he is the curator. She was waiting for him to finish work so they could go home together; she works at the museum part-time.

Mrs. Greenson is a few years older than Agnoli, in her middle forties, and the mother of four grown children. . . .

The museum job was everything her husband had always wanted, and they had moved to Santa Fe from Cincinnati even though it meant a cut in income at a time they could hardly afford it, just after the birth of their second child. Margaret Greenson, who had majored in math and anthropology in college (a "funny combination," she admits), found herself obliged to "take in bookkeeping the way women take in washing" to help set aside college tuition for their children. . . .

Under the circumstances, . . . she found herself "feeling angry almost all of the time at my children and my husband. It was as if everybody else was entitled to do what they wanted in life except Mother.". . .

She discovered a program associated with the University of Maryland for which she could work toward a degree at home and at the same time take a part-time job at the museum. . . .

She had come to hate bookkeeping, which had somehow grown into a symbol of a way of life she wanted to shed. "I have to work like a maniac now," she said, "but it's worth it. Twenty years ago I would have died at the prospect of getting a mail-order degree. But I think I have my priorities a little straighter now. My big fear, frankly, is that with life being so expensive, it will be back to the bookkeeping before I know it. I'm not sure I could take that. Somehow I feel I've used up my ability to compromise and always look on the bright side of things. But maybe it won't have to come to that.". . .

Choices and Tensions

The [Agnolis and Greensons] *are* typical in several respects. Both families gradually became aware that a greater range of life choices might be available to them than in earlier periods of their lives. Each of them strived to win greater freedom of movement and flexibility in their lives. And in each instance, the newer self-fulfillment values came in conflict with older, more traditional ones.

Under conditions of economic strain, the Agnoli marriage came apart. But it is clear that the economic constraints which discouraged Agnoli from moving to California did not wreck his marriage; they merely precipitated a crisis long in the making. For the Greensons, tighter economic conditions added to the pre-existing strain on a family struggling to take advantage of new life choices. Even under conditions in which both husband and wife seem genuinely responsive to each other, the new circumstances create stress.

As we shall see more clearly when we examine other life histories and surveys gathered for this study, the truly determined seekers of self-fulfillment are plunged into confusing predicaments even when they are affluent. . . . All of us have come to know of marriages that have broken up for reasons that would not have led to divorce a generation ago; of young people who have more choice than young people enjoyed in the past and yet cannot decide what to do with their lives; of men and women who, being discontent with themselves, transform their lives in the name of self-fulfillment, however disastrously this turns out for themselves and others. All around us we see signs of aimlessness and dissatisfaction with conventional choices. We see people unable to settle the basic questions of where to live, with whom, under what conditions and with what focus for one's time and life. Among people like the Agnolis who are involved in what I call "the strong form" of the self-fulfillment predicament, the search for self-fulfillment raises more fundamental questions than most people can take in stride without stumbling.

Experiments in Living

My interviews with Professor Agnoli and other middle-income people involved in self-fulfillment experiments remind me of types of adventures that used to be confined to the very wealthy. It is as if upper-crust life styles have been democratized and made part of the conventional psychoculture—but with an important difference between the life experiments of the wealthy and those of the rest of us.

Leaving aside the emotional wear and tear that affects us all with relative equality, the wealthy can afford, from a practical point of view, to make more than one mistake. When they take a risk and it fails, they can afford to walk away from it: for the very rich, being obliged to maintain several households or failing in a new career are not terminal dilemmas. The middle class, however, suffers all the emotional trauma of failed risks, and devastating practical consequences as well. People on tight budgets are plunged into instant hardship when marriages break up and former partners are obliged to support two households, usually on the same income that had barely sufficed for one. In the life experiments of the average American, there are no safety nets woven of excess dollars.

CHAPTER 5

Women's Issues in the 1970s

The Movement to Liberate Women

Judith M. Bardwick

Judith M. Bardwick, a professor of psychology, gives a brief outline of the issues surrounding the women's movement of the '70s. Some feminists demanded radical changes in society, while others were more moderate. Resistance to such changes was also divided in many ways. At times women, men, and young people did not want a change in the status quo. After looking at the complexity of the women's movement, Bardwick challenges the reader to also look into the future.

In the late 1960s and early 1970s radical feminists called for the end of marriage and capitalism, and advocated homosexuality and test-tube conceptions. The radicals were especially visible because they had learned how to shock us and therefore how to assure widespread coverage in the media. While such exposure led many to dismiss all feminists as crazy or irrelevant, its conspicuousness made the existence of a women's movement impossible to ignore. Equally important, the demands of mainstream feminist groups such as NOW (National Organization for Women) seemed tame in contrast; such goals as ending sex discrimination in social benefits and in employment, granting tax deductions for child care costs to working parents, estab-

Excerpted from *In Transition: How Feminism, Sexual Liberation, and the Search for Self-Fulfillment Have Altered Our Lives,* by Judith M. Bardwick. Copyright ©1979 Holt, Rinehart, and Winston. Reprinted and edited by permission of the publisher.

lishing more child care centers, providing equal educational opportunities, giving housing and family allowances to women at the poverty level—all of which would be revolutionary in effect—appeared rational, even tame.

It is hard to measure the impact of the radicals, since their accomplishments do not lend themselves to an easy accounting. We cannot ask, for example, How many legislators have they put into office? How many reforms have they been responsible for? Yet they seem to have provided much of the initial crucial energy of the movement.

But every movement must organize and set goals so that accomplishments and impediments are clear and concrete. The radicals, in general, did not do this, and that became the mission of the mainstream feminists. A movement may become less radical when its objectives have to be specified with realistic means to achieve them. It may also be true that a movement becomes less radical as its anger is dissipated by the energy required to organize.

Because both radical and mainstream feminists articulated the frustration and latent motivation for change that already existed among a significant percentage of women, feminism could and did become a major movement. It was led by women who had been educated to participate as individuals and as equals in the work world and who found themselves unable to do so. Their education prepared them to achieve and compete in the world outside the home. That women were being trained to work outside their traditional confined roles itself signified that an important social change had already occurred, but it had not been recognized or responded to by society. Victimized and angered, feminists transformed their individual frustrations into an ideology of change.

More than anything else, feminism is a psychological revolution based on women's insistence that they have a basic right to make choices and to be judged as individuals. The movement is a statement that women are not whatever their marital status is. Feminism is a statement by those whose lives had been organized by their responsibilities to others that they have the right to self-expression, to individual achievement, to independence. Since individualistic gratification—as well as economic independence—can be gained directly by success in an occupation, mainstream feminists have directed their major efforts to achieving parity in careers. As radical feminism declined and mainstream feminism became dominant, media portrayal of the movement became increasingly sympathetic. The emphasis on work success unwittingly lowered the status of women's traditional roles even further. As a result of the extraordinary success of feminism and its visibility, resistance to the movement was an inevitable secondary development. . . .

Resistance in Different Forms

Men who are confronted by angry wives will predictably feel resentment and then anxiety when their wives want to change the contract of their relationship, often after several years of marriage. Some men's resistance expresses both conscious fears that new demands will be made on them or that they will lose support, and less conscious anxieties that the changes their wives want have as much to do with their own inadequacy as with their wife's ambition.

A more complicated form of resistance stems from women having internalized the traditional norms. In this case women feel a conscious anger at their husbands, who, they insist, bound them to the home and prevented them from doing what was important to them. While these women are often aware of being scared about whether they could succeed in work or in school, they are not aware of the extent to which their choices in the past were governed by their own traditional values. Wives may therefore demand and want their husbands' attitudes and behavior to change, but at an unconscious level neither expect nor desire what they are requesting. We see this, for example, when a wife insists on the opportunity to earn money, the husband agrees, and the wife is then upset because she feels he is not willing to support her anymore.

Another source of resistance to feminist goals is the conservatism of children. They seem very resistant to changing ideas about what the sexes are supposed to do and be like. This is probably because their gender is the only thing about them that does not change as they grow up. In one experiment, for example, psychologist Marcia Guttentag attempted to change sexist attitudes in schoolchildren. Guttentag designed a six-week program intended to increase awareness of sexist issues. The program was given to over 1,000 children aged 5, 10, and 14 in three school districts in Boston. The focus was on sexual stereotypes in personality, work, and family responsibilities. The program emphasized the ideas that women can do any sort of work that men can, that men should enjoy their families, and that both sexes ought to have the personality qualities we admire.

Tests given before the experimental curriculum established that the majority of the children knew from the age of 5—from television, their peers, and what they saw at home—that boys and men are strong and do interesting things and girls and women are weak and silly and are best kept at home. These views were held by children of diverse ethnic, social, and economic backgrounds, and it made no difference whether their mothers were employed.

At the end of the program the researchers found that 10-year-old boys whose mothers worked and all 14-year-old boys, with employed or unemployed mothers, became notably more stereotyped, rigid, and outspoken about what women's roles ought to be. In contrast, many of the girls moved closer to feminist views, accepting the ideas that women can do a wide variety of jobs and can combine marriage and work.

In another effort to reduce children's sexism, Gale Mitchell designed a curriculum which she used with eighth- and ninth-grade students. She made up a country called Ruritania, in which two groups, the Schleeps and Greeps, lived. Her charts showed that Schleeps were 49 percent of the population, made up 50 percent of the college graduates and 60 percent of those working, held 97 percent of the major government jobs, controlled 82 percent of the money invested in business, earned almost double what Greeps did, could have almost any kind of job they wanted, and could get the training they needed for the employment they chose. The students were asked to describe what they would feel like if they were a Schleep or a Greep and what their life would be like.

The students were very angry about the enormous inequities—until the groups were described as male and female and the data as true for the United States. The girls either tended to become angrier or to back down, apparently because they were afraid of alienating the boys. Boys said it changed things to know the data referred to real sex differences. This was the way things ought to be. Mitchell found that the boys who expressed the strongest sexist prejudices were the poorer students, the "tough guys," and the athletes. Boys who were successful academically were much more flexible about sex roles.

The Counter Revolution

Another significant source of resistance to the women's movement, especially toward its focus on achievement in work, is many women's experience of the traditional roles as significant and creative. While many mothers of young children would welcome some help, most continue to want major responsibility in rearing their own small children. As long as this continues to be true (and as long as women are expected to raise their own children), women will reduce their work involvements at precisely the time when ambitious men are most fully involved in their careers.

Some women may therefore choose to remain within the traditional roles, at least for part of their adult life, because they find the responsibilities important and the work at least sometimes creative and pleasurable. Other women may limit their activities to a *confined* version of the traditional role for the negative reason that they are afraid to venture out of it. Thus, for diverse reasons, some women and men who are successful according to traditional criteria will not want these measures of successful adulthood changed.

While men have been the primary and obvious target of feminist *anger,* some women believe that traditional women have been the primary target of feminist *contempt.* This is because the most visible feminist position is that real parity will be achieved through success in work. This position implies the judgment that the roles of wife and mother are of less value than roles which are paid, and therefore that wives and mothers are of less value than employed women. While the mainstream feminist position is actually that everyone has the right to make choices and develop self-esteem in different ways, the focus is on increasing opportunity for career success. Many women who are unwilling to take this route and engage in this risk, many misunderstand the feminist message to be, "You are worthless and you have wasted your life."

Earlier expressions of a counter-revolutionary conservatism had little effect: MOM (Men Our Masters); HOW (Happiness of Womanhood); The Pussycats ("The lamb chop is mightier than the karate chop"). But Helen Andelin's *Fascinating Womanhood* has now sold over 400,000 hardback copies since it was published in 1965, and 11,000 teachers have given the author's eight-week course to 300,000 women in the past 14 years. *The Total Woman* by Marabel Morgan sold 370,000 hardback copies in 1974 alone, and Pocket Books paid $750,000 for the paperback rights.

The counter-revolutionary movement developed when feminist accomplishments and values were so visible that they were impossible to ignore. The counter-movement formed when the success of feminism created a large number of disturbed, anxious people. Much of the focus of the anti-feminist movement has been the fight against ratification of the Equal Rights Amendment (ERA) [which Congress had passed in 1972]. While anti-ERA forces coach their arguments in terms of threats to the family, the end of alimony, the possibility of women being drafted into the military, and the fascinating specter of unisex toilets, they are also expressing rejection of a movement they perceive as elitist, preoccupied with the goals of the career-oriented middle class, and contemptuous of housewives and the working class. When women vote against the ERA they may also be voting against a movement that they believe characterizes them as people who have been duped by society, who are brainless, passive, incompetent, and frightened. They are voting against values and heroines that make them feel unintelligent and unsophisticated. They are saying, "I am affirming the value of my life. The hell with you and your ERA."

Passage of the ERA would, in fact, be an explicit recognition of the need for such an amendment. It would then be hard to escape the interpretation that women need the protection of an amendment because they are significantly discriminated against. In this sense the ERA specifically acknowledges women's minority status as women, that is, as they have been discriminated against and confined to the traditional roles.

While anti-ERA groups express opposition to feminism, such books as *Fascinating Womanhood* and *Total Woman* go further. These books and the classes based on them purport to provide a solution to the anxiety provoked by the feminists' questions, giving women clear instructions on how to find happiness through subservience to their husbands. These specific and detailed programs provide scenarios to play and sentences to say, in which adult women are asked to pretend to be dumb, absentminded, childish, submissive but seductive, diffident, deferential, passive, weak, and opinionless. How acting out such roles can lead to self-esteem is unclear to me. I have equal difficulty imagining that men can respond to this contrived playacting with a surge of masculine confidence.

Many women apparently do find solace in these programs, which assure and support traditional women by saying that the choices they have made and the values they hold are correct, even moral, and sanctioned by God. In fact, these programs assert, the path to joy lies in following the old rules—but more strictly and extremely than before.

In addition to the comfort gained from simple rules that deny social change, the essential message is sustaining, since it proclaims that if man is a king, his wife is a queen.

It seems absurd but understandable that a movement devoted to upgrading the status of women is perceived as liberating by women ready to act on the new options and as sexist and denigrating by women who are not. To the latter, feminism appears to be a movement that scorns them and despises the central values of their lives. Imagine how threatening that is, since feminist values appear to them to be the dominant values in the media, in the nation. They are correct: pro-feminist values have become the majority opinion. . . .

Uncertainty About Gender Roles

The feminist movement, like many other movements, is clearest about what it is rejecting from the past. But the movement is not clear about what norms will replace those which have been rejected; new norms are hard to imagine. If the new norm is that henceforward each sex will do what it had previously been forbidden to do, thereby making gender irrelevant, this ostensible solution ignores the fact that changes in gender roles involve not simply changes in what people do but also changes in concepts of femininity and masculinity. It is hard to conceive of a more profound change.

Of course people do not experience the uncertainties and conflicts that stem from changing sexual identity in an abstract way. They wonder whether or not to marry, go to medical school, have children. Even simpler, they become concerned about who does the laundry or picks up the kids after school. While we can think of the latter as purely logistical decisions based on who has the time or the interest to do it, even discussion of what choices to make and who is to do what could not have arisen until people accepted the idea that women have a right to make important commitments outside the family because they have a right to a more egocentric sense of themselves. . . .

Aside from issues of gender, what happens to people when the changes in social values are so fundamental that their commitments necessarily change?

Uncertainty About Life

When there is extraordinary value change, the security that people gain from conforming to the expectations of their culture is endangered and identity crises are predictable. I mean this simply and concretely. When social values are changing, much less reversing, it becomes increasingly difficult to know what we may expect from others and they from us. It becomes more difficult to know what we should want and what we should become. In a period of profound social change people lose their existential anchors.

"Existential anchors" are the commitments and responsibilities that give life direction and meaning. Anchorage is found in the efforts, and tasks which come from commitment. In primitive economies anchorage comes from unending efforts to survive—to eat, to be warm, to cope with the violent onslaught of the elements. Freed by our affluence, we have sought commitment in the extended family, marriage, parenting, and work.

Sex roles have defined responsibilities in work, marriage, and parenthood. The roles of husband and wife, father and mother, have been one source of sexual identity. The specific tasks of the roles can be thought of as existential anchors. Anchors are commitments that tie us to reality because they force us to act on problems and tasks which are real. Grappling with the responsibilities of these roles, which have provided many of our most significant and permanent commitments, gave us our major routes toward achieving adulthood. Coping with these jobs gave us the feeling that we had secured an identity and earned maturity.

In societies that do not change rapidly people know what life was like and what their life will be. Their anchors are specific tasks—to build a house, kill a lion, have a child—and they are safeguarded by the essential stability of a society where rules are not changing and people have certain responsibilities that are known and accepted.

[In the 1960s] most women's identities were anchored in the stereotyped ideal of their family roles. In [the 1970s] extreme ideal this anchor is specifically rejected in favor of anchoring within one's self, as though one can have a self independent of relationships. The anchor of parenthood may be rejected for the anchor of work, that is, an identity based upon occupational success.

Looking for New Anchors

In their most exaggerated form, these ideals may contain a new danger. At least some existential anchors must be permanent to ensure that people have some sources of a stable identity. This occurs most easily if among the responsibilities the society defines as permanent commitments there are some tasks that need be accomplished only once because that achievement or commitment cannot be undone. Parenthood is probably the most permanent of the anchors; marriage once was. In some societies, belonging to a family is a significant anchor, but in our mobile society it has lost some of its importance. Can we find a stable anchor for our identities in work success? I cannot imagine any area more filled with risk. Success in work involves the fluctuating economy, bureaucracies, changing technology, competition—a myriad of factors over which we have no control. Work success involves risk. In work we are as good as the last thing we accomplished. That means that we may be successful and then again we may not. Identity based on work success cannot be a stable, once-accomplished, settled thing. It is always contingent.

Some find their most crucial anchors in their family. This is where they know who they are and what they must do. Part of their identity is secure in the role of wife, husband, child, mother, father. They do not have to recreate these relationships. While family responsibilities may be psychologically draining—and we have all had times when we wanted to get rid of such responsibilities—still, if we sense that these bonds are permanent, we have a crucial source of identity.

Especially because the competitive and risky work milieu is so unstable, the stability of reciprocal, permanent relationships, in which we know our responsibilities, makes them a crucial source of most people's anchorage. It is therefore not surprising that while people are divorcing at record-breaking rates, they are remarrying at extraordinary rates. People are seeking anchorage, hoping for permanence, if not in this relationship, perhaps in the next.

It should be clear that values have not simply changed; in some instances they have reversed. All of us who are trying to adapt to the new values need to create anchorage when the blueprints have not yet been drawn.

Where, then, are our anchors? This is no idle question. I think it is a central issue, the most imperative question in a society that is a maelstrom of changing technologies, ideals, and moralities.

The Faces of Feminism

Sheila Tobias

Looking back over the turbulent years of the late 1960s and 1970s, Sheila Tobias attempts to sort out some of the tensions within the feminist movement. Over the years feminism has been divided over several crucial issues. Should society view women as identical with men, or as different from men, but with equal rights? How should feminism view the family and mothering? Tobias explains how such simple questions caused major divisions in the movement. She was active in the feminist movement in the 1970s and has continued to explore the roles assigned to women in our culture. She is a leader in understanding the causes and effects of math anxiety in young women.

Initially, or so it appears in retrospect, most feminist theorists answered the question "Do women have to be the same as men to be equal?" with "probably so." Not maleness itself but the power men exercised was attractive to the high-achieving, mainly academic women who were writing theory at the time. Since gender differences were learned or "conditioned" by a society cast in a male model, unlearning and unconditioning were necessary first steps to equality. This is what liberation or emancipation meant: freedom from the constraints not just of gender stereotypes but also of gender itself, "free to be," as Letty Cotton Pogrebin wrote in her best-selling record album for children, "you and me." What the "liberated woman" would become, once free of stereotypes, was left somewhat to the imagination. After all, how could one know one's true self if that self had been artificially constructed in conformity to some gender ideal? Nevertheless, even when not explicitly stated, a genderless society seemed not only possible but also a desirable feminist outcome. Women were not essentially *different* from men, only *disadvantaged* in ways that an enlightened society could correct. . . .

Feminists who answered the sameness and equality question in the affirmative came to be known as "rights-oriented" or liberal feminists. For liberal feminists, writes Cynthia V. Ward in a recent recounting of the argument, "sex discrimination is an aberration, an externally imposed collectivization of women that violates liberal ideals of equal concern and respect for all persons as individuals." Feminism's task is to make this clear to men so that once unequal treatment is corrected, women's assigned (or constructed) group identity will also disappear.

According to rights-oriented feminism, government and society simply need to be informed that women's full rights are missing. Since the barriers to women's power and prestige are artificial, and since liberal society is basically "enlightened," legal rights will inevitably be equalized. And once this is accomplished, women's "true" selves will emerge, selves that are equal to men's in their all-important capacities for autonomy and rationality. Logically, then, there should be no long-lasting woman's point of view, no need to conserve women's group identity, no need even for a long-standing feminist movement. Once inequality disappears, so will the differences (read: disadvantages) that women experience. And so liberal feminism was poised to work its way toward its own annihilation.

Opposing views were not long in coming and rested on several distinctive levels of disagreement. Betty Friedan's plaint "Do we want to be equal to unfree men?" resonated with many of the 1960s counterculturalists streaming into the feminist movement, who found much to disavow in mainstream politics and culture. But the more serious challenge to rights-oriented liberal feminism and to the goal of a genderless society came from the work of Carol Gilligan on women's distinctive moral development, Nancy Chodorow's post-Freudian description of "womb envy" in men, Mary Field Belenky's and her colleagues' description of "women's ways of knowing," and dozens of popularizers of their writings from the mid-1970s onward. What these thinkers had in common was the view that woman's nature is not something to be replaced but something to be maintained, indeed celebrated, for the sake both of women and society.

Such theoreticians, writes Ward, challenged the imperfect realization of equal rights and the root concepts of individualism. "[They] believe that liberal ideas . . . are not merely the wrong way to end sexual inequality but help to perpetuate it since they reflect *male ways of being*." Radical feminists were also concerned that only women who are "similarly structured" to men—that is, career- and power-oriented women—would succeed when external barriers were removed. "The norm is already sex-specific," wrote Zillah Eisenstein in *The Female Body and the Law.* Echoing Schlafly, these thinkers—particularly those who are concerned with sexual abuse and exploitation—saw the removal of traditional protections as contributing to women's greater vulnerability.

What remains is a reality check: Can feminism embrace the Gilligan-Belenky-Chodorow position that celebrates gender differences (even speaks favorably of a woman's culture) and still achieve equality in what is a society dominated by male values? In the much celebrated Sears case *(EEOC v. Sears Roebuck and Company),* where a woman employee brought suit against the giant retail company, claiming employment discrimination, two feminist scholars, Rosalind Rosenberg and Alice Kessler-Harris, testified on opposite sides. Rosenberg, a professor of women's history at Barnard College, testified for Sears that women preferred low-risk, noncompetitive positions that did not interfere with family responsibilities. Kessler-Harris, director of women's studies at Rutgers University, made the case for women's sameness on every work-related dimension. The court ruled in favor of the employer. . . .

Rethinking the Family

"Over the last three decades, the nuclear family has been at the very heart of the battle between progressive and conservative forces in the U.S." writes Karen Kahn, editor of the feminist publication *Sojourner* in her introduction to a collection of essays on the family from that journal published in 1995. Kahn attributes this in part to the growing power and popularity of the religious Right, which promoted a pro-family ideology as part of its campaign against women's liberation, abortion, gay rights, and the other leftover "excesses" of the 1960s. But it is not only antifeminists who have come to the defense of the nuclear family. Within feminism itself—and feminist theory reflects this shift—there has been a sizable retreat from the original starting point on which liberal, radical, socialist, and Marxist feminists all agreed: that "the male-dominated, child-centered nuclear family was the single most important site of female oppression." That consensus no longer obtains.

Kahn does a masterful job of reconstructing feminism's original view of the family. For white middle-class feminists to whom Betty Friedan's *The Feminine Mystique* appealed, it was "the oppressive nature of the ideology of domesticity which had flung women out of the work force and into suburban homes." For radical feminists like Shulamith Firestone, ways had to be found, however extreme, to dismantle the patriarchal family. This was the reasoning behind her extreme notion that women should no longer gestate their young. The family was further censured by early feminists for being a microcosm of the patriarchal state and for helping to socialize children to fit into a "gendered" world. As Kahn reminds us,

As the primary site of gender socialization, the family was where girls and boys learned the rules of femininity and

255

masculinity . . . [girls] to gain fulfillment from taking care of others, . . . [boys] to wield . . . power. Moreover . . . families kept women economically dependent on men.

Not only were they expected to stay home and focus their entire lives on caretaking, women who did work were paid less than their male counterparts because they didn't need to support a family . . . [which made them] vulnerable to violence, battering and incest, and to poverty in case of abandonment and divorce.

Indeed, some radical feminist organizations felt so strongly about the reactionary nature of the family, as Molly Lovelock, another *Sojourner* writer, reported at the time, that they restricted the number of married women allowed into their political groups or made married women feel, in the early years, like "fish out of water."

Because of feminists' deep distrust of the male-headed, wife-subordinated family, insufficient intellectual attention was given in the early days to the complex economics of marriage and to the difficulties of finding suitable alternate arrangements for bringing up children. There was a flurry of excitement in 1970 when Pat Mainardi and others proposed a system for assigning "wages for housework." The Chase Manhattan Bank had at one point calculated that a typical Wall Street employee's wife worked 99.6 hours at home, for which $257.53 (1970 dollars) would be a fair weekly wage. But the question of who would pay the housewife's wage was never satisfactorily answered. The "family allowance" paid mothers by the British and some European governments is considerably less than $257.53 per week; for families not in poverty, it seemed hard to justify a government subsidy for the already well-off that would not burden the rest. Besides, on what basis would the subsidy be paid: income forgone by the mother who stayed at home (in which case the rich would get even richer) or numbers of children? With zero-population growth a concern during that same period, a money incentive for having more children was not likely to be popular. And the purer theoretical "solution"—namely, charging husbands (or even children in a delayed payment system) for the care of home and hearth—would further increase wives' and mothers' economic dependence on their families.

As for government-supported child care, the argument foundered over real differences of opinion as to whether what was "good" for working mothers was always equally "good" for children and over the total cost of providing day care for all working mothers. In the face of a growing need for day care, as more and more women with small children entered the workforce, it was always easy for the pro-family Right to exaggerate cost estimates by arguing that if the government was going to subsidize day care for mothers who worked outside the home, it should pay the equivalent for child care performed by individual mothers in the home. This mother subsidy caught feminists in one of the contradictions of their own thinking about the family: On the one hand, it provided at least in theory the "wages for housework" that some feminists had demanded, and on the other, it killed government-subsidized day care every time (which was its proponents' real intention) because it trebled the total estimated cost.

But the real challenge to the view that the family was the seat of the oppression of women came from feminists themselves and falls under four lines of rethinking. First, there was ever-growing and undeniable evidence that, while housework could be denigrated with some impunity, motherhood could not. Feminists quite as much as other women felt a special attachment to their children, which no amount of theorizing could deny. Second, a shift in sentiment occurred over surrogate motherhood occasioned by the Baby M case [explained below], which raised new threats to birth mothers owing to improvements in reproductive technologies that no one, including feminists, could have foreseen. Third, there was some rethinking about the family led by influential feminist thinkers, who gave ringing reendorsements of family life as unique and irreplaceable. And fourth, it was undeniably true that for African-Americans, Latinas, Chicanas, and women of other ethnic minorities living in a racially charged society, the family was often the only source of resistance and support. With 47 percent of African-American families and 23 percent of Hispanic families headed by women, the whole notion of a "patriarchal family" needed modification if a feminist theory of the family was to have any meaning for women of color.

These four "deviations" (if you consider the family-as-the-seat-of-oppression to be the correct analysis) must be viewed against the backdrop of a pro-family political ascendancy in the Reagan and Bush years. Two feminist books published in the mid-1980s can be taken as one measure of change. Kristin Luker's prize-winning study of pro- and anti-abortion advocates (among women), published in 1984, found that more than any other factor, a woman's attitude toward *motherhood* determined her stance on abortion. If motherhood was seen to be the most important and satisfying role open to her, she tended to be antichoice; if motherhood was seen as only one of several roles and a burden when defined as the only role, she tended to be prochoice. Clearly, there was no room for debate about the family on the Right.

But among feminists there was growing ambivalence. Writing about the family at about the same time as Luker was publishing her long-term study, a group of feminist scholars and theoreticians chose contributors who would give attention both to "the supportive and nurturant" as well as to "the oppressive side" of family life. Their title shows the loss of a feminist consensus on the family. They called their collection *Rethinking the Family: Some Feminist Questions* and acknowledged in their Introduction that they were "struggling" with a series of contradictions in feminist thinking about the family. Yet they held fast to the notion that agreement might be achieved and promised that a "more realistic and complex understanding [of] the family [would be] part of a larger program of social change."

Mothering and Motherhood

It is not as if feminists had ignored mothering altogether. Rather, in books such as *Woman's Estate* and *The Reproduction of Mothering,* authors Juliet Mitchell and Nancy Chodorow found evidence that the assignment of mothering varies from culture to culture and era to era and that mothering as a full-time occupation is only a modern industrial phenomenon. In the past mothers had to grow food as well as prepare it, construct clothing as well as select it, and with multiple pregnancies and many more children to bring up, spend much more time caring for their families. Thus, full-time mothering was never known in human history and might even be dysfunctional for all kinds of reasons. Indeed, Dorothy Dinnerstein in *The Mermaid and the Minotaur* and Nancy Chodorow in *The Reproduction of Mothering* found that women-exclusive mothering confined children as well as mothers in unhealthy ways. In 1976 poet Adrienne Rich offered a way out of the "good motherhood/bad motherhood" dilemma by suggesting that motherhood exists in two forms, its natural form, mostly a positive experience for both mothers and children, and its institutional form, from which its negative aspects flow. Throughout the 1970s, then, the discussion of motherhood among feminists was ongoing but still attentive to its negative side.

In 1981 Betty Friedan made public her growing doubts on the subject. Friedan had always been an integrationist as far as men were concerned; recall, she named NOW the National Organization *for* and not *of* Women. Nor was she a radical critic of the nuclear family. But in her 1981 book *The Second Stage,* she went further. She regretted that the family and, as she put it, "women's need to give and get love" had been "overlooked" by the movement. What caused Friedan to distance herself even from her own earlier writings and to call for a "second stage" were several: "the way the rhetoric of women's lib was being used to justify increased divorce, explosion of rape, battered children, and the moral delinquency of the 'me' generation; . . . the way judges were shortchanging women [in divorce settlements] who had given over their own wage-earning years to their family's well being; and . . . the agonizing conflicts young and not so young women are facing or denying . . . as they come up against the biological clock."

These concerns were real, but did they justify a dramatic remaking of the feminist agenda? Friedan thought so. She wanted to abandon the "personal is political" basis of feminist politics, to distance herself from what she now dubbed the "*feminist* mystique," and to accelerate feminism's "second stage." Her book is not as carefully argued as her others, but it bears mentioning because the need for the "second stage," in her view, rested *entirely* on feminism's failure to appreciate the family. The family, she wrote, had to be "the new feminist frontier and motherhood its joyous expression"—a far cry from the original feminist consensus on the family. Indeed, when Betty Friedan and NOW Legal Defense and Education Fund Coordinator Muriel Fox expressed these views at the 1979 National Assembly on the Future of the Family, some feminists accused Friedan and Fox of "reactionary family chauvinism."

But Friedan and Fox were not alone. Even radical theologian Mary Daly, who had shocked the country in the 1970s with her books challenging the maleness of God himself (*Beyond God the Father* and *Gyn/Ecology*), during this period wrote that the mother-child relationship is the primary relationship of all.

In 1987 a childless professional couple, William and Elizabeth Stern, contracted with Mary Beth Whitehead, a working-class mother, to carry to term a fetus fertilized by Stern's sperm. The contract was overseen by the Sterns' attorney, and a fee of $10,000 was settled upon. Further conditions governed the mother's health and prenatal care and the right of the Sterns to have the fetus aborted if amniocentesis showed the child to be in any way deformed. After the child was born healthy, to everyone's surprise the birth mother reneged on her contract and refused to hand the baby over to her legal "owners."

The case seems to have accelerated feminist rethinking on birthing, motherhood, and reproductive technology. Sociologist Barbara Katz Rothman, herself a mother, was driven to write a book entitled *Recreating Motherhood* in response to the decision on the part of the courts to award Baby M to the surrogate parents. Calling for a "feminist analysis of mothers and motherhood that is consistent with feminist politics and feminist theory," her book is a mélange of feminist and pronatalist thinking. In one section Rothman acknowledges that in a patriarchal society men *use* women to have *their* children, but, at the same time, she romanticizes pregnancy by talking about a "baby inside [that is] not so different from the baby outside." Such a blurring of the distinction between the fetus and the child could be used to undermine the legal case for abortion, especially when Rothman concludes that aborting a fetus is a means of "ending the relationship" between mother and child.

By supporting the primacy of the birth mother's claim in the Baby M case, Rothman and other feminists who took that same position found themselves side by side with conservatives and religious fundamentalists. To be sure, they (in Rothman's words) had taken "very different paths to get there and [were] headed in very different directions." Only the feminists, for example, noted that in the argument over which would be the "fittest" family, money, class, and race loomed large. The Sterns were well educated and well off; Mary Beth Whitehead was neither. But if theory is to generate political alignments, these differences may not matter much. To justify the birth mother's rights, feminists found themselves reclaiming "maternal instincts."

By the end of the 1980s, the wheel seemed to have come full circle. While feminist theoretician Sara Ruddick, in the widely published and republished essay "Maternal Thinking," argued that the "most revolutionary change" in the institution of motherhood would be to include men equally in every aspect of child care, elsewhere in that same essay she asserted that "maternal thought exists for all women in a radically different way than for men." "It is because we are daughters, nurtured and trained by women that we early receive maternal love with special attention to its implications for our bodies, our passions, and our ambitions." Moreover, she argued, the assimilation of men into child care is *not* the primary social goal for mothers. Rather (echoing the "women-are-morally-superior-to-men" arguments of the suffrage era), with women in power the public realm will be "transformed by maternal thought."

Mothering, Careers, and Self-Fulfillment

Joyce Maynard

During the 1970s, a new push in society for each person to find self-fulfillment, particularly in a career outside their home, caused a dilemma among many women. Such a choice collided with their choices and responsibilities as mothers. In this selection, Joyce Maynard describes one woman's struggle to find her place in the world. As she looks at herself, she also looks at the confusion felt by many men and women in the '70s. While she feels a new freedom to choose between various lifestyles, she also feels that such freedom is a burden. Earlier in her life, Maynard wrote for the *New York Times*. At the time of this article, she lived and wrote in the slower-paced environment of New Hampshire.

I n New York the other day, a young man stopped me on the street to ask if the baby on my back was real. Evidently there is a fad now for carrying baby dolls in backpacks, following the small vogue, a few years ago, for wearing maternity-simulating pillows under one's dress. My own stomach grew unfashionably large, however, before my daughter was born, and now that she's four months old, she's rarely taken for a baby doll. Indeed, once this fellow got a better look at my grouchy, sweaty daughter, there was no need to tell him that I wasn't a trend-follower, just a mother.

And there's nothing very fashionable about that. Not, at least, among women of my age—24, or women with careers, women looking for success and (something our mothers never spoke of) self-fulfillment. More and more, they tell us, these women are choosing not to have children, or not to have them, at any rate, until they're older, more "established." Every month I read the class notes in my husband's Yale Bulletin and observe how few babies have been born to alumni under 30. They write about their work and their studies, not their children. I ran across a checklist recently of 50 questions to determine whether or not a couple is ready for a child. Once, it was a foregone conclusion: you got married, you had kids. Now, there are books and seminars on the subject. The decision to have a baby is worked on like a tax return.

My husband and I speak all the time with friends and total strangers who agonize over the question and grill us on what life is like with Audrey. They talk about having a baby, they have been talking about it for years. The number 35 looms before them as the age by which the wife had better have the baby, if she's going to. But they feel frightened of what that tiny 7-pound package will do to their lives.

An Irreversible Step

And even when they decide to take that huge and irreversible step toward parenthood, they speak of it so often as an interruption, a necessary but inconvenient detour from their true course. You take a few months out, maybe, for pregnancy, and a few months caring for an infant, and then (aided, with luck, by a good nanny) you get back on the track, with one extra piece of baggage. Interviews with the current crop of female stars convey the same message. "Next year," says one—who must keep slim for her appearances on "Charlie's Angels"—"is our year for a baby."

There's no getting around it, having a baby—unless you write a book about it afterward—slows down your career. Interrupts things so much that some women simply won't have one, like a frankly ambitious newspaper colleague of mine who once said she didn't want to find herself beaten out on a story because she had kids at home and some other reporter didn't. I used to write for her newspaper, and now I'm home, worrying about diaper rash, so I guess I'm one of the ones who will never be first on the scene of a crime, never assigned to cover wars or earthquakes. And I can't pretend, holding my sleeping daughter and hearing one of my child-less friends tell me about her work, that I don't, sometimes, grieve for my career, my freedom, my fulfillment.

Pampers and Work

In the supermarket one day, as I piled boxes of Pampers in my cart, with Audrey, beaming, propped up in front be-tween two bags of onions, an acquaintance asked me sym-pathetically if I was getting any "real" work done yet. I knew what he meant, of course, and said, a little defen-sively and a bit too loud, that I was, that Audrey is a "good" baby—by which one always means a baby who sleeps well and interferes as little as possible with the busi-ness of one's former child-free life. But the truth is that I write less now, and launder more.

Probably because of that kind of encounter and the need to prove how little interruption having a baby brought about, Audrey and I set out together for New York last week. I was going to write about houses of prostitution in Manhattan. I was going to get inside, pretend I was apply-ing for a job, maybe. I was going to hear lots of seedy sto-ries and write about the mob. My daughter, hiccuping qui-etly in her Easy Rider backpack, wasn't going to get in my way at all.

For three days we skulked around in New York City, try-ing to make contact with someone who could get me in, collecting stories of strange exploits carried out at fancy East Side addresses and of dangerous characters whose names I was advised to forget. Audrey was less "good" than usual, so I had to dance with her a lot, but didn't let that stop me from my "real" work. Up at 2 a.m. for a night feeding, I talked on the phone to the operator of a chain of brothels, with Audrey sleeping at my breast. "I could tell you tales that would curl your hair," the voice said over the receiver. "You'll probably have to stick around for a few weeks, but you can get a great story," said my detective friend the next afternoon. But Audrey, by the fourth day, was cranky and constipated. I missed my husband, thought how nice it would be to do a load of laundry, and decided to give up and drive home, where I sit now, facing a stack of diapers and a baby who will wake soon, wanting to play.

If we'd filled out that questionnaire about "Are You Ready for a Baby?" before I got pregnant last year, and if we'd followed what it told us, I would still have money for $30 haircuts and silk blouses, still be able to eat dinner alone with my husband without having to ask him to cut up my chicken because I'm holding the baby. I would have a thick folder of newspaper clippings with my by-line on them now. I would be a much better reporter. And we would not have Audrey.

The Jump

I don't imagine that what we chose would be right for everyone. Still, it does seem to me that there's absolutely no way—no matter how many experts you consult—to predict how a child will change your life. There is only so much about sky diving you can learn on the ground. Past a point, confronting parenthood too, there is nothing for it but to jump. Once having jumped, though, no couple should think of going back, ever, to the way things used to be in their "real life." For myself, I never really pictured us as "taking time out" to have Audrey. She is simply with us, and part of my advancement in my career as a person.

Attitudes Toward Women in the Workplace

Nancy E. McGlen and Karen O'Connor

In the 1970s, many people modified their views about working women. Should women stay at home and care for their husbands and children? Should women seek careers that will span their whole lives? How should women with small children view their responsibilities? Simple answers to such questions were slipping away. In this selection, the authors seek to understand the answers various segments of the American population gave in public opinion polls.

The popularity of the women's movement in the 1970s and its focus on a woman's right to work, have facilitated the positive attitude on behalf of the public toward married working women. By the end of the 1970s, the vast majority of the public had come to accept paid employment of married women. For example, in 1978, large majorities of those interviewed who had a high school or a college education approved of a married woman working even if her husband was able to support her—there was a gain of 18 percent in only nine years. Among certain categories of respondents, notably working women, the college educated, and the young, support for married working women was overwhelming. Eighty-four percent of all employed women approved compared to only 66 percent of all housewives. Among college-educated working women under thirty, 98 percent endorsed this prac-

Excerpted from *Women's Rights: The Struggle for Equality in the Nineteenth and Twentieth Centuries*, by Nancy E. McGlen and Karen O'Connor (New York: Praeger, 1983). Copyright ©1983 by Praeger Publishers. Reprinted with permission from the authors.

tice. Only among the elderly or those less-educated was approval for women workers considerably lower. These figures seem to indicate that the public was largely supportive of the employment of married women.

The Role of Women in the Workforce

Acceptance of the idea that participation in the labor force is not exclusively a man's right, however, is tempered by the view that a salaried position is of primary importance for men but only secondary for women. For example, it appears that most people still believe that a married woman should accept a job outside of the home *only* if she is not taking a job away from a man. As recently as 1977 when asked, "If there are a limited number of jobs, do you approve or disapprove of a married woman holding a job in business or industry when her husband is able to support her?" levels of support in all segments of the population for married working women plummeted. Overall, 64 percent disapproved (62% of all men, 66% of all women), while, as expected, working, college-educated women, and young women were much more supportive of the employment of married women even if jobs were limited. Yet, the highest approval rate even among these groups was only 60 percent. When these figures are compared to 1946 responses to the same question, we find only a 20 percentage point improvement in 30 years. Furthermore, 38 percent of respondents questioned in 1976 favored laying-off married women first if a company was forced to cut back. Thus, given high unemployment rates in the 1980s, there is a strong likelihood of a reversal in public support for the employment of married women.

Not only do significant segments of the population still expect women to give up their jobs in times of shortage, many also cling to the view that employment of a married woman is acceptable so long as it does not infringe upon her husband's career. For example, in 1977 when queried about whether "it was more important for a wife to help her husband's career than to have one herself," 57 percent of all respondents agreed. Interestingly, more women than men (60 versus 53 percent) thought that a man's career should come first. The view of many that a woman's career is secondary is also revealed by the widely held view that "it is much better for everyone involved if the man is the achiever outside of the home and the woman takes care of the home and family." In fact, only 31 percent of the male and 37 percent of the female respondents disagreed with this statement. Likewise, in 1979, 77 percent of all women and 68 percent of all men were in accord with the view that a woman should give up her career if her husband has to relocate. And, in another poll, two-thirds of the sample responded that they believed that a woman should reject a job promotion if it meant she and her husband would have to relocate.

There is, however, some evidence that this view may be changing. For instance, in 1964 among some groups of college-educated women, more than 80 percent believed that it was more important to help their husband's career than to have one themselves; however, by 1977, more than 50 percent of all working women with a high school education or better rejected the view that it was better for the man to be the achiever as did majorities of young (under 30) high school and (under 50) college-educated women. Additionally, another [early 1980s] study found that a growing number of young women today think that it is acceptable for a woman to work even if her husband objects. The husband's job, however, is not the only factor that historically has been considered more important than a woman's career. Since the early days of the Industrial Revolution, taking care of one's children always has been assumed to be a woman's primary role in life. Thus, paralleling our findings with respect to political participation, our findings in this area show that the public always has held reservations about working women with child-care responsibilities.

The History of Working Mothers

Early in the Industrial Revolution, in England and in some parts of the United States, whole families often were hired for factory work, apparently with public approval. By the mid-1800s, however, public sentiment was anything but favorable toward working mothers. As already discussed, the evils of factory life and the toll it took on working women and their families were an important rationale for much of the progressive legislation enacted in the early 1900s. Although most married women who worked left their jobs upon the birth of their first child, the National Consumers' League and others tried to limit the hours of women's work to assure that those who had to work would be able to spend some time with their families.

The almost universal practice of women leaving their jobs after the birth of their first child was in keeping with the educated public's view that the roles of mother and employee were incompatible. Even in the 1920s, an era of relatively high support for working women, the majority of professional women saw their choice as either marriage and a family *or* work. During this period, only 19.3 percent of all professional women were married, and most viewed a family and a profession as mutually exclusive.

In the 1930s and 1940s, one of the most frequently voiced objections to married women working was that the practice posed potential harm to children. Even in the 1960s, when more than 30 percent of all mothers with children under sixteen were employed outside the home, a sample of married men cited child neglect as their main objection to the growing practice of a woman with children working.

As we have already noted, the mothers who were employed outside the home in the 1950s, especially those with young children, tended to cite economic need as their motivation for working. While most of these women wanted to stay on the job, many apparently suffered guilt about neglecting their parental role. Overall, working mothers were no more likely than nonworking mothers to report *ever* having had feelings of inadequacy as a parent, but they did report experiencing these feelings more frequently. Working mothers also were more likely to report that they did not spend enough time with their children. It appears that the role conflict between working and motherhood was most unsettling for mothers of preschool children. In fact, working women with younger children were more likely to report negative or ambivalent self-perceptions.

New Attitudes About Working Mothers

Although the 1960s and 1970s saw a massive increase in the number of mothers working, as revealed in Table 1, altering public sentiment toward the employment of young mothers has been a more gradual process. Leading forces in this process include working women themselves and perhaps, the women's movement. Karen O. Mason et al., report that between 1964 and 1970, the proportions of women in certain subgroups of the population who thought a working mother could establish just as warm and secure a relationship with her children as a mother who did not work rose significantly with the change being sharpest for educated women. By 1977, almost half of a national sample agreed with this view, as revealed in Table 2. Although not indicated in Table 2, among women who worked, there was particularly strong sentiment that such a warm relationship between children and a working mother was possible. Indeed, among college-educated working women, more than 88 percent agreed with the statement. Similarly, working mothers of the 1970s, seemed to experience less guilt about the influence of their work on their ability to be parents. They still were more likely than full-time homemakers, however, to report that they did not spend enough time with their children. Yet, another survey found many working mothers (43%) felt that they made up for this deficiency by improving the quality of the time they spent with their children.

The relative influence of a woman's own work experience and the women's movement in shaping this attitudinal change is difficult to gauge. The importance of labor force experience is evident from the figures showing that working women at all education levels are more likely than men or nonworking women to report a belief that working

Table 1: Labor Force Participation Rates of Married Women, Husband Present, by Presence and Age of Own Children: Selected Years, 1950–1982

Participation rate
(percent of population in labor force)

Year*	Total	With no children under age 18	With children under age 18		
			Total	6 to 17, none younger	Under 6
1950	23.8	30.3	18.4	28.3	11.9
1955	27.7	32.7	24.0	34.7	16.2
1960	30.5	34.7	27.6	39.0	18.6
1965	34.7	38.3	32.2	42.7	23.3
1970	40.8	42.2	39.7	49.2	30.3
1971	40.8	42.1	39.7	49.4	29.6
1972	41.5	42.7	40.5	50.2	30.1
1973	42.2	42.8	41.7	50.1	32.7
1974	43.0	43.0	43.1	51.2	34.4
1975	44.4	43.9	44.9	52.3	36.6
1976	45.0	43.8	46.1	53.7	37.4
1977	46.6	44.9	48.2	55.6	39.3
1978	47.6	44.7	50.2	57.2	41.6
1979	49.4	46.7	51.9	59.1	43.2
1980	50.1	46.0	54.1	61.7	45.0
1981	51.0	46.3	55.7	62.5	47.8
1982	51.0	46.2	56.3	63.2	48.7

*Data were collected in April of 1951–1955 and March of all other years.

Note: Children are defined as "own" children of the women and include never-married sons and daughters, stepchildren, and adopted children. Excluded are other related children such as grandchildren, nieces, nephews, and cousins, and unrelated children.

Source of data: U.S. Department of Labor, Bureau of Labor Statistics, Perspectives on Working Women, June, 1980, p. 4, and Howard V. Hayghe, Office of Current Employment Analysis, Bureau of Labor Statistics, oral report.

mothers can be adequate parents. Yet, the fact that this view is so much stronger among all college-educated women suggests the ideology of the women's movement may be having additional, independent impact on the attitudes of these women. Interestingly, men in all segments of the population are much less likely to agree that a working mother can have relations with her children as good as those enjoyed by nonworking mothers. The differences between the sexes are perhaps most telling among the college educated and the young. In the former category, 78 percent of the women but only 53 percent of the men in 1977 believed such a situation was possible. Among people aged 30 to 40, many of whom no doubt have children, the gap was an astounding 34 percentage points. A remarkable 70 percent of the women but only 36 percent of the men believed

Table 2: Attitudes Toward Working Mothers: 1977

| | Education | | | | | |
| Age | Less than High School | | High School | | Some College | |
	Men	Women	Men	Women	Men	Women
Under 30	53	64*	57	64	63	79*
31–40	58	57	44	69*	59	91*
41–50	33	37	24	56*	64	82*
51 or Older	27	32	33	52*	29	60*
Overall	35	40	42	60*	53	78*

*Statistically significant at .05 level or greater.

Note: Figures represent the percent agreeing (strongly and/or just agree) with the following statement. "A Working mother can establish just as warm and secure a relationship with her children as a mother who does not work."

Source of data: The National Opinion Research Center, General Social Survey, 1977. Figures compiled by the authors.

that working would have no impact on a working mother's relations with her children. These disparities between the sexes on both questions about working mothers suggest the strong possibility of conflict between parents over the issue of mothers working.

A related question about the impact of a working mother on preschool children produces a similar pattern of responses, but there is much greater agreement by all segments of the population that this situation would have negative consequences for the child, as revealed in Table 3. More than two-thirds of those interviewed in 1977 (73% of all men and 62% of all women) felt a preschool child suffered if his or her mother worked. Among educated young adults, there was a considerable difference of opinion between the sexes about the impact of employment on small children, even though most sociological research supports the notion that little harm and perhaps some good comes to small children when mothers work. In fact, in 1978, only 23 percent of the public *disagreed* with a statement that women with young children should *not* work outside of the home unless it is financially necessary. Thus, as in the realm of politics, we can predict that many women will forego, if economically possible, seeking positions outside of the home while they have young children to care for rather than act counter to the sentiments of their husbands, society, or their own beliefs regarding the impact of their employment on their ability to be a good mother.

This review of the public's attitudes toward the relative importance and place of women's work outside the home helps us to understand the lower commitment of women, especially in the past, to salaried employment. Quite simply, prior to 1940, employment was looked upon only as something to do before they took up their *real* life's work—being wives and mothers. Even after 1940, when the prospect of two stages of work-force participation seemed more likely and resistance on the part of the public to married women working diminished, the place of work in most women's lives was no doubt less important than their parental and

Table 3: Attitudes Toward Working Mothers of Preschool Children: 1977

	Education					
	Less than High School		High School		Some College	
Age	Men	Women	Men	Women	Men	Women
Under 30	57	47*	37	45	31	63*
31–40	32	46	36	46	34	71*
41–50	19	24	18	42*	36	41
51 or Older	10	19*	22	30	24	43
Overall	22	27	29	40*	31	56*

*Statistically significant at .05 level or greater.

Note: Figures represent the percent disagreeing with the following statement: "A preschool child is likely to suffer if his or her mother works."

Source of data: The National Opinion Research Center, General Social Survey, 1977. Figures compiled by the authors.

spousal roles. Even today, many women and an increasing number of men consider their own marketplace activity as secondary to a family and marriage. However, there is evidence that women, especially young women, are increasingly rejecting these cultural views about the place of work in women's lives. Many are preparing for and committing themselves to a lifetime of paid employment. A 1979 Virginia Slims public opinion poll reports that nearly half—46 percent—of all women preferred an outside job to homemaking (an increase from 35% in 1974). This desire to work apparently is not limited to women who already are working. Among nonworking women, 73 percent of those under thirty and 62 percent of those in their thirties plan to work in the future. Even among mothers under thirty, 44 percent report they would probably look for a job if daycare facilities were available.

Among certain classes and age groups, the proportion of

respondents favoring work over traditional roles is striking. In 1976, for example, 3 percent of working women desired to be full-time housewives. In 1957, this figure was 20 percent. Similarly, when female high school seniors were asked about families in which there were no children, only 24 percent viewed an arrangement in which the husband would work and the wife would stay home as either desirable (5 percent) or acceptable (19 percent). Forty percent viewed this option as unacceptable. Interestingly, more male seniors clung to traditional role divisions as the desirable or acceptable options. Only 15 percent of them found the family in which the wife was a full-time housewife unacceptable; twelve percent actually rated it desirable.

Attitudes of High School Students

Paralleling the attitudes of the general public were the attitudes of these same high school seniors who were more likely to find the traditional division of labor more desirable or acceptable when the presence of preschool children was introduced into the scenario. Even then, however, 87 percent rated the option of part-time work by wife and full-time work by husband as at least somewhat acceptable. Increasing acceptance of women's employment though has not necessarily been accompanied by a change in attitudes about men and work. Among the high school seniors who reported support for female workers, few found it even somewhat acceptable for a husband not to work or to work part time even if his wife was employed.

Although stereotypical attitudes continue to exist, many women see themselves as long-term members of the labor force. This increased commitment to full, life-time work activity, moreover, does not seem solely a function of financial need. While majorities of women give economic reasons for going to work, polls of employed wives in the mid-1970s found that 82 percent would continue to work even if they did not have to earn a living. Just nineteen years earlier, only 58 percent of a similar group of women reported this kind of commitment.

Women not only want to work but they increasingly want a good job and a career. A national study of women workers done in the early 1970s found that women were as likely as men to want jobs that were interesting, challenging, and intellectually demanding. Similarly, the 1980 Virginia Slims poll reported that 36 percent of employed women and 45 percent of employed men were concerned about achieving success in their careers. The poll also found an increase from 39 percent in 1970 to 45 percent in 1979 in the proportion of women who planned to make their jobs full-time careers. This increased commitment and interest may well produce some improvement in women's position in the marketplace. We can speculate that as more young women reject the notions that they will work only briefly and that their work is secondary to their roles of mother and wife, the likelihood will be greater that these women will also reject their second-class status in the labor market.

Abortion Rights for Women: *Roe v. Wade*

Dan Drucker

In the early '70s a number of issues related to abortion were hotly debated. What are the rights of a pregnant woman? Does the fetus have rights? Does society have any role or responsibility in situations in which a woman wants an abortion? Should tax dollars support the decision to abort or discourage such a decision? This selection quickly reviews important court cases and some of the issues surrounding abortion in the '70s.

O ne dictionary defines *abortion* as "the expulsion of the fetus before it is viable or able to survive outside the womb." In legal terms abortion is an "intentionally induced miscarriage." The procedure may be accomplished in one of several ways: through the use, for instance, of any instrument, surgical or otherwise, including the hand, that applies external force; or through the administering of any drug, chemical substance, or potion.

After many months of expert testimony, the United States Supreme Court determined in 1973 that "there is no medical or scientific proof that life is present from conception." The belief is solely a religious concept, based on ancient philosophies and recorded in 430 B.C. as part of the ancient Hippocratic Oath. The Court further concluded that, "we need not resolve the difficult question of when life begins, when those trained in the respective fields of medicine, philosophy and theology are unable to arrive at any consensus. The judiciary at this point in the development of man's knowledge is not in a position to speculate as to the answer."

The relevant argument over the abortion issue is strictly a question of its constitutionality. Is the Constitution deficient on issues pertaining to women, and specifically abortion? Do women have the inalienable constitutional right to procure an abortion?

In the landmark abortion decision of 1973, did the justices of the Supreme Court act properly by invalidating century-old abortion laws in effect in many states? Prior to 1973 the only "legal" abortion procedure performed was to save the life of the mother. Under no circumstances could abortion be performed legally for any other reason. Since forbidding abortion is based solely on religious and philosophical feelings of morality, there remains no scientific or legal basis for banning the procedure. Based on that reasoning, the Court handed down its landmark decision.

Prior to the Supreme Court ruling on abortion, "back alley" abortion clinics flourished, literally victimizing thousands of desperate women who wished to terminate unwanted pregnancies. An estimated 750,000 illegal abortions were performed annually in the United States, under conditions best described as deplorable and unsanitary. Many women were permanently maimed and in some cases even died under the hands of untrained practitioners.

The Rules Change in 1973

On January 22, 1973, the United States Supreme Court, in a landmark decision, ruled on the constitutionality of abortion by handing down judgments on two "test" abortion cases. The first, *Roe vs. Wade,* challenged abortion laws of the state of Texas, enacted in 1857 and never amended. The second case, *Doe vs. Bolton,* questioned the constitutionality of Georgia's abortion statutes, enacted in 1876 and slightly modified in 1968. The Court replaced the invalidated statutes with a uniform system clearly identifying stages of pregnancy in trimesters and the "legal" enforcement one can expect during each trimester. During the first trimester (up to the 12th week of pregnancy), the abortion decision is left to the pregnant woman in consultation with her physician; the state is powerless to intrude in the decision or procedure. The state can require a written consent from the pregnant woman, certifying that she is of a certain age and maturity in giving informed consent. During the second trimester (from the 13th to the 24th week of pregnancy), the state has a justifiable interest in the abortion procedure and may impose regulations if necessary; however, the regulation cannot be overly restrictive and must be related to interests of maternal health. Sometime during the 24th to the 27th week, at the beginning of the third trimester, viability occurs (the fetus is capable of independent survival outside the womb). It is primarily because of viability that the state has a compelling interest in the abortion decision, and may choose either to regulate the procedure strictly or completely proscribe it, unless the health of the pregnant woman is in danger. However, even at this late stage of pregnancy, the state is forbidden from making any medical determination as to the probability of fetal viability; that remains a medical judgment. Essentially the Court stipulated that abortion should be a medical decision, regardless of the stage of pregnancy. However, states were allowed to retain an interest in the procedure, but the interest of the state would be limited to concerns of maternal health, and if restrictions were imposed, they could not be overly burdensome.

The landmark Supreme Court ruling on abortion was a complete overhaul of abortion laws in effect in a number of states, which allowed abortion only to save the life of the mother. A few of the states had previously granted permission for an abortion if the pregnancy was a result of rape or incest, but elective abortion was not permitted.

In the years following the landmark ruling on abortion, there have been many challenges made by fundamentalist religious groups and conservatives, but the basic structure of the original judgment stands as firm as it did in 1973. This can be attributed primarily to the philosophical balance of the Court, virtually unchanged in the years following the abortion decision. However, in recent years some of the moderate justices have retired from the bench, many of whom had played a major role in the landmark abortion decision. Many of the justices today are "new breed" jurists who follow a more fundamental, conservative philosophy. The shift in the Court's ideology could have a profound effect on future challenges to current abortion laws.

Interpretation of the Constitution

The United States Constitution is written in a manner allowing for broad interpretations; a good example of this is applying the wording of the Fourteenth Amendment's Due Process Clause to a woman's right in terminating an unwanted pregnancy. The manner in which a particular law is defined depends largely on the individual's interpretation. There are often no correct or incorrect ways of defining a point of law. For instance, on the issue of abortion and the application of the wording contained within the Fourteenth Amendment's Due Process Clause ("nor shall any state deprive any persons of life, liberty or property, without due process of law"), three justices interpret the clause differently: Justice Harry Blackmun avers that the right said to be possessed by the pregnant woman to choose to terminate her pregnancy, would be found in the concept of personal liberty, embodied within the Fourteenth Amendment's Due Process Clause; Justice John Paul Stevens says that the Constitution does not specify or mention the right of personal choice in matters of family life (abortion); and Justice William Rehnquist has written that the only conclusion possible is that the drafters of the Constitution did not intend to have the Fourteenth Amendment withdraw from the states the power to legislate with respect to the issue of abortion. Challenges to abortion laws also have been based on violations of the Fourth Amendment (adopted 1791), which states, "The right of the people to be secure in their persons, houses, papers, and effects, against unreasonable searches and seizures, shall not be violated and no warrants shall issue, but upon probable cause, supported by oath or affirmation, and particularly describing the place to be searched, and the persons or things to be seized," and the Ninth Amendment (adopted 1791), which proclaims, "The enumeration in the Constitution, of certain rights, shall not be construed to deny or disparage others retained by the people.". . .

Other Court Decisions

Prior to 1973, in some states a woman did not have the "right" to have an abortion without first obtaining permission from her husband. During the debate of this issue, the Court cited the Missouri case of *Planned Parenthood vs. Danford* (1976) as a prime example of denying a woman her right to have an abortion. The Missouri law under discussion required that the woman's husband first give his approval if the procedure was to be performed during the first twelve weeks of pregnancy, unless the procedure was needed to save her life. The statute was ruled unconstitutional by the Supreme Court. When the Missouri legislators enacted the statute, they reasoned that most of the important decisions in a marriage are agreed to by both husband and wife, including family planning, artificial insemination, and voluntary sterilization. Also, adopting a child requires joint consent. Since so many decisions require joint consent, why should abortion be treated differently, when it is perhaps the only decision that is irreversible? The opposition argued that there could be problems if the father of the child could not be located at the time of the abortion procedure.

Planned Parenthood vs. Danford was again cited for the argument over restricting minor children from seeking an abortion without parental permission. The abortion restriction in the Missouri case included all minors, regardless of their maturity.

For their argument in favor of restricting abortion for adolescents, the state legislature reasoned that minors are prohibited from purchasing firearms, tobacco, or alcoholic beverages without parental permission, as well as viewing sexually explicit material. Since abortion is irreversible, the Missouri legislature felt that it should be added to the list of restrictions adolescents must face.

Lawmakers, however, displayed an even deeper concern in restricting abortion for minors because they felt that an immature wrong decision could lead to lifelong emotional and physical problems.

But the opposition argued that minors could be tested for venereal disease and treated for drug abuse without parental knowledge. The statute was ruled unconstitutional because it failed to separate "mature" minors from "immature" ones; some adolescents are emotionally ready to make rational decisions at earlier ages than others; individuals must be judged independently. Emancipated and married minors must be given separate consideration. . . .

Prior to 1973, many states had preconditional hospital requirements before an abortion procedure could be performed. The state of Georgia had the severest of requirements. All women desiring to terminate an unwanted pregnancy had to appear before a hospital committee charged with the responsibility of approving the abortion after certain requirements were met. Approval or denial was a result of majority vote of the committee. In addition to the approval of the hospital committee, the woman had to obtain as many as six consensual opinions before the procedure could be performed. All of these legalities were problematic for a procedure where timing was of the utmost importance.

Medical Judgments

Viability is a medical concept that specifies a certain time within the gestation cycle when the fetus is capable of independent survival outside the mother's womb. Viability of the fetus varies with each patient but can be expected somewhere between the 24th and the 28th week of pregnancy. Fetal viability is a matter of great concern for the medical and legal community because of the serious ramifications that occur if a viable fetus is aborted. It is essential for physicians to approximate the date viability will occur. One method is in estimating the size of fetal growth by determining the size of the patient's uterus.

In the 1973 case of *Roe vs. Wade,* the United States Supreme Court held that when viability is reached, a state may exercise concern over safeguarding fetal survival by preventing the abortion procedure, unless it can be proved the health of the mother is in jeopardy. Even in this late stage of pregnancy, a state is forbidden from making any determination as to the viability of the fetus; that remains a medical decision.

Public Funding

Critics of abortion thought it highly improper to use public funds by allowing Medicaid recipients to have elective abortions. Legislation designed to restrict abortions for indigent women on welfare was introduced into Congress in 1976 by Congressman Henry Hyde. The bill and subsequent law became known as the Hyde Amendment. The amendment gave Congress the power to prohibit the use of federal funds to reimburse costs of elective abortions to indigent women under the Medicaid program by adjusting the annual budget of the Department of Health, Education, and Welfare, with exceptions based on individual appeals. Medicaid, however, continues to provide funding for natural childbirth. The Equal Rights Clause of the Fourteenth Amendment does not require states participating in the Medicaid program to pay for elective abortions, even though they have a policy of providing funding for natural childbirth. In 1980 the language of the Hyde Amendment was amended and broadened to include emergency abortion funding for pregnancy that was a result of rape or incest, or placing a woman's life in jeopardy.

The Supreme Court acknowledged that providing funds for natural childbirth but refusing it for abortion is an attractive incentive for natural childbirth. A question over the constitutionality of the use of public funds which provide benefits to some while at the same time refusing them to others is raised.

In conclusion, the Supreme Court stipulated that states have a legitimate interest in seeing to it that abortion like any other surgical procedure is performed under circumstances ensuring maximum safety for the patient. The interest extends to the performing physician and his staff, the facilities involved, the availability of after-care, and adequate provisions for any complications or emergency that may occur. The risk to a woman's health increases as the pregnancy advances to full term. Thus, states retain a definite interest in protecting the woman's health when an abortion is proposed at a later stage of pregnancy. A state's interest also extends to protection of prenatal life. Only when the life of the mother is at stake, balanced against the life she carries within her, should the interest of the embryo or fetus not prevail.

CHAPTER 6

From the 1970s into the Future

AMERICA'S DECADES

Did The Women's Movement Lose Direction?

Christina Hoff Sommers

Looking back on the women's movement from the vantage point of the 1990s, Christina Hoff Sommers concludes that something has gone wrong. She writes that the "First Wave" feminists wanted equality for women and wanted to build a society of cooperation. However, the "Second Wave" feminists (who, Sommers believes, have dominated the movement's leadership in the 1980s and 1990s) want to "self-segregate" women from men, and recognize a permanent state of tension between women and men. Sommers concludes that the women's movement has lost its faith in liberalism. Sommers uses the term "liberalism" in the tradition of the nineteenth century, which meant: an assumption that rational discussions lead toward the truth, that individualism is good, that democracy is better than authoritarian leadership, and that governments should provide equal opportunity, not equality of results. Sommers teaches philosophy at Clark University. She has written a number of articles and books dealing with women's studies and ethics.

A surprising number of clever and powerful feminists share the conviction that American women still live in a patriarchy where men collectively keep women down. It is customary for these feminists to assemble to exchange stories and to talk about the "anger issues" that vex them.

One such conference—"Out of the Academy and Into the World with Carolyn Heilbrun"—took place at the Graduate Center of City University of New York in October 1992. The morning sessions were devoted to honoring the feminist scholar and mystery writer Carolyn Heilbrun on the occasion of her voluntary retirement from Columbia University after thirty-two years of tenure. I had just then been reading Marilyn French's *The War Against Women*, which Ms. Heilbrun touts on the cover as a book that "lays out women's state in this world—and it is a state of siege."

Intelligent women who sincerely believe that American women are in a gender war intrigue me, so a day with Ms. Heilbrun and her admirers promised to be rewarding. I arrived early, but so did an overflow crowd of more than five hundred women. I was lucky to get a seat. . . .

Jane Marcus, of the City University of New York, called the afternoon "Anger Session" to order, introducing herself as "an expert on anger" and thanking Heilbrun for teaching her "to use my rage in my writing." She introduced the other panelists as angry in one way or another: Alice Jardine of Harvard University's French department was "angry and struggling." Brenda Silver of Dartmouth had been "struggling and angry since 1972." Catharine Stimpson, a former vice-provost at Rutgers and recently selected to head the distinguished MacArthur Fellows Program, was introduced as "an enraged and engaged intellectual."

Gloria Steinem took the microphone and explained why *she* was enraged: "I have become even more angry . . . the alternative is depression." To deal with patriarchal schools, she recommended an "underground system of education," a bartering system in which a midwife could exchange her services "in return for Latin American history." Steinem believes things are so bad for contemporary American women that we might have to consider setting up centers for training political organizers.

For someone like me, who does not believe that American women are in a state of siege (and so lacks the basis for the kind of anger that drives out depression), the conference was depressing. It was clear that these well-favored women sincerely felt aggrieved. It was equally clear to me that the bitter spirits they were dispensing to the American public were unwholesome and divisive.

For whom do these "engaged and enraged" women at the conference speak? Who is their constituency? It might be said that as academics and intellectuals they speak for no one but themselves. But that would be to mistake their mission. They see themselves as the second wave of the feminist movement, as the moral vanguard fighting a war to save women. But do American women need to be saved by anyone?

The women at the Heilbrun conference are the New Feminists: articulate, prone to self-dramatization, and chronically offended. Many of the women on the "Anger" panel were tenured professors at prestigious universities. All had fine and expensive educations. Yet, listening to them one would never guess that they live in a country whose women are legally as free as the men and whose institutions of higher learning now have more female than male students.

It was inevitable that such single-minded and energetic women would find their way into leadership positions. It is unfortunate for American feminism that their ideology and attitude are diverting the women's movement from its true purposes.

The presumption that men are collectively engaged in keeping women down invites feminist bonding in a resentful community. When a Heilbrun or a Steinem advises us that men are not about to relinquish their hegemony, the implicit moral is that women must form self-protective enclaves. In such enclaves women can speak out safely and help one another to recover from the indignities they suffer under patriarchy. In such enclaves they can think of how to change or provide alternatives to the "androcentric" institutions that have always prevailed in education and the workplace. The message is that women must be "gynocentric," that they must join with and be loyal only to women.

The traditional, classically liberal, humanistic feminism that was initiated more than 150 years ago was very different. It had a specific agenda, demanding for women the same rights before the law that men enjoyed. The suffrage had to be won, and the laws regarding property, marriage, divorce, and child custody had to be made equitable. More recently, abortion rights had to be protected. The old mainstream feminism concentrated on legal reforms. In seeking specific and achievable ends, it did not promote a gynocentric stance; self-segregation of women had no part in an agenda that sought equality and equal access for women.

Most American women subscribe philosophically to that older "First Wave" kind of feminism whose main goal is equity, especially in politics and education. A First Wave, "mainstream," or "equity" feminist wants for women what she wants for everyone: fair treatment, without discrimination. "We ask no better laws than those you have made for yourselves. We need no other protection than that which your present laws secure to you," said Elizabeth Cady Stanton, perhaps the ablest exponent of equity feminism, addressing the New York State Legislature in 1854. The equity agenda may not yet be fully achieved, but by any reasonable measure, equity feminism has turned out to be a great American success story.

Heilbrun, Steinem, and other current feminist notables ride this First Wave for its popularity and its moral authority, but most of them adhere to a new, more radical, "Second Wave" doctrine: that women, even modern American women, are in thrall to "a system of male dominance" variously referred to as "heteropatriarchy" or the sex/ gender system. According to one feminist theorist, the sex/ gender system is "that complex process whereby bi-sexual infants are transformed into male and female gender personalities, the one destined to command, the other to obey." Sex/gender feminism ("gender feminism" for short) is the prevailing ideology among contemporary feminist philosophers and leaders. But it lacks a grass roots constituency.

The New Feminists claim continuity with the likes of the eighteenth-century feminist Mary Wollstonecraft or later feminists like the Grimké sisters, Elizabeth Cady Stanton, Susan B. Anthony, and Harriet Taylor. But those giants of the women's movement grounded their feminist demands on Enlightenment principles of individual justice. By contrast, the New Feminists have little faith in the Enlightenment principles that influenced the founders of America's political order and that inspired the great classical feminists to wage their fight for women's rights.

The idea that women are in a gender war originated in the midsixties, when the antiwar and antigovernment mood revivified and redirected the women's movement away from its Enlightenment liberal philosophy to a more radical, antiestablishment philosophy. The decisive battles of the sexual revolution had been won, and students here and on the Continent were reading Herbert Marcuse, Karl Marx, Franz Fanon, and Jean-Paul Sartre and learning how to critique their culture and institutions in heady new ways. They began to see the university, the military, and the government as merely different parts of a defective status quo.

Betty Friedan and Germaine Greer would continue to offer women a liberal version of consciousness raising whose aim was to awaken them to new possibilities of individual self-fulfillment. But by the midseventies, faith in liberal solutions to social problems had waned, and the old style of consciousness raising that encouraged women to seek avenues of self-fulfillment rapidly gave way to one that initiated women into an appreciation of their subordinate situation in the patriarchy and the joys and comforts of group solidarity.

Having "transcended" the liberalism of Friedan and the fierce individualism of Greer, feminists began to work seriously on getting women to become aware of the political dimension of their lives. Kate Millett's *Sexual Politics* was critical in moving feminism in this new direction. It taught women that politics was essentially sexual and that even the so-called democracies were male hegemonies: "However muted its present appearance may be, sexual dominion obtains nevertheless as perhaps the most pervasive ideology of our culture and provides its most fundamental concept of power."

The New Feminists began to direct their energies toward getting women to join in the common struggle against patriarchy, to view society through the sex/gender prism. When a woman's feminist consciousness is thus "raised," she learns to identify her personal self with her gender. She sees her relations to men in political terms ("the personal is the political"). This "insight" into the nature of male/female relations makes the gender feminist impatient with piecemeal liberal reformist solutions and leads her to strive for a more radical transformation of our society than earlier feminists had envisioned.

It is now commonplace for feminist philosophers to reject the Enlightenment ideals of the old feminism. According to the University of Colorado feminist theorist Alison Jaggar, "Radical and socialist feminists have shown that the old ideals of freedom, equality and democracy are insufficient." Iris Young, of the University of Pittsburgh, echoes the contemporary feminist disillusionment with the classically liberal feminism of yesteryear, claiming that "after two centuries of faith . . . the ideal of equality and fraternity" no longer prevails:

> Most feminists of the nineteenth and twentieth century, including feminists of the early second wave, have been humanist feminists. In recent years, a different account of women's oppression has gained influence, however, partly growing from a critique of humanist feminism. Gynocentric feminism defines women's oppression as the devaluation and repression of women's experience by a masculinist culture that exalts violence and individualism.

The University of Wisconsin philosopher Andrea Nye acknowledges that the liberal agenda had been successful in gaining women *legal* freedoms, but she insists that this means very little, because "the liberated enfranchised woman might complain that democratic society has only returned her to a more profound subordination."

The loss of faith in classically liberal solutions, coupled with the conviction that women remain besieged and subject to a relentless and vicious male backlash, has fumed the movement inward. We hear very little today about how women can join with men on equal terms to contribute to a universal human culture. Instead, feminist ideology has taken a divisive, gynocentric turn, and the emphasis now is on women as a political class whose interests are at odds with the interests of men. Women must be loyal to women, united in principled hostility to the males who seek to hold fast to their patriarchal privileges and powers.

This clash of "old" and "new" feminism is itself nothing new. Here is the British feminist and novelist Winifred Holtby writing in 1926: "The New Feminism emphasizes the importance of the 'women's point of view,' the Old Feminism believes in the primary importance of the human being. . . . Personally I am . . . an Old Feminist." The old feminism has had many exponents, from Elizabeth Cady Stanton and Susan B. Anthony in the middle of the nineteenth century to Betty Friedan and Germaine Greer in our own day. It demanded that women be allowed to live as freely as men. To most Americans, that was a fair demand. The old feminism was neither defeatist nor gender-divisive, and it is even now the philosophy of the feminist "mainstream."

The New Feminists, many of them privileged, all of them legally protected and free, are preoccupied with their own sense of hurt and their own feelings of embattlement and "siege." When they speak of their personal plight they use words appropriate to the tragic plight of many American women of a bygone day and of millions of contemporary, truly oppressed women in other countries. But their resentful rhetoric discredits the American women's movement today and seriously distorts its priorities.

Indeed, one of the main hallmarks of the New Feminism is its degree of self-preoccupation. Feminists like Elizabeth

Stanton and Susan B. Anthony were keenly aware of themselves as privileged, middle-class, protected women. They understood how inappropriate it would be to equate their struggles with those of less fortunate women, and it never occurred to them to air their personal grievances before the public.

Reflections on the 1970s:
A Personal View

Lawrence Wright

In this selection Lawrence Wright takes a very personal look at his values developed in the 1970s and how these changed once he contemplated having a child. Wright's personal reminiscence reveals greater insight into the 1970s and the impact that decade had on the future. In addition to writing about his personal experiences, Wright has been a faculty member at the American University of Cairo and the writer-in-residence at the University of Georgia.

A pproaching thirty, Roberta and I began to think of children. No one we knew had them. No one we knew really wanted them. In the age of the Pill, "accidents" didn't happen the way they used to, and if they did, the Supreme Court had ruled that abortions were a constitutional privilege. In the past, the age of cumbersome and imperfect contraception, children had been almost inevitable, a penalty of spontaneous carnality. Now they were optional; we could be childless without being chaste or even very careful. The brief moment between courtship and parenthood had become elastic, and in our case it had already stretched across five years of married life, but we began to feel the pressure of middle age and mortality. If we were going to have children, now was the time.

These deliberations felt entirely new. My parents had

dived into childbearing with characteristic postwar fervor. For them, marriage was a license to get on with what they really wanted in life, which was several children as soon as possible. My father married my mother six weeks after he met her, and by the time he was shipped off to Europe he had accomplished his biological task. That first baby was born dead, but by the time my father came home from Korea in 1952, his three children were waiting for him. "It seems rather strange now," my mother had said to me, "but nearly everyone wanted to have a baby. Somehow the fact that the father might never return made the wives even more eager to have a child. It must be some sort of biological instinct to preserve the race."

Children, Self, the World

My generation felt a different urge. The planet was already too crowded, too polluted; we lived with the prospect of nuclear apocalypse. Bringing babies into such a world seemed irresponsible and cruel. When I saw people my age with two or three children, I quietly condemned them. They must be greedy, naive, obtuse. I certainly didn't envy or admire them. They were the wrong people to have children; the right people were people like me, who knew better.

These were all rationalizations of a culture that had turned against children. I wasn't really planning my own family on the basis of world population growth or the likelihood of nuclear war. Children made me nervous. I was uncertain how to behave around them. As an adult I thought that the introduction of children into restaurants or movie theaters was a savage breach of etiquette. Their mere presence was a rebuke. In a purely animal sense, Roberta and I understood that we were designed to procreate, nurture, and die, leaving our progeny behind, but as a twentieth-century man and woman we felt a different imperative, which was to get ahead. Children were dead weight, a renunciation of our modern-adult lives.

This was a contemporary moment: deciding to go off the Pill. It was a decision to be chewed over at length during late-night dinners we would never enjoy again, or idly speculated upon some lazy Sunday morning when we were cuddled up in bed with the newspapers—how could we choose to surrender such quiet pleasures for the chaos of children? We were not afraid of the big responsibilities of parenthood; it was the day-to-dayness, the dreary moments of standing in line at the grocery store with a bawling infant, the countless diaper changings, and the middle-of-the-night feedings that wore down our imagination. At the same time, we had a primitive longing for consequences. We wanted our marriage to have an object other than companionship. We were ready to get on with the serious moments of life. We wanted—what? To create our own people, to become a family and not just a married couple. And so we went off the Pill. It was like taking off the final vestment, becoming naked in a thrilling way known only to the ancients; one felt exposed to the sky and the whims of the gods.

Now that I was a prospective parent, I looked at the world through a different lens. To have children, or even to imagine having them, required certain political adjustments. One need not become more conservative, although it seemed every parent did, but one must become less blithe. One must focus on schools and property taxes and interest rates, and upon the background wash of pornography and violence and drug use. Tolerance ebbed. I wanted to clear a safe space for my children, but safety was expensive and hard to find. I began to dream about money. For the first time in my life I looked at the Dow Jones industrial averages and saw a connection between the capitalist economy and the rest of my life. I did not really approve of these changes in myself, because conservatism, even in my hesitant turning toward it, was a movement backward, to the Dallas of my childhood. It was tied in my mind to square values, religious extremism, racism, and rabid anti-Communism. Nonetheless, I was beginning to see myself not as a liberal bohemian writer but as an uninvested, uninsured, marginal American.

Revolution and Religion

This was a time when my values were being shaken for other reasons as well. Charles Manson had taken the radical chatter of revolution, the fantasy literature of Heinlein and Hesse, the interior mysteries of the Beatles' music—all of them secret signposts of my generation—plus a kind of idle, collective feeling that we were all more like each other than we were like our parents, and he had breathed it all horribly to life. He had forged a hippie commune into a gang of murderers. They killed between thirty-five and forty people, most of them not wealthy or well known or even much missed, but because they had killed actress Sharon Tate (who was eight months pregnant), and coffee heiress Abigail Folger, and hairstylist Jay Sebring, and a wealthy grocer named Leno LaBianca, and his wife (they stuck a fork in her abdomen), and because they had scribbled on the walls in their victims' blood the radical slogan of the day, "Death to Pigs," Manson became a hero in the radical community. "Offing those rich pigs with their own knives and forks, and then eating a meal in the same room—far out!" cheered Bernardine Dohrn at a Students for a Democratic Society (S.D.S.) convention. During a recess in the Chicago Seven trial, Yippie leader Jerry Rubin went to Los Angeles to speak to Charles Manson in jail. "I fell in love with Charlie Manson the first time I saw his cherub face and sparkling eyes on TV," Rubin wrote. Manson became an underground hero. He had his own column in the *Los Angeles Free Press. Rolling Stone* described him as "this smiling, dancing music man [who] offered a refreshing short cut, a genuine and revolutionary new morality that redefines or rather eliminates the historic boundaries between life and death."

Until then, when I spoke of revolution it was nothing more than an emphatic way of speaking of economic and political changes. I did not mean murder. After the Manson killings, I began to speak more carefully. I pulled back from the easy loathing of the middle class, which had become habitual in the writings of the underground press. Being a liberal had always involved having certain sentimental ties to the radical Left. After Manson, those ties snapped.

It's strange that my generation would find so much significance in assassinations and sensational murders. But we lived in an age of symbolic action. Manson was important to us because we saw in him the degeneration of our own lives and thinking. He had fostered the idea that he was Jesus, which his disciples truly seemed to believe. One underground paper published a sketch of Manson nailed to the cross, with a plaque above his head that said HIPPIE. There had always been, in the hippie movement, a spiritual yearning, a search for the countercultural Jesus, who was not clutched by the capitalists and the hypocritical, warmongering middle class. One could reject Jesus, but to accept and worship Manson suggested the insanity that yawned ahead when old values were thrown aside without new ones to replace them. It showed the bankruptcy of the revolutionary agenda, which was calling not for a new order but for chaos. When one of Manson's followers, Lynette ("Squeaky") Fromme, dressed up in a Little Red Riding Hood outfit and tried to shoot Gerald Ford in the genitals, it seemed to me that symbolic action had raced into new territory, the age itself had broken loose from anything like familiar reality, and the weird gesture had become paramount.

The airports were filled with religious extremists, but they were strangely different from the hot-eyed fanatics I had known in Dallas. They were selling not salvation but bliss. There was a monastic allure about the cults, which beckoned even to reasonable people who felt bewildered by their lives and wanted to retreat from complexity. One could shave one's head and put on saffron robes and sell Tootsie Rolls on the street corner. I felt a similar urge at times, but it was like the small compulsion one feels to jump out of windows when one is high, high off the ground. It was a call to the withered spirit to take flight from the towers of material desire to the self-effacement that awaits like a concrete slab. And of course one knew friends who made the leap.

The cults reconstructed the idea of the family so that it ran horizontally across the generations, and not vertically from one generation to the next. People wanted to be together without the burdens of children and aging parents. It seemed to me a way of staying in school, a dormitory life that might last—well, if not forever, at least for longer.

There was a gravitation from radical politics to radical religion. Loss of faith in the one led to a search for faith in the other (perhaps this is a cycle). Rennie Davis, for instance, cofounder of S.D.S., a man whose politics I had followed with interest, went to India in 1973 and became an acolyte of the sixteen-year-old guru, Maharaj Ji; Davis said he would "crawl across the face of the earth to kiss the feet of the Perfect Master." The line between matters that were properly spiritual and those that were necessarily political had become smeared. How were we supposed to deal with Third World insurgencies, now that our confidence had been shaken in Vietnam? During the Nicaraguan revolution, when the Sandinistas were fighting in the suburbs of Managua, the dictator Anastasio Somoza was hiding in his bunker, and an American delegation was desperately trying to negotiate peace, another American group of fifty transcendental meditationists booked a room in the Intercontinental Hotel and tried to levitate for peace. Newsmen found them hopping around the ballroom "like frogs." They said they had been sent by the Maharishi Mahesh Yogi to persuade Somoza to surrender his weapons and follow TM. Was this the future of the resistance?

I could criticize these religions because they seemed to me so transparently bogus, so rash and dramatic—and in the cases of Manson and, later, of Jim Jones, cults of personality, not of the spirit, which could become so crushingly evil. And yet I too felt spiritually empty. The prospect of parenthood made me feel it all the more keenly. I disagreed with what my parents had told me about God, but as a child I had been reassured by their belief. Now my belief in the supernatural was limited to an embarrassed half-acceptance of certain truths of astrology.

This was not a religion one could pass on to children. It did not answer questions about how and why we are here. It did not make one feel a part of a larger effort. I could face being an adult without answers to these questions, but as a parent I wanted to give my children the same religious comforts I had experienced as a child, even if they rejected them. Agnosticism was a chilly prospect for children, no matter what their sign.

And yet having children, the deliberate act of creation, was such an act of faith that it mocked my doubt. I thought about the resolution I made as an undergraduate, as I was wading through the existential philosophers, never to have children until I understood the purpose of life (undergraduates are allowed to think categorically). The point of life can't be just to go on and on, aimlessly, one generation producing the next, with no goal in mind. That is what I told myself, fiercely, at the age of twenty. At thirty, I was ready to accept that life must be perpetuated, regardless of its object, and that the act of making more life was both grave and joyful, a godlike power, the most severe responsibility and the closest approach to divinity I was likely to have.

John Gordon Wright was born April 10, 1976. His sister, Caroline Murphy Wright, came five years later, on October 20, 1981.

Lessons from Vietnam

Walter H. Capps

Many books and articles have been written about America's involvement in Vietnam. Walter Capps, a professor of religious studies at the University of California at Santa Barbara, suggests that during the Cold War era, America was torn between two mythical views of the world: Armageddon and Eden. Armageddon divided the world between the forces of good and evil: America was good and communism was evil. In Eden, America and the ideals of liberty and justice would eventually spread over the world, creating universal harmony. Capps explains that Vietnam brought an end to the image of Eden. No longer did Americans hope to bring peace and prosperity to the world by simply spreading democratic ideals. The Armageddon myth continued into the 1980s and did not end until the collapse of Communist Russia.

The radical differences between the expectations of Armageddon and the impulses of Eden provide the framework for much of what has happened within the United States, and throughout the world, in the post-World War II era. Some of the time, for some of the people, motivation has come from Armageddon, while for others the compulsions have been those of Eden. The one encourages a readiness to confront the adversary; its temper is tough, res-

---

olute, defensive, self-protective. The other exhibits an interest in enunciating the underlying harmony; it speaks of maintaining the essential components of the living environment while proclaiming the blessings of global harmony.

The two agendas, therefore, differ markedly. The basic distinction is, in Irving Kristol's words, between "the patriotic temper, the politics of national assertion," and the "social democratic temper, the inward-looking politics of compassionate reform." Both have been present in the American collective consciousness from the beginning, and for long periods there was balance between them. For most of the post-World War II era, however, the inhabitants of Eden and the advocates of Armageddon have been at such severe odds that it has been as if there were two United States of America, competing with each other for supremacy and the allegiance of the citizenry. Within the counterculture, the Eden mentality found ascendancy, while during the following period, a time of counterrevolution, the mood of national assertiveness reemerged. The trauma of Vietnam was a product of the projection of this fundamental quarrel onto the battlefield; what became most visible during the war was America in conflict with America—the dark night within the nation's soul. The war remains unfinished because the quarrel has not been resolved.

How did it happen this way? What forces gave the drama such orientation?

Dean Acheson, secretary of state under President Truman, offered some reminiscences that illuminate these questions. Writing in a book appropriately titled *Present at the Creation,* Acheson stated that it took some while for Americans to recognize that "the whole world structure and order that we had inherited from the nineteenth century was gone" after World War II. What replaced it, Acheson observed, was a struggle "directed from two bitterly opposed and ideologically irreconcilable power centers"— the world's great superpowers, whose rivalry had a pervasive influence upon all significant subsequent events.

Nearly thirty years later, Richard Nixon described the

fundamental challenge in almost the same language that Acheson had used:

> The old colonial empires are gone. The new Soviet imperialism requires a new counterforce to keep it in check. The United States cannot provide this alone, but without strong and effective leadership from the United States, it cannot be provided at all. We cannot afford to waffle and waver. Either we act like a great power or we will be reduced to a minor power, and thus reduced we will not survive—nor will freedom or Western values survive.

The United States certainly wished to have it both ways: to retain some semblance of the world structure that it inherited from the nineteenth century (enough, that is to say, to support strong alliances between former colonial powers, the majority of which continued to identify themselves as allies within the "free world"), and at the same time, to make certain that the contest with the Soviet Union would be played out in its favor.

As it happened, the beginning of strong United States involvement in Vietnam coincides exactly with the beginning of the construction of this postwar U.S. foreign policy. Similarly, the period in which the United States' presence was felt in Vietnam—from September 2, 1945, to May 1, 1975—coincides exactly with the period in which these foreign-policy objectives were being enunciated. Thus it was to be expected that American policy toward Vietnam would reflect the tension between these two competing principles.

Blindly Looking at the World

From Harry Truman to Gerald Ford, all framers of American foreign policy had to act as if the principles were compatible in order to speak in clear and resolute terms about America's interests in Vietnam. Each said that the United States was in Southeast Asia because of its deep desire to maintain a benevolent and workable world structure. Each explained that the extension of American power and influence into Southeast Asia had been encouraged by humanitarian concerns. Each defended American involvement on the grounds that it had been requested by people seeking emancipation from oppression, saying that people wishing to take their place among the strong and self-reliant nations of the modern world had sought the counsel and assistance of the world's leader. All these expressed motives were in full keeping with the legacy of images that had been utilized across the centuries to describe what America stands for. That same legacy could be tapped to show that American involvement in Vietnam corresponded to the best within the national character.

It took but a short additional step for John F. Kennedy to look to Vietnam as the potential testing ground in Southeast Asia for the heretofore remarkably successful American-styled democratic system. Lyndon Johnson merely followed the sequence, adding his own particularities, when he spoke with enthusiasm about making the Mekong Delta as resourceful as the valley of the Tennessee River. Naturally Johnson also looked ahead to the time that the goals of the Great Society would be transmitted to Indochina, after the local skirmishes there had been brought to resolution.

As such high hopes and confidences were repeated, the American leadership provided assurances that our motives were pure. "We seek no territory for ourselves," Johnson reiterated. Ostensibly, America had not become active in Vietnam to promote selfish ambitions, to advance its own desires, or even to protect its vested interests. All that it attempted could be justified on the basis of the cardinal principle—the need to maintain a stable and benevolent world order.

Unfortunately, this professed altruistic motive became hopelessly entangled with the discordant twin objective of winning the competition with the rival power center. Before long, it became inevitable that the second objective would be taken as the means to insure the realization of the first. An expectation grew that stable world order could be achieved if the United States could win the contest with the

Soviet Union, now simply referred to as the adversary. Logically speaking, the two principles were interdependent from the very moment following the end of the Second World War when foreign policy was being reformulated.

By the time that John F. Kennedy gave his Inaugural Address on January 20, 1961, each of the two principles could be expressed in the words of the other: "Let every nation know, whether it wishes us well or ill, that we shall pay any price, bear any burden, meet any hardship, support any friend, oppose any foe, in order to assure the survival and the success of liberty." This was a large promise, to be made good within the intrinsic conflicts of those postwar realignments that had been set in motion even as Ho Chi

 **Views of Vietnam**

"I regard the war in Indochina as the greatest military, political, economic, and moral blunder in our national history."

—George McGovern

"Unless the United States shakes the false lessons of Vietnam and puts the 'Vietnam syndrome' behind it, we will forfeit the security of our allies and eventually our own. This is the real lesson of Vietnam—not that that we should abandon power, but that unless we learn to use it effectively to defend our interests, the tables of history will be turned against us and all we believe in."

—Richard Nixon

"The era of self-doubt is over."

—Ronald Reagan
(Commencement Address,
U.S. Military Academy,
West Point, May 27, 1981)

Walter H. Capps, *The Unfinished War: Vietnam and the American Conscience.* Boston: Beacon, 1982.

Minh was declaring Vietnamese independence.

Accordingly, when crucial choices were placed before American decision-makers, the outcome was inevitable. Certainly most U.S. Presidents wished to have it both ways—to keep the two objectives in harmony and balance. When they couldn't, however—when the twin ambitions became manifestly incompatible and contradictory—the leaders found most support in advancing the American cause against its primary competition. No American President could afford politically to be soft on communism, so each felt obliged to push the get-tough policy to prominence. In doing so, each allowed the ideological struggle to assume critical and strategic dominance, and whenever this occurred, the "patriotic temper" (promoting "the politics of national assertion") gained mastery over the "inward-looking politics of compassionate reform." The same temper won out in the leaders' attitude toward the nation's involvement in Vietnam: Vietnam was the testing ground not simply for the free-enterprise system, but for the conflict in American will and resolve, manifested for the entire world, including the American citizenry.

If the United States had not invested the situation in Vietnam with rivalry with Communist powers, the tragedy might have been avoided. If it had perceived the conflict as a civil war, it would have had no good reason to become involved. If it had seen the situation simply as a clash between colonialists and nationalists, it might not have entered military engagement. But because it viewed the war as part of the fundamental conflict between the world's two great superpowers, the United States eventually felt a responsibility to commit its forces. The quality and intensity of that commitment was nurtured by the religious sanctions of the patriotic temper and the Manichaean mythology by which the rivalry was expressed. In this rendition, America was placed on the side of good, in opposition to evil. Light was pitted against darkness, freedom against bondage, America against anti-America—yes, even God against the Devil.

Within a relatively brief span of time, therefore, the postwar world became sharply polarized, exhibiting all of the characteristic invitations for takeover by an Armageddon mentality. By the time of the Gulf of Tonkin Resolution in 1964, the way had been cleared by Korea in 1950, the Berlin blockade in 1961, and the Cuban missile crisis in 1963. All of these challenges had been met successfully, to America's advantage. Vietnam was simply next in the series. The nation could be confident that the problem would be solved in a relatively short time. But by now the equations were inexact.

To be sure, Ho Chi Minh espoused the Communist philosophy and had strong loyalties to both China and the Soviet Union. He had been trained in the teachings of Marx and Lenin and was thoroughly committed to Marxist thought and the Communist social and political program. Yet the plot the Americans envisioned bore only generalized application to the actual drama in Vietnam. U.S. leadership tried to direct the scenes with little or no knowledge of local circumstances and incentives. It tried to erect in South Vietnam a government which the people clearly resisted. It wished to promote certain Western forms of democratic decision-making among a people who had had no preparation and had shown no strong inclinations for them. It possessed only slight acquaintance with the indigenous sociocultural matrix, based on a combination of Confucian, Taoist, Buddhist, and native religious influences and organized according to ancient Chinese mandarinic systems. It was as if the plot had been written by someone who had not yet visited the territory and had been imposed much more because of the plight of the outsiders than because it concerned the affairs of the Vietnamese. . . .

Loss of Innocence

In his masterful book *The American Adam*, R.W.B. Lewis explores the variety of ways in which the imagery of the New World is treated in American literature. The discovery of America as the occasion for a new Adam and a second chance for humanity has been treated by Hawthorne, Melville, Whitman, Browne, Emerson, and Thoreau as well as by more contemporary writers such as Faulkner, Salinger, and Bellow. Central to their imagery, according to Lewis, is the quest for innocence, which makes claims on a renewed or recaptured innocence, as this has been expressed through a recurrent revitalization of Adam traditions throughout American literature.

The Vietnam War is about innocence too, not the quest for innocence, but the loss of American innocence. Through it the imagery of the restorative and re-creative power of the New World—Lyndon Johnson's "last best hope for mankind"—was plunged again and again into what Lewis calls "the spurious disruptive rituals of the actual world." After this experience, assumptions of innocence could never be the same again. No clear-eyed, wide-open sense that as Americans, we are here to make the world a better place. No vigorous sense of trust and confidence. No Billy Budd. No opportunity for undiminished heroism. No new or recent esteemed warriors. No John Wayne. No Joe DiMaggio. Only the sounds, the confusion, the self-doubt and self-hate, and the need to get back on track.

Chronology

1969
First U.S. astronauts land on the moon.

1970
Environmental Protection Agency (EPA) is established.

1971
The "Pentagon Papers," demonstrating a long history of secret American actions in Vietnam, are published, generating public distrust of the federal government.

1972
Richard Nixon visits China to improve political and trade relations.

Nixon visits Russia and signs ABM and SALT I treaties to limit the arms race.

Men associated with the White House are caught breaking into the Democratic Party offices at the Watergate building; Nixon is linked with these and other illegal activities, but no clear evidence against Nixon is brought to light.

Nixon is re-elected by a landslide vote.

1973
Supreme Court's decision in *Roe v. Wade* gives women a constitutional right to abortion.

Truce is signed with North Vietnam to negotiate the end of the Vietnam War.

Watergate hearings in Congress begin investigating Nixon and his staff.

Happy Days television series begins.

War in Middle East leads to an Arab oil embargo, and gasoline prices climb.

Vice President Agnew resigns; Gerald Ford appointed the new vice president.

1974

Saturday Night Live television series begins.

OPEC (Organization of Petroleum Exporting Countries) is able to push world oil prices higher.

President Nixon resigns under imminent impeachment, Ford becomes president.

1975

Last Americans and American supporters are evacuated from the U.S. embassy in Saigon.

South Vietnam falls to the Communists and is unified with North Vietnam.

1976

America celebrates its two-hundredth birthday.

Jimmy Carter is elected president.

1977

Panama Canal treaty is signed, awarding eventual control to Panama.

1978

Camp David agreement between Egypt and Israel, the first face-to-face negotiation between Israel and an Arab neighbor.

1979

Iranian revolution leads to an oil crisis.

American embassy in Iran is invaded and hostages are taken.

1980

Ronald Reagan is elected president.

1981

Hostages in Iran are freed after 444 days of captivity.

For Further Reading

Harry S. Ashmore, *Hearts and Minds: A Personal Chronicle of Race in America.* Washington, DC: Seven Locks, 1988.

Francis J. Beckwith and Todd E. Jones, eds., *Affirmative Action: Social Justice or Reverse Discrimination?* Amherst, NY: Prometheus, 1997.

Clayborne Carson et al., *Eyes on the Prize, Civil Rights Reader: Documents, Speeches, and Firsthand Accounts from the Black Freedom Struggle, 1954–1990.* New York: Viking, 1991.

Harry Castleman and Walter J. Podrazik, *Watching TV: Four Decades of American Television.* New York: McGraw-Hill, 1982.

Frank Coffey and Joseph Layden, *America on Wheels: The First 100 Years: 1896–1996.* Los Angeles: General Publishing, 1996.

Charles W. Colson, *Born Again.* Old Tappan, NJ: Chosen/Fleming H. Revell, 1976.

Robert J. Dworak, *Taxpayers, Taxes, and Government Spending: Perspectives on the Taxpayer Revolt.* New York: Praeger, 1980.

Curtis W. Ellison, *Country Music Culture: From Hard Times to Heaven.* Jackson: University Press of Mississippi, 1995.

Adam Fairclough, *To Redeem the Soul of America: The Southern Christian Leadership Conference and Martin Luther King, Jr.* Athens: University of Georgia Press, 1987.

Jo Freeman, *The Politics of Women's Liberation: A Case Study of an Emerging Social Movement and Its Relation to the Policy Process.* New York: Longman, 1975.

Michael Harrington, *Decade of Decision.* New York: Simon & Schuster, 1980.

Louis Harris, *The Anguish of Change.* New York: Norton, 1973.

Gordon Harrison, *Earthkeeping: The War with Nature and a Proposal for Peace.* Boston: Houghton Mifflin, 1971.

Maureen Harrison and Steve Gilbert, eds., *Abortion Decisions of the United States Supreme Court: The 1970s.* Beverly Hills, CA: Excellent, 1993.

Hal Himmelstein, *Television Myth and the American Mind.* New York: Praeger, 1984.

Paul Johnson, *Modern Times: The World from the Twenties to the Eighties.* New York: Harper & Row, 1983.

Paul M. Kattenburg, *The Vietnam Trauma in American Foreign Policy, Nineteen Hundred and Forty-Five Thru Nineteen Hundred and Seventy-Five.* New Brunswick, NJ: Transaction, 1980.

Dean M. Kelley, *Why Conservative Churches Are Growing: A Study in Sociology of Religion.* New York: Harper & Row, 1972.

Stephen M. Krason, *Abortion: Politics, Morality, and the Constitution: A Critical Study of Roe v. Wade and Doe v. Bolton and a Basis for Change.* New York: University Press of America, 1984.

Jerrold H. Krenz, *Energy: From Opulence to Sufficiency.* New York: Praeger, 1980.

Christopher Lasch, *The Culture of Narcissism: American Life in an Age of Diminishing Expectations.* New York: Norton, 1979.

Herbert I. London, *Closing the Circle: A Cultural History of the Rock Revolution.* Chicago: Nelson-Hall, 1984.

Richard Maltby, *Passing Parade: A History of Popular Culture in the Twentieth Century.* New York: Oxford University Press, 1989.

Donella H. Meadows et al., *The Limits of Growth.* New York: Universe, 1972.

James T. Patterson, *Grand Expectations: The United States, 1945–1974.* New York: Oxford University Press, 1996.

Thomas R. Peake, *Keeping the Dream Alive: A History of the Southern Christian Leadership Conference from King to the Nineteen Eighties.* New York: Peter Lang, 1987.

Burton Yale Pines, *Back to Basics: The Traditionalist Movement That Is Sweeping Grass-Roots America.* New York: William Morrow, 1982.

James A. Reichley, *Religion in American Public Life.* Washington, DC: Brookings, 1985.

Thomas Richards, *The Meaning of Star Trek.* New York: Doubleday, 1997.

Janet Ward Schofield, *Black and White in School: Trust, Tension, or Tolerance?* New York: Teachers College Press, 1989.

John Oliver Wilson, *After Affluence: Economics to Meet Human Needs.* San Francisco: Harper & Row, 1980.

Index

314